AT WAR WITH ACADEMIC TRADITIONS
IN AMERICA

AT WAR WITH
ACADEMIC TRADITIONS
IN AMERICA

BY

A. LAWRENCE LOWELL
PRESIDENT EMERITUS OF HARVARD UNIVERSITY

GREENWOOD PRESS, PUBLISHERS
WESTPORT, CONNECTICUT

PREFACE

ONE who has spent a long time in any undertaking finds it natural to record for his own satisfaction the aspirations that have sustained him, the plans and the methods under which he and his colleagues worked. Throughout these papers the guiding idea was to inspire in university and college life a greater desire and respect for scholarship, and especially creative scholarship, for in America these seemed to the writer far undervalued. To him and to many others it appeared that our country was not contributing what it might to creative thought; that American institutions of higher learning were, as a rule, unduly interested in numbers of students, teachers and courses as compared with the quality of the product; that their methods were too mechanical, and that for credits in courses there should be substituted, in part at least, more personal incentive, more careful selection of students, and a better system of measurement.

The endeavor involved a conflict with traditions, not, indeed, old, yet firmly intrenched and hard to dislodge. On the side of students and parents the chief object in going to college was often social rather than intellectual; and on the side of teachers and administrators throughout the country the taking of courses was treated as the essential means of education from the primary school through the university, the measure of success to be applied being the credits accumulated therein and the degrees obtained thereby. To the writer it seemed that even theses and examinations for the doctorate were too much based on such a preparation; and that a system of this kind, while effective for mass production of a moderate grade, was in many cases inaccurate as a measure of attainment, and, what was worse, unsuited to recruit and stimulate the highest type of scholar.

Associated with this tradition was the prevalent assumption that undergraduates could hardly be expected to take true scholarship seriously, and that the only place to acquire it was in the graduate schools, which in fact had become almost wholly seminaries for teachers in universities, colleges, and secondary schools. Now, for young men to spend in the process of their education four — or for that matter any number — of their formative years in an atmosphere where scholarship was not held by them in high repute was clearly unfortunate; and to assume that teachers alone can have a deep aspiration for intellectual pursuits seemed a grave injury to the whole community.

Moreover, any substantial improvement must obviously begin with the college, on which the other parts of the university rest, and from which, in one way or another, they recruit their material; and here a change began with the report of a committee in 1903, whereof Dean Briggs was the Chairman and the writer one of the members. Questionnaires were sent to the instructors, and to a large number of students who had taken courses the year before, asking about the methods of instruction, the reasons for the election, and the hours devoted to study. The answers were full, frank, and interesting, but showed that the average amount of study in Harvard College was discreditably small. The result was the stiffening of many courses; and this was followed later by changes recorded in this book.

Strangely enough the belief, then not uncommon, that knowledge should be sought because of its utility, or because men wanted it, and not for any inferior motive, had an unexpected effect. Among the less worthy incentives were classed mere ambition, the desire to excel, the pride of victory — and they were little encouraged, whereas the direct usefulness in one's career in life was given prominence; and that a poor youth should strive for rank in order to obtain a scholarship he needed to continue his education was regarded as a higher type of motive than proving one's worth and the sense of achievement; with the result that among undergraduates the respect for high scholarship was small. The students themselves conducted their athletics on the opposite principle, for they appealed to two motives, the ambition for personal fame, and the collective impulse of service for their institution. They developed intercollegiate competitions, and ruled out players who received pay, on the ground that they were professionals. The effect was an exaggerated prominence of college athletics unparalleled in the history of education. From the standpoint of applied psychology the students proved themselves wiser than their teachers. Surely none of these motives are bad; they are all natural, good, and worthy of appeal if they will promote the object desired.[1]

To the writer it seems that many of the attempts made of late years to improve conditions savor of treating symptoms rather than causes. If the student is indifferent toward a subject he is invited to select something else that is less objectionable because it requires less effort; whereas the profit in his development lies to a large extent in the habit of hard mental thought. All true advance in training his brain being the product of self-education, with guidance and help, the vital matter is to incite him to voluntary exertion, arduous and exacting, but pursued with the desire of a mastery over difficulties; and to a youth worthy of higher education this is more interesting as well as more remunerative than less severe work. Nor is it essential, or always wise, to show a connection between his studies and his future vocation, for this is often illusory, and the purpose is not to provide him with knowledge that he can use directly hereafter, but to develop his capacity to the utmost. He is himself the object, the only true unit, of the whole process; any special knowledge may fade away, but the man's cultivated faculties remain, to be used throughout his life as his work demands. To some ex-

---

[1] "But weightier still are the contentment which comes from work well done, the sense of the value of science for its own sake, insatiable curiosity and, above all, the pleasure of masterly performance and of the chase. These are the effective forces which move the scientist. The first condition of the progress of science is to bring them into play." — Prof. L. J. Henderson, Preface to *Claude Bernard* (New York: Macmillan, 1927).

tent this is true even in the professional schools, where too much stress is sometimes laid upon information, as compared with the grasp of principles.

To bring about a distinct improvement in the respect and desire for high scholarship in college was especially difficult, and was declared by some observers impossible, because the end sought was a distinct change of attitude, and the objective hard to make clear to the students. There could be little appeal, as in professional or vocational schools, to immediate utility. Like all efforts to elevate morale it was somewhat intangible, and to anyone who does not perceive the aim clearly the means employed may seem artificial; and in fact any one of them alone might have little value, for they are not detached devices, each contrived for a specific purpose, but — although adopted separately when the time was ripe — parts of one consistent whole. They are, indeed, not another mechanism, but an attempt to provoke an attitude of mind, a collective type of thought, a desire and determination, and are to be judged as such. The methods adopted for attaining the result are by no means the only ones that could be used; perhaps they are not the best, but they appeared suited to the conditions at Harvard, and they were shaped by the combined labors of many men, learning by experiment, — although exposed herein by one spokesman who even in preparing what he said was often helped by the criticism of others.

The work has been long, and since much of it partook of the nature of argument for a cause, constant repetition of the themes was inevitable, but in what follows an attempt has been made to avoid this as much as possible. To arrange the papers by subjects was found hopeless, because many of them covered more than one topic, but for the convenience of anyone interested in some special phase a synopsis of subjects follows the table of contents. For the same reason it was impossible without confusion to arrange the articles reprinted and the annual reports together chronologically, for the former were mainly discussions of principles, while the latter were in large part statements of what had been done; and even when referring to the same subject the two were often far apart in time. In the annual reports there is, indeed, much exposition of principles, but usually such as had, or were shortly expected to have, an immediate application. For example, criticism of graduate work comes early in the reprinted articles, but late in the annual reports, since little could be done until conditions in the college were improved, and when this was well advanced too short a time remained for the great task of making the graduate work all that it might be. At most the needs could be indicated and the Society of Fellows established.

Perhaps this preface may end with a remark made at the Tavern Club in Boston after the writer had quitted office:

"Any constructive labor is in the nature of a work of art, and no one is more aware of the defects of what he has done than the artist himself. When he has finished his picture, as well as his skill permits, he takes it and hangs it up beside the altar, saying, I am sorry that it is not better, but in the time for work allotted it is the best that I could do."

A. LAWRENCE LOWELL

BOSTON
October 16, 1934

CONTENTS

TOPICS

AT WAR WITH ACADEMIC TRADITIONS IN AMERICA

THE CHOICE OF ELECTIVES

THE HARVARD MONTHLY, OCTOBER, 1887

FOR a score of years the college has been surrendering the selection of the studies to be pursued by undergraduates more and more into the hands of the students themselves, and in so doing it has, in fact, made three assumptions, upon the correctness of which the wisdom of this policy must depend. The first assumption is that the student will work harder upon a subject selected by himself than upon one which has been prescribed for him by the faculty. The second is that he will choose a course of study corresponding more closely with his individual needs than any curriculum that can be fixed by the college, and the third is that the responsibility cast upon the student and the experience which he will gain by exercising it will be themselves potent factors in his education. The first of these assumptions is, no doubt, correct, but the second and third are true only in case the student has knowledge enough of his own mental strength and weakness and sufficiently clear views upon the general principles of education to make a really wise selection, and in case he is willing to give the subject a serious and careful consideration.

Now it may be very true that the student's experience in college will teach him a great deal about his own mental needs; that he will learn each year more about education; and that he will finally appreciate the responsibility involved in the choice of his electives; but all this is not enough, because it is a great mistake, as everyone will admit, for a student to change his plan of study at each successive year. It is highly important that he should choose his electives throughout his college course upon some definite system that he has carefully thought out, and yet in his freshman year when that system must be formed he has no experience of electives, and as a rule no general views upon education and a very imperfect knowledge of his own mental needs. It is absurd to suppose that a list of electives alone will furnish him with the required knowledge, or that the sense of responsibility which always sits lightly upon the undergraduate will inspire him with wisdom in arranging his course of study. As well might one imagine that a sick man in an apothecary's shop would be moved to choose the medicine he required from the appearance of the bottles on the shelf. It is necessary, therefore, if the elective system is to be a success, that the student should be encouraged to think about his course of education, and that in choosing his electives he should have the benefit of the wisdom and experience of his instructors. Some method of fitting the undergraduate to exercise the responsibility cast upon him is, indeed, an essential feature of the system, and it is clear that the father can furnish little or no assistance in the matter, for even if he has had the benefit of a college training himself, his experience is at least a quarter of a century old, and in view of the great changes that have taken place in the college in that time, his advice to his son would be of very little value today. It remains for the college, therefore, to devise some other way of reaching the desired result. Perhaps the choice of electives might with advantage be made the subject of one or more themes, and much good might be done by a few lectures delivered by members of the faculty. It is not, in fact, so important that the views of the lecturers should agree as it is that the student should be induced to think upon the matter, and that he should have some clear opinions to consider. No doubt in choosing their electives the undergraduates are largely actuated by the ease or "softness" of the course, and with a few of them the desire to get through college with the least possible amount of work is the only motive. With these and with the propriety of subjecting them to a more severe discipline I am not concerned here. They form in any class a very small proportion of the members, for the great majority of men, while not intending

to do more than a certain amount of work, choose their
courses with a real desire to get an education, and, indeed, if
this were not true the whole elective system would be an
absurdity from the very start.

At the threshold of an inquiry into the principles which
ought to guide a student in the choice of his electives, the
question presents itself: what is the object of the college
course? And until that question is answered it is impossible
to proceed a step further. The question may be answered in
various ways, and has been the cause of a great deal of difference of opinion, but inasmuch as a discussion of the matter
would be very long, and lead us far out of our way, I shall
simply assume that the object of the undergraduate department of the University is to give an education, and without
attempting an exact definition of this term, I understand it to
mean a general training of the mind as distinguished from the
acquisition of specific information which is expected to be of
any definite use in after life.

Such a training of the mind may be looked at from two
sides, one of which concerns the strength and soundness of
the mental fibre, and the other the breadth and elasticity of
the mind. What I mean by mental fibre is easily explained.
No one who has been in a railroad station when the car-
wheels were being tested by a blow with a hammer has failed
to recognize the great difference even among those wheels
which are passed as safe. One of them when struck gives a
confused, harsh sound, and another a clear musical ring.
Now there is as much difference between a well-trained and
an ill-trained mind as there is between these two car-wheels;
a difference which is evident just as soon as an idea strikes the
mind; and it is one of the first objects of a college education
to produce that quality of mental fibre which makes it easy
for a man to analyse all propositions presented to him; to accept what truth there is in them and to reject the error; that
enables him to form clear and correct opinions, and to develop systematic and profound conceptions of things; that

gives him, in short, the habit of thinking clearly and deeply. There is no royal road to this result. It can be obtained only by constantly using the mind upon subjects which call out its full powers, and it is, therefore, essential that the college student should undergo a rigorous mental training in some department of study. It is a matter of secondary importance what subject he selects for this purpose provided it is one that requires hard mental work. All branches of science are good, and so are the various forms of metaphysics and of law. Mathematics is excellent if one has any taste for it, and so are history and literature if they are really well taught. Modern languages, as distinguished from philology and literature, do not call upon the reasoning powers enough to be the main subject of mental training, and the same may be said of fine arts and music, unless under a remarkable teacher. It is to be remembered that I am now dealing with a course of study which is to be pursued, not with a view to the knowledge acquired, but for the sake of the training of the mind, and I think that this training is much more certainly obtained by working upon a single subject until one has thoroughly mastered its principles and is completely familiar with them, than by devoting a smaller amount of time to a variety of topics. How much time ought to be given in this way to one subject, in view of the many departments of knowledge with which every educated man ought to have some familiarity, it is very hard to say. The amount will vary with each individual, according to his natural aptitude and the extent to which his mind has already been opened by previous study. Perhaps as a rough estimate we should not be far wrong in saying that it ought rarely to be less than one-third of the time given to electives, and never more than a half, and it ought in all cases to be divided among the college years in about equal proportions.

We have been considering so far only one half of an education. There remains the half of what I have called the breadth and elasticity of the mind, for although the knowledge how to use one's mental powers and the capacity of thinking clearly and deeply are a part and indeed the essential foundation of all intellectual training, they are not in themselves a complete education. There are, indeed, few spectacles so melancholy as that of a man of strong and acute mind who can see things only from one narrow standpoint, and who thinks that no study but his own is worthy of the attention and study of mankind. It is unfortunately only too common to see men eminent in their own department whose knowledge is so limited that they are not even aware of their own incapacity to deal with subjects lying outside of their ordinary line of thought. A really cultivated man is one who looks at the world from many points of view and who understands and appreciates the ideas of all classes of thinkers not only of his own day but also of former times. In this way alone is it possible to have broad and comprehensive views and to keep the mind open so that information may flow in through all possible channels. This does not mean that an educated man ought to know the details of every branch of learning. On the contrary such a feat is an impossibility, and with the increase in the mass of the world's knowledge the attempt to approach it even distantly becomes every day more futile. But it is nevertheless true that a thorough education ought to make a man familiar with the fundamental conceptions that underlie the various departments of human knowledge, and with the methods of thought of the persons who pursue them. Nor is this as difficult a task as it would at first sight appear, for there are running through every study certain deep-seated principles which must be grasped before any real progress can be made, and when these are once mastered it is comparatively easy to understand the subject. Now it is astonishing how readily a man who has been so trained as to be thoroughly familiar with the principles underlying one subject can get hold of those underlying another. A student, therefore, who undergoes a rigorous training in one department of study can, with a relatively small expenditure of time, acquire a considerable amount of familiarity with several more.

I have said that every thoroughly educated man should be familiar with the fundamental conceptions, and the methods of thought, which belong to each of the departments of human learning, and for this purpose these departments may be divided into certain large classes. The methods of thought in all branches of physical science, for example, are very much alike and differ radically from those to be met with in the study of literature or of metaphysics. A division of subjects on this basis will readily occur to everyone, and without attempting a philosophical classification it may be laid down that every student ought to devote a part of his time to the study, at least, of science, of philosophy, of history, of literature, and of art or of music if he has an ear for it.

In addition to the courses taken for this object there is another which I should prescribe for a different reason. I am strongly of opinion that no student ought to graduate without a considerable knowledge of the government of his country, and in fact, I should go so far as to claim that a course on this subject equal, at least, to one hour a week for a year ought to be among the studies required by the college. It is perhaps unnecessary to say that quite apart from college work every student ought to devote a large amount of time to reading good literature.

It is impossible, in a short article, to go into details and point out why certain branches of science or philosophy and certain periods of history are more valuable than others for the purpose of a general education; one or two hints, however, on the choice of electives may be useful, and here I must ask the reader to bear in mind the distinction I have drawn between the subject which is to be pursued as the chief basis of mental training, and which is to be gone into very thoroughly, and the other courses which are to be taken for the sake of acquiring breadth of view, and are studied less elaborately, because an elective which is quite suitable for the

first purpose may be entirely out of place for the second. A
course, for example, devoted to a minute examination of the
reign of Edward I might be extremely valuable as a part of
an extensive study of history, but to a student who intended
to take only one or two electives in this department it would
not be as useful as a course which gave a good general grasp
of a longer period. I remember a graduate who complained
that when in college he thought some scientific course would
be a benefit to him, and felt an attraction towards botany,
but that on consulting the list of electives in the subject, he
found Course I all about cryptograms, Course II all about
gymnosperms, and so on throughout the list.[1] So that while,
if he took the whole series, he would, no doubt, graduate with
an excellent knowledge of botany, any single course would be
of but little value, if, indeed, of any use to him at all. In this
case botany would have been all very well if he meant to
make it his chief subject of study, but if not it would have
been better to choose an elective in some other branch of
science.

One word more about the choice of electives. It is not uncommon for an undergraduate to be guided in his selection
by a desire to help himself in the study of his future profession. In fact the instructor in a scientific course told me on
one occasion that he could pick out the members of the class
who intended to be doctors by the way they devoted themselves to the part of the course which dealt with human
anatomy. Such a method of choosing electives seems to me
a very great mistake, because the courses in college are not
given with a view to technical instruction, and, therefore, a
man can get from them little or nothing that will save him
time in learning his profession, and because the details, even
of a strictly technical course isolated in the middle of college

[1] The catalogue shows that the electives in botany are not open to any such
reproach now, and probably they never were. The anecdote is used of course
only as an illustration, and is not intended as a criticism of the botanical
courses.

work, are certain to be so much forgotten by the time a man begins his professional studies that a great deal of time will be found to have been wasted and the student will discover that he has worked at a great disadvantage. If a man really cannot afford the time for a complete college education he had far better spend three full years on college work and then go into a professional school than attempt to piece out a year of study on his profession during his college term. By taking a course in law or medicine, for example, he can acquire very little except a general familiarity with legal or medical methods of thought. But this will come to him fast enough when he enters the professional school, and in order to get it in college he sacrifices his opportunity to become familiar with philosophical, scientific, or historical methods of thought, as he might otherwise do, and to just that extent he narrows his intellectual basis. Of course in saying this I am not referring to such a matter as learning German for the sake of its usefulness in a medical career. That is a case of studying German, not medicine, and it is not done at a disadvantage compared with a subsequent study of the language while learning the profession. It usually involves, also, the study of a certain amount of literature and does not tend to give the man an exclusively medical way of seeing the world. But I should include such a subject as Roman Law in the list of courses to be avoided by one who proposes to be a lawyer.

To examine this matter of the choice of electives thoroughly, and discuss fully the various problems it presents would require a complete treatise on education. In a single article it is impossible to do more than touch upon the prominent outlines of the subject, and the writer is conscious how rough and imperfect a sketch he has made and how much that is important has been entirely omitted. But these very imperfections and omissions will have been useful if they result in provoking argument, for it is above all important that this subject should be discussed both by the students and the faculty far more fully than it has been hitherto. If the suggestions in this article succeed in accomplishing this result; if they succeed in drawing attention to the importance of making the undergraduate work out for himself a rational system of choosing his electives and of giving him the benefit of the experience of the faculty in so doing, and if the views here expressed contribute to some extent towards forming a general opinion in the college about the principles on which electives ought to be chosen, then this article will have done its work whether the theory presented in it is accepted or whether another is developed in its place.

COLLEGE RANK AND DISTINCTION IN LIFE

ATLANTIC MONTHLY, OCTOBER, 1903

THERE is a tradition in England — very wholesome for undergraduates — that university honors are a premonition of an eminent career. They are even associated in the popular mind with cabinet office, and men point to Peel, Palmerston, Gladstone, Lowe, Northcote, Harcourt, and many more to prove that the general impression is well founded. The list includes, indeed, most of the great figures in English public life during the Victorian era who were graduates of Oxford or of Cambridge. Nor are we entirely without similar examples in this country. If we take the alumni of Harvard, and classify as honor men those who stood in the first seventh of their class, who received honors at graduation in any special subject, or who won a Bowdoin Prize; then in the honor list of Harvard there figure the President of the United States, the only Harvard men in his cabinet and in the Supreme Court, the Ambassador to England, and the last Governor of the Commonwealth who graduated from the college. Nor would it be difficult to cite many examples among the successful professional and business men. Yet, the impression is certainly common here that high scholars rarely amount to much afterwards, and that the competitive trial of life does not begin until college days are past.

It seems worth while, therefore, to determine by statistics the relation between rank in college and success in after life. Attempts to do this have been made of late, and one of them has recently been published under the title High-Grade Men; In College and Out, by Professor Edwin G. Dexter, in the Popular Science Monthly for March, 1903. In it the author compares the subsequent careers of the members of the

Φ. B. K. — the society of high scholars — with the careers of other graduates, and he gives figures, taken from twenty-two colleges, to the effect that the proportion of the former who have proved to be high-grade men in the world is nearly three times as large as that of the graduates taken as a whole.[1] He examines, also, two large New England colleges, the percentage of whose living graduates that have achieved success is 2.2, and shows that the percentage among the men who ranked in the first tenth of their class is 5.4; while in the second tenth it is 2.9; in the third tenth, 2.5; in the fourth and fifth, 1.8; and in the rest of the class, 1.9. In one of these colleges he considers the first four scholars in each class, and finds that their percentage of success is very much larger still.

As his test of success in life Professor Dexter has relied upon the names that appear in Who's Who in America. No doubt, like every other compilation of the kind, this book leaves out many people who ought to be included, and inserts many names that ought to be left out; but in dealing with a large number of cases such personal errors affect the validity of the result very little, unless they are caused by some systematic error, some false standard or criterion in estimating men. Now the editors of this work intended it to be a catalogue of all men of mark in the country, and yet, if used for the purpose of measuring success in life, it is certainly subject to a systematic error. While it attempts to include every man who has achieved a position of great eminence of any kind, it pays far more attention to success in some fields than in others. Its list covers all authors, an undue proportion of college professors, and perhaps for our purpose too many men, also, who hold high public office in the

---

[1] In the case of Harvard, at least, Professor Dexter has by mistake included among the Φ.B.K. men the members of the society who have been elected some years after graduation on the ground of reputation achieved out of college. This vitiates his ratio of success as between Φ.B.K. and other graduates, — which in Harvard he puts at nearly five to one, — but the error is, no doubt, too small to affect his general conclusion.

nation or in the state. Hence, as a measure of success in life, it tends to favor those who devote themselves to scholarship or public affairs as compared with men who expend their energies on professional and especially on mercantile pursuits. It gives particular prominence to scholarship, and as this is an occupation for which high scholars in college are peculiarly fitted, the book cannot be considered a fair test of the relation between college rank and general success in after life. So far as mere fame is concerned, however, the position is somewhat different. The reputation won in the practice of a profession or in business fades more rapidly than that achieved by the pen or by public service. The writers and statesmen of half a century ago have been forgotten far less than the successful lawyers, doctors, and merchants. Who's Who is, therefore, a much better test of distinction than of success in life; although in any case the results it yields must be looked upon as approximate, not absolute. At present, however, it is the only statistical measure that can be applied, and hence the figures taken from it have no little value, even if we cannot regard them as numerically exact.

Bearing these facts in mind, an effort has been made to discover the relative distinction in after life, as shown by Who's Who,[1] of those men who were scholars or athletes at Harvard as compared with other graduates of the college. With that object the records of the classes have been studied from 1861 to 1887 inclusive. The first of these classes was taken as the point of departure, because from that date the rank lists were easily found, and because if we go further back the proportion of members who have died becomes large. On the other hand, the reasons for ending with the class of 1887 were the fact that after that year the practice of ranking the high scholars in numerical order was given up, and the consideration that a very small part of the graduates would have an opportunity to attain distinction within less than fifteen years after leaving college.

[1] Edition of 1902.

The total number of men who graduated from Harvard College during the twenty-seven years, 1861–87, was four thousand and eleven, of whom three hundred and one, or one in thirteen and three tenths, are named in Who's Who. The chance, therefore, that the average graduate will attain the distinction that this implies is one in thirteen and three-tenths. Or — since a number of the graduates have died — it would be more accurate to say that this fraction represents the average chance that he will be living and possessed of such dignity some thirty years after graduation. Inasmuch, however, as there is no reason to suppose that the mortality of high and low scholars, athletes and others, is markedly different, the deaths may be neglected for purposes of comparison, and it will be convenient to speak of the chance of distinction in terms of the ratio of the total number of graduates to those in Who's Who at the present day.

If now we turn to the high scholars, and take the men who graduated in the first seventh of their classes during the same period, we find that they number five hundred and seventy-three, of whom eighty-two are in Who's Who; so that their chance of distinction is a trifle better than one in seven, or nearly twice as great as that of the average graduate. Moreover, if, instead of comparing them with the whole body of graduates, we compare them only with the men in the remaining six-sevenths of the class, we find that the chance of the latter is one in fifteen and seven-tenths, or decidedly less than half as great as that of the men in the first seventh of the class.

One would naturally suppose that the chance of the very highest scholars would be better still, and so in fact it is. Out of the twenty-seven first scholars there are seven, or more than one in four, in Who's Who; out of the second scholars three; of the third scholars five; and of the fourth scholars six. These numbers are, of course, so small that accident plays a large part in the result; but, speaking roughly, it may be said that the chance of distinction for any one of the first four scholars is about one in five, as against one in seven for the men in the first seventh of the class, and about one in sixteen for the rest of the class.

In considering the causes of the greater chance of distinction among the high scholars, many elements must be taken into account. The large proportion of men with university honors among the prominent English statesmen is due, in no small degree, to the fact that their honors opened to them while young the doors of the House of Commons, and an early start has always been an enormous advantage in a parliamentary career. Lord Palmerston quotes his tutor as saying to him, at about the time he came of age, that having done exceedingly well in his examinations he ought to expect shortly a seat in Parliament; and, in fact, he obtained one before long. It is impossible to compute how many Lord Palmerstons the State Department has lost by our failure to imitate this salutary tradition. In America, and certainly at Harvard, college rank is no help to a man in starting either in public life, in a profession, or in business. Rank is, no doubt, a help toward an academic post, and thus assists indirectly to the literary eminence which is most noticed in Who's Who; but this alone is clearly not enough to account for the difference in subsequent distinction between the high scholars and their classmates. To some extent, at least, the college career of the high scholars works as a principle of selection, or as a preparation, of the fittest. The high scholar wins distinction in after life mainly because he is naturally better fitted, or because his training makes him more fit, to win it. Both of these things are probably true. The taking of rank is a test of natural qualities, and tends also to develop those qualities. It is, in fact, impossible to distinguish between the two; nor is it necessary for our purpose to do so, seeing that their results are the same.

Let us suppose — to make the matter plain — that to bring distinction four things must be combined. Let us say industry, intelligence, adaptability, and opportunity, and that the average chance that any one of them falls to a man's lot is one half. Then the chance that all four will be combined is one in sixteen. This would be the chance of distinction for the average man. But if we know that a man possesses one of them, the chance of his having the other three is one in eight, and this would be that man's chance of distinction. If he possess two the chance of his having the other two, and therefore his chance of distinction, is one in four. Now, let us suppose that the fact of ranking in the first seventh of the class shows that a man possesses, or has acquired, industry. In that case his chance of distinction would be one in eight, or twice as great as that of the average member of the class. If in the same way we suppose that the first scholar in the class must possess both industry and intelligence, his chance would be one in four, or four times as large as the average chance of his classmates. Of course the problem is by no means so simple as our suppositions would make it appear. The possible combinations of qualities and accidents that will bring distinction are indefinitely variable and complex. Nor are these qualities independent of one another, for the presence of one quality affects the probability of the existence of another; so that even if we knew the average chance of the presence of each separate element, it would be well-nigh impossible to calculate the chance of a successful combination. Still, the principle is true, although we cannot apply it by means of vulgar fractions, and the known presence of one or more important qualities increases a man's chance above the average — and the more he possesses the better his chance.

But it may be suggested that while all this is true, while it is admitted that the high scholars possess industry, and that it is an element of chance in their favor, they have no monopoly of it. There are many men in the class who possess it, and other valuable qualities besides, but who do not feel impelled to display them in the form of a struggle for marks. Their gifts may be exercised on other objects in which they are interested, or may not be called forth at all until college days are over and men are aroused by contact with the problems of the outer world. The conclusion deduced is that rank as an indication of future achievement amounts to little or nothing. Herein lies a fallacy. It is the fallacy which gives rise to the common belief that because a first scholar is rarely the most distinguished man in his class, and is commonly not distinguished at all, therefore he has no better chance of distinction than any one else. It is the old fallacy of the favorite and the field. The favorite may have a better chance than any one of the other horses, and yet the odds may be that some horse will beat him. If, as most people unconsciously do, we compare the chances of the first scholar on one side, and all the rest of the class on the other, the odds are overwhelmingly in favor of the latter. But if we were to compare the chances of the first scholar and those of any other one man, let us say the fiftieth scholar, it would be easy to show that the chances of the first scholar were very much the better; and, in fact, the impression left on the mind after such a comparison would probably be that the particular man selected — the fiftieth — attained distinction with singular rarity. To revert to the numerical example. If the chance of distinction of the first scholar is one in four, and that of the average student is one in sixteen, then, if the class contains one hundred and sixty men, their collective chances are forty times as great as that of the first scholar; and yet his chance is four times as great as that of the average student, or of any single student drawn by lot.

Another common fallacy arises from comparing the test of rank with other tests, such as the opinion of a man's comrades. It is often said that this last is the better test, and the inference is often unconsciously drawn that the former is of no value. The error here is obvious. Rank may prove the presence in one man of certain requisite qualities, and hence an unusual chance of distinction, and yet the presence of the same or other qualities may be known by different means to exist in an even higher degree in some other man, whose chance is therefore better still; but this in no way affects the fact that both are in better case than the average man.

So far our statistics have been drawn only from the general rank list, but very valuable results may be obtained from the honors won in special fields of college work. The Bowdoin Prize for an English essay is an old institution at Harvard, and while far less work is needed to win it than to attain a high general average of marks for the whole college course, it requires a serious effort for a time and abilities of a high order. During the years under consideration, — that is from 1861 to 1887, — one hundred and thirty-three men won this prize, of whom twenty-nine, or one in four and six-tenths, are to be found in Who's Who. Their chance is, therefore, nearly as good as that of the first scholar in the class.

Still more interesting are the results to be derived from a study of the honors given at graduation for excellence in special subjects, such as classics, philosophy, history, etc. These were established first in 1869, and during the nineteen years from that time through 1887 they were obtained by three hundred and seventy-five men, of whom seventy-one, or one in five and three-tenths, are in Who's Who. Some of these men, for supposed peculiar merit, were given highest honors; and of the eighty-one students who attained to that grade, no less than twenty-nine, or more than one in three, are in Who's Who. In order to compare these results with those already found by a study of the general rank list it is necessary to revise our figures by taking them for the same nineteen years; because the graduates of those years, being more recent, have naturally reached a somewhat smaller share of distinction than the classes that have been longer out of college, although the difference is not, in fact, great. The proportion of men in Who's Who from the different categories of graduates in the classes from 1869 to 1887, inclusive, is as follows:

Total graduates	224 out of	3239	or one in 14.46
First seventh of class	67	473	7.05
First scholar *	7	19	2.71
First four scholars	16	76	4.75
Bowdoin Prize men	18	89	4.94
Honors in special subjects	67	379	5.66
Highest special honors	28	93	3.33

* None of the first scholars in the eight classes from 1861 to 1868 happen to be in Who's Who, so that the proportion for the nineteen years from 1869 to 1887 is considerably larger than for the whole period from 1861.

From this table it will be seen that scholarly attainment of every kind in college tends to be followed by distinction in after life, though not to an equal degree. The proportion of names in Who's Who is decidedly larger among the men who took honors in special subjects than among men, to about the same number, taken in the order of rank on the general scale. It is one in five for the former, but it is only one in seven for the first seventh of the class. In fact the proportion among the men with special honors is nearly equal to that of the first four scholars, although the former are five times as numerous. For the students who graduate with highest honors the chance of distinction is extraordinary. It is better than one in three, being about the same as that of the first scholars for these nineteen years, and much above that of any other men. We are irresistibly led to the conclusion that the work done for honors in a special subject is a better preparation, or a better test of ability, than that which confers rank on the general scale. It is probably safer to regard it as a better test of ability, and the reasons why it should be so are evident to any one familiar with the methods of instruction and examination. Mere talent for acquisition, quickness, and memory count somewhat less, while thoroughness, power of reasoning, and originality count for more.

The same remark applies to the Bowdoin Prize, for, taking the whole period from 1861 to 1887, this gives a chance of subsequent distinction almost equal to that of the first scholar, and better than that of any other class of men save the winners of highest honors.

One would naturally suppose that the question of pecuniary aid might have an important bearing upon the relation of rank in college to distinction in life. At Harvard, where undergraduate scholarship has met, unfortunately, with scant recognition among one's fellows or in the outer world, the ordinary man has little inducement to study for marks; but the scholarships are allotted mainly by rank, and hence the student in need of aid must work hard in his courses in order to obtain it. Under such conditions one might expect to find that the men of means who took high rank were gifted with a peculiar energy and love of work that would give them an advantage over other high scholars who studied because they were obliged to do so. But this does not appear to be the case. Of the men in the first seventh of the class, about three-fifths held money scholarships during the years from 1861 to 1887, and the proportion of them in Who's Who is almost the same as that of the other two-fifths who had no such inducement to work. Either the struggle on the part of the scholarship men to get to college and remain there works as a selection of the really vigorous, or the discipline involved develops a strength of character that stands them in good stead throughout their life.

But after all, the scholar is not the only type of man of mark in college whose subsequent career is worth following. The athlete is a far more prominent figure. What is the relation between his fame in college and his distinction in after life? In undertaking to examine the question the writer believed, and expected to find, that any success in college, intellectual or physical, would be an indication of natural vigor, and therefore increase to some extent the chance of distinction in any subsequent career; but this proves to be true only in part. In the case of the three great athletic bodies, the crew, the baseball nine, and the football eleven, we have no data to work with so accurate as those which the college rank lists furnish in regard to scholars, because until very recent times their records of membership were not carefully made and preserved. Still, it is believed that the lists compiled by Mr Thompson, of the Harvard Union, are so nearly correct that any errors are not likely to affect the general result.

Take first the crews. We find that during the twenty-seven years from 1861 to 1887 they comprised eighty-two different men, of whom six, or one in thirteen and two-thirds, are in Who's Who. This, it will be observed, is very nearly the same as the proportion for the total graduates of the college during the same period, and it has remained fairly constant throughout. The members of the crew would appear, therefore, to have about the same chance of the kind of distinction implied in Who's Who as the average members of the class. That is, intellectually speaking, they are neither better nor worse than their classmates. When we come to the captains of the crew, we should expect to find men chosen on account of superior force or intelligence. We should, therefore, expect them to win a greater share of distinction in the world than the average of their classmates; and this proves to be the fact. Of the seventeen captains of the crew during the twenty-seven years in question, three, or one in five and two-thirds, are to be found in Who's Who. The numbers dealt with are, of course, so small that accident plays a very large part, — a part large enough to make the results untrustworthy as a basis for any theory. Still, so far as they go, they would indicate that the chance of the kind of distinction implied by Who's Who is as great for the captains of the crew as for the high scholars in the class, and the men who take special honors, and greater than for the average of the men who rank in the first seventh of the class. So far, our results are not very different from those we might have been led to expect; but when we turn to the other teams we reach quite different conclusions.

Baseball began with the Class of 1866, and from the twenty-two classes down to and including 1887 there were drawn one hundred and two members of the nine, of whom seven, or one in fourteen and a half, are included in Who's Who. At first sight this seems to show that, intellectually speaking, the members of the nine have been fair average specimens of the class; but when we examine the matter a little more closely we find that a great change has taken place. Six out of the seven baseball men whose names appear in Who's Who belong to the three classes of 1867, 1868, and 1869. During the eighteen years that followed there were seventy-two players on the nine, of whom only one is in Who's Who. The contrast is very surprising until we examine more carefully the names of the men who played upon the nine in the early days. In the four classes from 1866 to 1869, there were thirty members of the nine, of whom six, as we have said, or one in five, are in Who's Who; but these were days in which scholars played upon the nine. In fact, one member of the nine in each of five consecutive classes in those days was in the first seventh of his class; and of the thirty men already mentioned, three were in the first seventh of their class, while two more took special honors; and thus it happens that of the six men in Who's Who in the first four years, four are men who distinguished themselves by scholarship in college. Since that time the scholars have ceased to play ball, or the nine have ceased to study; for of the one hundred and eleven men recorded as members of the nine from 1872 through 1898, there was only one man who took honors in any subject, no man who won a Bowdoin Prize, and through 1887 (when the rank list was given up) only one man in the first seventh of his class.

Perhaps the reason for such change may be found in the very improvement of the game. A higher amount of skill is required than of old, and this means more training and more time expended. So that while it was possible in the early years for men like James Barr Ames, Francis Rawle, and Francis Greenwood Peabody to be proficient both with bats and books, this has become well-nigh an impossibility today.

The case of the baseball captains is even more surprising. Their names are not given for the first few years; but from 1874, when the list begins, down to the present day, there does not appear in Who's Who the name of a single captain of the nine.

The record of the football team tells much the same story, except that it opens after the days were passed when men combined scholarship with athletics. Mr Thompson's football records start with the class of 1874; and from that time through 1887 there were ninety-three members of the eleven, of whom three, or one out of thirty-one, are found in Who's Who; while of the seven captains, not one appears in that work. Of late years the result has been more promising, for of the fifty-five men who have been upon the team from 1888 to 1898, two are in Who's Who, and one of these was a captain. As in baseball after the early years, so among the football men the record of scholarship at college has not been brilliant. In all the years from 1874 to 1898 there were, out of the one hundred and forty-eight men upon the team, only two men who took special honors, two who took a Bowdoin Prize, and two who were in the first seventh of the class. In one case, however, all three kinds of honors were attained by the same man. So that out of the one hundred and forty-eight men, four attained some distinction in scholarship. Curiously enough, no one of the four appears in Who's Who.

These statistics would tend to show that while the chance of the kind of distinction recorded in Who's Who is about the same for the crew as for the average of the class, and is much greater for the captains of the crew, it is for the football and baseball men far less than for the average graduate. Such a result cannot be attributed entirely to the fact that high scholars no longer play upon the nine or upon the eleven, for this is equally true of the crew. In fact, from 1861 to 1898 no member of the crew won a Bowdoin Prize, or stood in the first seventh of his class, and only one took final honors in any subject; but the oarsmen proved in other ways that they possessed in as great a degree as the average of the class the qualities that make for distinction. Why should not this be true of the baseball and football men also?

To contrast the proportion of college athletes and high scholars found in Who's Who might well be thought unfair on the ground that the criterion of eminence used in that book tends to favor scholarship as compared with success in the professions or in business, and tends, therefore, to give a distinct advantage to men who were scholars in college. This might explain, in part at least, why the high scholars should appear in Who's Who in greater numbers than the athletes; but it does not explain why the athletes should appear in it less than the average graduate. There is no obvious reason why the athletes should not distinguish themselves in later life, whether through scholarship or otherwise, as frequently as the other members of the class who are not scholars. If they do not do so it would seem that a principle of selection must be at work in the case of the nine and the eleven which eliminates men of intellectual abilities and tastes. The time that one must devote to such sports is greater than in the case of the crew, and this apparently discourages men who who have other interests.

That the members of the teams should attain in after life a smaller share of distinction than the average of their classmates, by whatever criterion it is measured, was a surprise to the writer, and is certainly a matter for regret. It is one of many indications that athletics have become too much an end in themselves, distinct from the current of college life; that the pursuit has become so absorbing, the amount of practice required so great, as to entail a sacrifice of other things in order to play on the team. This is due partly to the professional character of all American sports, which tend peculiarly to the development of a very high degree of technical skill, and partly to a distribution of the college year which throws work and play into the same periods. Division of labor, and specialization of occupation, is an important element in the progress of the world, but men can carry it too far in the training of their brains and bodies in college.

DIVISION OF UNDERGRADUATES
INTO RESIDENTIAL COLLEGES (OR HOUSES)

Part of Address at Yale University on April 19, 1907

Printed in the Harvard Bulletin

It would appear, however, that bringing young Americans together for a common education from every section of the country is at this present day pre-eminently the problem of the endowed universities, and especially of the larger ones; for, while some of the smaller colleges draw their students from a wide area, the larger institutions are peculiarly fitted to work on a national scale. Their very size means a wider constituency, and hence a more complete mingling of young men from all over the country. They are best adapted for the great function of helping to form a national type of manhood, because they have a better chance of drawing students in large numbers from every part of the land. But if size gives opportunities, it involves also difficulties. In a small college the individual is in less danger of being lost; the young man without aggressive personality is less likely to be ignored or submerged. Character and self-reliance are more developed by being a man of mark in Ravenna than by belonging to the mob in Rome; and what is more to our purpose, a body that is too large for general personal acquaintance tends to break up into groups whose members see little of one another. The citizen of a good-sized town has usually a wider acquaintance than the dweller in a big city.

In the social life of a college, as in other things, there is for any one form of organization an economic scale which gives the best results. Beyond that the social body becomes fissiparous, and thereby loses the benefits of size. What is worse, the lines of cleavage naturally follow the associations formed before coming to college; and hence a man from a distance, who has no friends already there, may well fail to become intimate with the men whom it is most important that he should know both for their sake and his own. In many places the social life of the students is regulated by fraternities, to some one of which almost every undergraduate belongs; and such a system may work well enough in a small college, or in one where the students come from a limited area, so that everyone has a chance of being known. But in the large endowed universities that system, or any system of societies or clubs, is incapable of supplying an opportunity for the best kind of social life to the great mass of students. Nor if it could include them all would it be a fortunate arrangement, because here again we should be met by the tendency to divide on the lines of previous association and one of the chief advantages of a great university, that of throwing together men from every part of the country, would be in great part lost.

Now, the larger colleges grow, the more pronounced this difficulty must inevitably become. In the largest of them it is already felt; in others it can be foreseen; and before many years have passed it will present a very pressing problem. With the rapid growth of the number of people who can afford to send their sons to college, with the ever greater need of education as a prerequisite to getting a good start in life, and with the tendency to require a college degree before beginning the study of a profession, there is every reason to believe that the total number of college students in the United States will increase very fast. If, therefore, the undergraduate departments of the larger endowed universities maintain their hold upon public confidence, it seems not unreasonable to suppose that in the space of a generation they may triple or quadruple in size; and before that happens the question of student life must be solved, or will have solved itself, for better or worse.

The problem is so to organize the students as to mix together on an intimate footing men of all kinds from all parts of the country. The obvious solution is to break the undergraduate body into groups like the English colleges, large enough to give each man a chance to associate closely with a considerable number of his fellows, and not so large as to cause a division into exclusive cliques. It must be understood, of course, that this applies only to the social life, not to the instruction, which would remain a university matter as heretofore. Such a suggestion of breaking up the student body has often been made, and something of the kind must be done sooner or later if we are to maintain our old ideas of the value of college life. Incidentally it would have the effect of provoking internal emulation which we sorely need. The socialistic, or for this purpose it is more appropriate to say the Christian, spirit that has come over the world has affected profoundly our undergraduates. Of late years an appeal to purely individual objects has less effect upon them than it did formerly. A student likes to feel that he is striving not for his own selfish fame alone, but for the glory of the organization to which he belongs, and hence a rivalry between a number of colleges would add a powerful incentive to effort in many lines.

But it is not enough to suggest that the undergraduate body can advantageously be divided into groups; the difficulty comes in arranging how the groups can be formed; and here we get very little light from European experience. The German universities, and those that have followed their model, are collections of professional schools training men to be clergymen, lawyers, physicians, and teachers or professors. They have nothing corresponding to the liberal culture at which our college purports to aim. That phase of education is supposed to be completed at the gymnasium. In England, on the other hand, where the universities have developed the ancient traditions in a very different way, the social conditions are such as to preclude the chief difficulty that confronts us. Oxford and Cambridge are doing a work of the same nature as our undergraduate departments, and they are made up of colleges such as I am now discussing; but the bulk of their students are drawn from a single class in the community; men of a different class who want that kind of education usually going to London, or to one of the provincial universities. This fact, together with the inducement of scholarships, and the tendency to be guided by inherited associations, causes the students to distribute themselves among the colleges in a very satisfactory way. The men who have grown up together as boys, or who come from the same region do not collect unduly in one college. In America we should have quite a different result if we allowed the boy to select his group on first coming to the university. He would almost certainly go to the group or college where the men were that he knew already, or at least to a place where he would not feel too much of a stranger. The students would be mainly segregated on the basis of origin, of geographical sections, of preparatory schools, of home surroundings; and thus we should have — as people have said — a college for western men, a college for southern men, a college for millionaires. Now this is the very worst scheme of division that could possibly be devised. It would accentuate and intensify the unfortunate lines of cleavage in the student body that are now beginning to appear. It would stereotype and perpetuate them. It would erect barriers to prevent a student from associating readily with the very men that he ought to be thrown with. What we need, on the contrary, is a system of grouping that will bring into each group men from different parts of the country, men with different experience, and as far as possible social condition. In short, what we want is a group of colleges each of which will be national and democratic, a microcosm of the whole university. This may not be an easy feat to accomplish, but I believe it can be done. Perhaps the freshman year, which is in any case a period of transition, could be advantageously used as time for mixing the students together, and bringing out their natural sympathies and affinities before they make their final selection of a college. But whether this solution be adopted or not, the problem is one that is, or shortly will be, common to the leading endowed universities in the eastern states, and they must all solve it sooner or later in some way if they are to maintain their undergraduate departments, and make them of the highest value to the nation.

INAUGURAL ADDRESS

DELIVERED IN FRONT OF UNIVERSITY HALL, ON WEDNESDAY FORENOON,
OCTOBER 6, 1909

REPRINTED FROM THE HARVARD GRADUATES' MAGAZINE, DECEMBER, 1909

AMONG his other wise sayings, Aristotle remarked that man is by nature a social animal; and it is in order to develop his powers as a social being that American colleges exist. The object of the undergraduate department is not to produce hermits, each imprisoned in the cell of his own intellectual pursuits, but men fitted to take their places in the community and live in contact with their fellow men.

The college of the old type possessed a solidarity which enabled it to fulfil that purpose well enough in its time, although on a narrower scale and a lower plane than we aspire to at the present day. It was so small that the students were all well acquainted with one another, or at least with their classmates. They were constantly thrown together, in chapel, in the classroom, in the dining-hall, in the college dormitories, in their simple forms of recreation; and they were constantly measuring themselves by one standard in their common occupations. The curriculum, consisting mainly of the classics, with a little mathematics, philosophy, and history, was the same for them all; designed, as it was, not only as a preparation for the professions of the ministry and the law, but also as the universal foundation of liberal education.

In the course of time these simple methods were outgrown. President Eliot pointed out with unanswerable force that the field of human knowledge had long been too vast for any man to compass; and that new subjects must be admitted to the scheme of instruction, which became thereby so large that no student could follow it all. Before the end of the nineteenth century this was generally recognized, and election in some form was introduced into all our colleges. But the new methods brought a divergence in the courses of study pursued by individual students, an intellectual isolation, which broke down the old solidarity. In the larger institutions the process has been hastened by the great increase in numbers, and in many cases by an abandonment of the policy of housing the bulk of the students in college dormitories; with the result that college life has shown a marked tendency to disintegrate, both intellectually and socially.

To that disintegration the overshadowing interest in athletic games appears to be partly due. I believe strongly in the physical and moral value of athletic sports, and of intercollegiate contests conducted in a spirit of generous rivalry; and I do not believe that their exaggerated prominence at the present day is to be attributed to a conviction on the part of the undergraduates, or of the public, that physical is more valuable than mental force. It is due rather to the fact that such contests offer to students the one common interest, the only striking occasion for a display of college solidarity.

If the changes wrought in the college have weakened the old solidarity and unity of aim, they have let in light and air. They have given us a freedom of movement needed for further progress. May we not say of the extreme elective system what Edmond Scherer said of democracy: that it is but one stage in an irresistible march toward an unknown goal. We must go forward and develop the elective system, making it really systematic. Progress means change, and every time of growth is a transitional era; but in a peculiar degree the present state of the American college bears the marks of a period of transition. This is seen in the comparatively small estimation in which high proficiency in college studies is held, both by undergraduates and by the public at large; for if college education were now closely adapted to the needs of the community, excellence of achievement therein ought to be generally recognized as of great value. The transitional nature of existing conditions is seen again in the absence, among instructors as well as students, of fixed principles by which the choice of courses of study ought to be guided. It is seen, more markedly still, in the lack of any accepted view of the ultimate object of a college education.

On this last subject the ears of the college world have of late been assailed by many discordant voices, all of them earnest, most of them well informed, and speaking in every case with a tone of confidence in the possession of the true solution. One theory, often broached, under different forms, and more or less logically held, is that the main object of the college should be to prepare for the study of a definite profession, or the practice of a distinct occupation; and that the subjects pursued should, for the most part, be such as will furnish the knowledge immediately useful for that end. But if so, would it not be better to transfer all instruction of this kind to the professional schools, reducing the age of entrance thereto, and leaving the general studies for a college course of diminished length, or perhaps surrendering them altogether to the secondary schools? If we accept the professional object of college education, there is much to be said for a readjustment of that nature, because we all know the comparative disadvantage under which technical instruction is given in college, and we are not less aware of the great difficulty of teaching cultural and vocational subjects at the same time. The logical result would be the policy of Germany, where the university is in effect a collection of professional schools, and the underlying general education is given in the *Gymnasium*. Such a course has, indeed, been suggested, for it has been proposed to transfer so far as possible to the secondary schools the first two years of college instruction, and to make the essential work of the university professional in character. But that requires a far higher and better type of secondary school than we possess, or are likely to possess for many years. Moreover, excellent as the German system is for Germany, it is not wholly suited to our Republic, which cannot, in my opinion, afford to lose the substantial, if intangible, benefits the nation has derived from its colleges. Surely the college can give a freedom of thought, a breadth of outlook, a training for citizenship, which neither the secondary nor the professional school in this country can equal.

Even persons who do not share this view of a professional aim have often urged that in order to save college education in the conditions that confront us we must reduce its length. May we not feel that the most vital measure for saving the college is not to shorten its duration, but to ensure that it shall be worth saving? Institutions are rarely murdered; they meet their end by suicide. They are not strangled by their natural environment while vigorous; they die because they have outlived their usefulness, or fail to do the work that the world wants done; and we are justified in believing that the college of the future has a great work to do for the American people.

If, then, the college is passing through a transitional period, and is not to be absorbed between the secondary school on the one side and the professional school on the other, we must construct a new solidarity to replace that which is gone. The task before us is to frame a system which, without sacrificing individual variation too much, or neglecting the pursuit of different scholarly interests, shall produce an intellectual and social cohesion, at least among large groups of students, and points of contact among them all. This task is not confined to any one college, although more urgent in the case of those that have grown the largest and have been moving most rapidly. A number of colleges are feeling their way toward a more definite structure, and since the problem before them is in many cases essentially the same, it is fortunate that they are assisting one another by approaching it from somewhat different directions. What I have to say upon the subject here is, therefore, intended mainly for the conditions we are called upon to face at Harvard.

It is worth our while to consider the nature of an ideal college as an integral part of our University; ideal, in the sense not of something to be exactly reproduced, but of a type to which we should conform as closely as circumstances will permit. It would contemplate the highest development of the individual student — which involves the best equipment of the graduate. It would contemplate also the proper connection of the college with the professional schools; and it would adjust the relation of the students to one another. Let me take up these matters briefly in their order.

The individual student ought clearly to be developed so far as possible, both in his strong and in his weak points, for the college ought to produce, not defective specialists, but men intellectually well rounded, of wide sympathies and unfettered judgment. At the same time they ought to be trained to hard and accurate thought, and this will not come merely by surveying the elementary principles of many subjects. It requires a mastery of something, acquired by continuous application. Every student ought to know in some subject what the ultimate sources of opinion are, and how they are handled by those who profess it. Only in this way is he likely to gain the solidity of thought that begets sound thinking. In short, he ought, so far as in him lies, to be both broad and profound.

In speaking of the training of the student, or the equipment of the graduate, we are prone to think of the knowledge acquired; but are we not inclined to lay too much stress upon knowledge alone? Taken by itself it is a part, and not the most vital part, of education. Surely the essence of a liberal education consists in an attitude of mind, a familiarity with methods of thought, an ability to use information rather than in a memory stocked with facts, however valuable such a storehouse may be. In his farewell address to the alumni of Dartmouth, President Tucker remarked that "the college is in the educational system to represent the spirit of amateur scholarship. College students are amateurs, not professionals." Or, as President Hadley is fond of putting it: "The ideal college education seems to me to be one where a student learns things that he is not going to use in after life, by methods that he is going to use. The former element gives the breadth, the latter element gives the training." [1]

But if this be true, no method of ascertaining truth, and therefore no department of human thought, ought to be wholly a sealed book to an educated man. It has been truly said that few men are capable of learning a new subject after the period of youth has passed, and hence the graduate ought to be so equipped that he can grasp effectively any problem with which his duties or his interest may impel him to deal. An undergraduate, addicted mainly to the classics, recently spoke to his adviser in an apologetic tone of having elected a course in natural science, which he feared was narrowing. Such a state of mind is certainly deplorable, for in the present age some knowledge of the laws of nature is an essential part of the mental outfit which no cultivated man should lack. He need not know much, but he ought to know enough to learn more. To him the forces of nature ought not to be an occult mystery, but a chain of causes and effects with which, if not wholly familiar, he can at least claim acquaintance; and the same principle applies to every other leading branch of knowledge.

I speak of the equipment, rather than the education, of a college graduate, because, as we are often reminded, his education ought to cease only with his life, and hence his equipment ought to lay a strong foundation for that education. It ought to teach him what it means to master a subject, and it ought to enable him to seize and retain information of every kind from that unending stream that flows past every man who has the eyes to see it. Moreover, it ought to be such that he will be capable of turning his mind effectively to direct preparation for his lifework, whatever the profession or occupation he may select.

This brings us to the relation of the college to the professional school. If every college graduate ought to be equipped to enter any professional school, as the *Abiturient* of a Ger-

[1] *Annual Report*, 1909, p. 22.

man *Gymnasium* is qualified to study under any of the faculties of the university, then it would seem that the professional
schools ought to be so ordered that they are adapted to receive him. But let us not be dogmatic in this matter, for it is
one on which great divergence of opinion exists. The instructors in the various professional schools are by no means of
one mind in regard to it, and their views are of course based
largely upon experience. Our Law School lays great stress
upon native ability and scholarly aptitude, and comparatively little upon the particular branches of learning a student has pursued in college. Any young man who has brains
and has learned to use them can master the law, whatever his
intellectual interests may have been; and the same thing is
true of the curriculum in the Divinity School. Many professors of medicine, on the other hand, feel strongly that a
student should enter their school with at least a rudimentary
knowledge of those sciences, like chemistry, biology, and
physiology, which are interwoven with medical studies; and
they appear to attach greater weight to this than to his
natural capacity or general attainments. Now that we have
established graduate schools of engineering and business administration, we must examine this question carefully in the
immediate future. If the college courses are strictly untech-
nical, the requirement of a small number of electives in certain
subjects, as a condition for entering a graduate professional
school, is not inconsistent with a liberal education. But I will
acknowledge a prejudice that for a man who is destined to
reach the top of his profession a broad education, and a firm
grasp of some subject lying outside of his vocation, is a vast
advantage; and we must not forget that in substantially con-
fining the professional schools at Harvard to college graduates
we are aiming at the higher strata in the professions.

The last of the aspects under which I proposed to consider
the college is that of the relation of undergraduates to one
another; and first on the intellectual side. We have heard
much of the benefit obtained merely by breathing the college

atmosphere, or rubbing against the college walls. I fear the walls about us have little of the virtue of Aladdin's lamp when rubbed. What we mean is that daily association with other young men whose minds are alert is in itself a large part of a liberal education. But to what extent do undergraduates talk over things intellectual, and especially matters brought before them by their courses of study? It is the ambition of every earnest teacher so to stimulate his pupils that they will discuss outside the classroom the problems he has presented to them. The students in the Law School talk law interminably. They take a fierce pleasure in debating legal points in season and out. This is not wholly with a prospect of bread and butter in the years to come; nor because law is intrinsically more interesting than other things. Much must no doubt be ascribed to the skill of the faculty of the Law School in awakening a keen competitive delight in solving legal problems; but there is also the vital fact that all these young men are tilling the same field. They have their stock of knowledge in common. Seeds cast by one of them fall into a congenial soil, and like dragon's teeth engender an immediate combat.

Now no sensible man would propose today to set up a fixed curriculum in order that all undergraduates might be joint tenants of the same scholastic property; but the intellectual estrangement need not be so wide as it is. There is no greater pleasure in mature life than hearing a specialist talk, if one has knowledge enough of the subject to understand him, and that is one of the things an educated man ought so far as possible to possess. Might there not be more points of intellectual contact among the undergraduates, and might not considerable numbers of them have much in common?

A discussion of the ideal college training from these three different aspects, the highest development of the individual student, the proper relation of the college to the professional school, and the relation of the students to one another, would appear to lead in each case to the same conclusion: that the best type of liberal education in our complex modern world aims at producing men who know a little of everything and something well. Nor, if this be taken in a rational, rather than an extreme, sense, is it impossible to achieve within the limits of college life. That a student of ability can learn one subject well is shown by the experience of Oxford and Cambridge. The educational problems arising from the extension of human knowledge are not confined to this country; and our institutions of higher learning were not the first to seek a solution for them in some form of election on the part of the student. It is almost exactly a hundred years ago that the English universities began to award honors upon examination in special subjects; for although the mathematical tripos at Cambridge was instituted sixty years earlier, the modern system of honor schools, which has stimulated a vast amount of competitive activity among undergraduates, may be said to date from the establishment of the examinations in *Literis Humanioribus* and in mathematics and physics at Oxford in 1807. The most popular of the subjects in which honors are awarded are not technical, that is, they are not intended primarily as part of a professional training; nor are they narrow in their scope; but they are in general confined to one field. In short they are designed to ensure that the candidate knows something well; that he has worked hard and intelligently on one subject until he has a substantial grounding in it.

For us this alone would not be enough, because our preparatory schools do not give the same training as the English, and because the whole structure of English society is very different from ours. American college students ought also to study a little of everything, for if not there is no certainty that they will be broadly cultivated, especially in view of the omnipresent impulse in the community driving them to devote their chief attention to the subjects bearing upon their future career. The wise policy for them would appear to be that of devoting a considerable portion of their time to some one subject, and taking in addition a number of general courses in wholly unrelated fields. But instruction that imparts a little knowledge of everything is more difficult to provide well than any other. To furnish it there ought to be in every considerable field a general course, designed to give to' men who do not intend to pursue the subject further a comprehension of its underlying principles or methods of thought; and this is by no means the same thing as an introductory course, although the two can often be effectively combined. A serious obstacle lies in the fact that many professors, who have reaped fame, prefer to teach advanced courses, and recoil from elementary instruction — an aversion inherited from the time when scholars of international reputation were called upon to waste their powers on the drudgery of drilling beginners. But while nothing can ever take the place of the great teacher, it is nevertheless true that almost any man possessed of the requisite knowledge can at least impart it to students who have already made notable progress in the subject; whereas effective instruction in fundamental principles requires men of mature minds who can see the forest over the tops of the trees. It demands unusual clearness of thought, force of statement, and enthusiasm of expression. These qualities have no necessary connection with creative imagination, but they are more common among men who have achieved some measure of success; and what is not less to the point, the students ascribe them more readily to a man whose position is recognized, than to a young instructor who has not yet won his spurs. Wherever possible, therefore, the general course ought to be under the charge of one of the leading men in the department, and his teaching ought to be supplemented by instruction, discussion, and constant examination in smaller groups, conducted by younger men well equipped for their work. Such a policy brings the student, at the gateway of a subject, into contact with strong and ripe minds, while it saves the professor from needless drudgery. It has been pursued at Harvard for a number of years, but it can be carried out even more completely.

We have considered the intellectual relation of the students to one another and its bearing on the curriculum, but that is not the only side of college life. The social relations of the undergraduate among themselves are quite as important; and here again we may observe forces at work which tend to break up the old college solidarity. The boy comes here sometimes from a large school, with many friends, sometimes from a great distance and almost alone. He is plunged at once into a life wholly strange to him, amid a crowd so large that he cannot claim acquaintance with its members. Unless endowed with an uncommon temperament, he is liable to fall into a clique of associates with antecedents and characteristics similar to his own; or perhaps, if shy and unknown, he fails to make friends at all; and in either case he misses the broadening influence of contact with a great variety of other young men. Under such conditions the college itself comes short of its national mission of throwing together youths of promise of every kind from every part of the country. It will, no doubt, be argued that a university must reflect the state of the world about it; and that the tendency of the times is toward specialization of functions, and social segregation on the basis of wealth. But this is not wholly true, because there is happily in the country a tendency also toward social solidarity and social service. A still more conclusive answer is that one object of a university is to counteract rather than copy the defects in the civilization of the day. Would a prevalence of spoils, favoritism, or corruption in the politics of the country be a reason for their adoption by universities?

A large college ought to give its students a wide horizon, and it fails therein unless it mixes them together so thoroughly that the friendships they form are based on natural affinities, rather than similarity of origin. Now these ties are formed most rapidly at the threshold of college life, and the set in which a man shall move is mainly determined in his Freshman year. It is obviously desirable, therefore, that the Freshmen should be thrown together more than they are now.

Moreover the change from the life of school to that of college is too abrupt at the present day. Taken gradually, liberty is a powerful stimulant; but taken suddenly in large doses, it is liable to act as an intoxicant or an opiate. No doubt every boy ought to learn to paddle his own canoe; but we do not begin the process by tossing him into a canoe, and setting him adrift in deep water, with a caution that he would do well to look for the paddle. Many a well-intentioned youth comes to college, enjoys innocently enough the pleasures of freedom for a season, but released from the discipline to which he has been accustomed, and looking on the examinations as remote, falls into indolent habits. Presently he finds himself on probation for neglect of his studies. He has become submerged, and has a hard, perhaps unsuccessful, struggle to get his head above water. Of late years we have improved the diligence of Freshmen by frequent tests; but this alone is not enough. In his luminous Phi Beta Kappa oration, delivered here three months ago, President Wilson dwelt upon the chasm that has opened between college studies and college life. The instructors believe that the object of the college is study, many students fancy that it is mainly enjoyment, and the confusion of aims breeds irretrievable waste of opportunity. The undergraduate should be led to feel from the moment of his arrival that college life is a serious and manysided thing, whereof mental discipline is a vital part.

It would seem that all these difficulties could be much lessened if the Freshmen were brought together in a group of dormitories and dining-halls, under the comradeship of older men, who appreciated the possibilities of a college life, and took a keen interest in their work and their pleasures. Such a plan would enable us also to recruit our students younger, for the present age of entrance here appears to be due less to the difficulty of preparing for the examination earlier, than to the nature of the life the Freshman leads. Complaints of the age of graduation cause a pressure to reduce the length of the college course, and with it the standard of the college degree. There would seem to be no intrinsic reason that our school boys should be more backward than those of other civilized countries, any more than that our undergraduates should esteem excellence in scholarship less highly than do the men in English universities.

The last point is one that requires a word of comment, because it touches the most painful defect in the American college at the present time. President Pritchett has declared that "it is a serious indictment of the standards of any organization when the conditions within it are such that success in the things for which the organization stands no longer appeal effectively to the imaginations of those in it." [1] We may add that, even in these days, indictment is sometimes followed by sentence and execution. No one will deny that in our colleges high scholarship is little admired now, either by the undergraduates or by the public. We do not make our students enjoy the sense of power that flows from mastery of a difficult subject, and on a higher plane we do not make them feel the romance of scholarly discovery. Every one follows the travels of a Columbus or a Livingston with a keen delight which researches in chemistry or biology rarely stir. The mass of mankind can, no doubt, comprehend more readily geographical than scientific discovery, but for the explorer himself it would be pitiful if the joy of the search depended on the number of spectators, rather than on zeal in his quest.

America has not yet contributed her share to scholarly creation, and the fault lies in part at the doors of our universities. They do not strive enough in the impressionable years of early manhood to stimulate intellectual appetite and ambition; nor do they foster productive scholarship enough among those members of their staffs who are capable thereof. Too often a professor of original power explains to docile pupils the process of mining intellectual gold, without seeking nuggets himself, or when found showing them to mankind.

---

[1] "The College of Freedom and the College of Discipline," *Atlantic Monthly*, November, 1908, p. 609.

Productive scholarship is the shyest of all flowers. It cometh not with observation, and may not bloom even under the most careful nurture. American universities must do their utmost to cultivate it; by planting the best seed, letting the sun shine upon it, and taking care that in our land of rank growth it is not choked by the thorns of administrative routine.

If I have dwelt upon only a small part of the problems of the university; if I have said nothing of the professional and graduate schools, of the Library, the Observatory, the laboratories, the museums, the gardens, and the various forms of extension work, it is not because they are of less importance, but because the time is too short to take up more than two or three pressing questions of general interest. The university touches the community at many points, and as time goes on it ought to serve the public through ever increasing channels. But all its activities are more or less connected with, and most of them are based upon, the college. It is there that character ought to be shaped, that aspirations ought to be formed, that citizens ought to be trained, and scholarly tastes implanted. If the mass of undergraduates could be brought to respect, nay, to admire, intellectual achievement on the part of their comrades, in at all the measure that they do athletic victory; if those among them of natural ability could be led to put forth their strength on the objects which the college is supposed to represent; the professional schools would find their tasks lightened, and their success enhanced. A greater solidarity in college, more earnestness of purpose and intellectual enthusiasm, would mean much for our nation. It is said that if the temperature of the ocean were raised, the water would expand until the floods covered the dry land; and if we can increase the intellectual ambition of college students, the whole face of our country will be changed. When the young men shall see visions, the dreams of old men will come true.

COMPETITION IN COLLEGE

Address at the Columbia Chapter of Φ. B. K., June 1, 1909

Reprinted from the Atlantic Monthly, June, 1909

WE ARE TOLD with wearisome reiteration, until it vexes us even as a thing that is raw, that America produces few great scholars who are pioneers in the domain of thought; that in exploiting a continent we have been too busy to explore the mysteries of natural science or the mind of man. So far as this charge is true, and we cannot deny that it has some foundation, it is commonly ascribed to our rapid industrial development, with the consequent attractiveness of material pursuits which draw our most promising youth away from the paths of learning. But must not our schools, and above all our universities and colleges, take their share of blame? It is our privilege to magnify the importance of education, but in doing so we must assume responsibility, not only for the benefits conferred thereby, but also for any evils that may flow from errors committed.

Education has many sides and many functions; otherwise it would not be the fascinating pursuit that it is. Both in discussion and in practice, we take account of imparting knowledge, and of training the mind; but in our zeal for these essential matters we seem, perhaps, to have neglected a not less important function, that of sifting out the minds capable of great intellectual achievement. Is it not possible, in short, that we have paid attention too exclusively to teaching, and too little to recruiting young men of the highest promise? This ought we to have done, and not to leave the other undone, for both are needed in keeping educational work at a high level. Every one who has had personal experience in a university must be aware that the standard maintained is due quite as much to the calibre of the students as to that of the instructors. The success of our law schools, for example, must be attributed not only to the capacity of the professors, and to the direct effect of their method of teaching, but in no less degree to the fact that these schools attract the most ambitious and vigorous college graduates.

Vast as the improvement in educational methods has been, it is not clear that the process of sifting is as effective as it used to be. The old classical school, with its rigid curriculum, was inelastic, unadaptable to individual needs, and is said to have been repellent and dulling to the ordinary child; but none the less it seems to have sorted out the boys with intellectual aptitudes and steered them toward higher education. The same thing was probably true of the old-fashioned college. The minimum, and indeed the average, amount of study has risen very much since those days. No doubt the ordinary student was more indolent then, and acquired less mental training, but it may be doubted whether there is now so great an incentive to superiority in scholarship. If that be true, our colleges are not performing so well as they did in the past the function of intellectual selection.

But have we not a new institution created to supply that very need? The Graduate Schools in our universities, that consummate product of the last thirty years, are designed to be real nurseries of scholars. They were surely intended to recruit the intellectual flower of the youth, fitting them to be leaders and teachers of the next generation; and when Johns Hopkins opened its doors it became a mecca for young men who aspired to high places among the learned. Since that time Graduate Schools have multiplied, their students have increased beyond expectation, and with their growth in popularity they have "faded into the light of common day." They certainly contain men of the finest type, but the bulk of their students are not of first-rate quality, and much of the instruction consists in burnishing rather soft metal. In the best of them the standard is very high so far as training and knowledge are concerned; quite as high, perhaps, as is wise, for it cannot be raised indefinitely without risk to one of the functions performed by these schools. They are, in fact, attempting to serve two objects, which are not necessarily identical in America: the education of productive scholars and of teachers; and there is some danger that in the process one or both of these objects may suffer.

The Graduate Schools of our universities contain in the aggregate some six thousand students, all preparing themselves, according to the popular impression, to be great scholars. But with any such conception the figures are monstrous. If we could turn out a score of men a year with any serious chance of eminence we should do well. The great bulk of the students have no delusions of this nature. All but a few of them are being trained to teach; to diffuse knowledge, not to add to it; to be live wires, not to be dynamos. We talk of their all doing research work, but that term covers a multitude of operations. The original thesis they are required to present for a degree proves that a student can handle original material, not that he can construct with it anything really new; it shows a familiarity with the sources of knowledge, but it does not show capacity for productive scholarship.

Our method of attracting students to the Graduate Schools is defective. If you want to generate energy you must have a resistance to be overcome. If you desire to recruit men of force and ambition, there must be a great prize to be won by facing an obstacle, just as, when you want to recruit strong characters, you must call for sacrifice. In our Graduate Schools we pursue to some extent a contrary policy, for we subsidize men freely with scholarships. By so doing we are in danger of making the Graduate School the easiest path for the good but docile scholar with little energy, independence, or ambition. There is danger of attracting an industrious mediocrity, which will become later the teaching force in colleges and secondary schools. Such a policy is due in part to a feeling that a large number of students is needed to justify the expenses of our graduate instruction; and in part to a less laudable spirit of intercollegiate rivalry. A long list of graduate students is regarded as a proof that a university is fruitful in its highest work of training the great scholars of the future, but unfortunately mere numbers prove nothing of the kind. Yet the popular assumption is not unnatural, because it is hard even for men engaged in education, and it is impossible for the general public, to distinguish between quality and quantity in an institution with which they are not thoroughly familiar.

While, therefore, the instruction in our Graduate Schools is admirable, our success in recruiting for them students of the strongest intellectual fibre is by no means so great. This is the vital point, for although eaglets are raised best in an eagle's nest, yet there is a better chance of producing them by setting eagle's eggs under a hen, than hen's eggs under an eagle. But how are the eagle's eggs to be collected? How are young men of intellectual power to be drawn into the Graduate School? My answer is that young men must be attracted to the pursuit of scholarship while undergraduates in college, and success in doing this depends upon the extent to which intellectual appetite and ambition are stirred there. It depends, moreover, not only upon the intensity with which a few men are stirred, but also upon the diffusion of that attitude among the mass of undergraduates.

The intellectual feast spread by the Graduate Schools does little, therefore, to create an appetite for learning. It feeds hungry scholars, but it does not make them. Craving for scholarship must be formed in college, and is deeply affected by the general atmosphere there. Important as this is for the recruiting of great scholars, it is of not less consequence in giving an intellectual tone to all the alumni wherever their paths in life may lead; but from that point of view the present situation is far from perfect.

It is safe to say that no member of a faculty is satisfied with the respect in which scholarship is held by the great body of college students today. Every one complains in his heart, although in public he is apt to declare that the conditions in his own college are better than they are elsewhere. In fact, we know little enough about the state of affairs in our own institutions, and are quite in the dark when we presume to draw comparisons with other places. This is a case where measuring ourselves by ourselves, and comparing ourselves among ourselves, is not wise. In spite of divergencies in detail, the problem is essentially the same everywhere, and any college that helps to solve it will confer a benefit upon the whole country. Nor is it enough if we are better than our fathers were, if the average amount of study in college is greater, and the minimum much greater, than it was. In the community at large the general activity has increased prodigiously; even elegant indolence is by no means so fashionable as it used to be. Our colleges ought, in a movement of this kind, to set the pace, not follow it; and they must not rest satisfied until they create among their students a high standard of achievement.

When the elective system was first introduced, its advocates believed that it would have a powerful selective influence, by offering to each student ampler opportunity for self-development in the branches of learning that he might prefer. The opponents of the system did not deny this, but complained that the undergraduate was not capable of judging what was best for him, and that to follow his own bent would lead to a one-sided development. In the plans of men, the indirect, and therefore unforeseen, consequences are often more important than those which form the subject of discussion. The elective system — which has to a greater or less extent penetrated almost all our colleges — did, indeed, furnish an opportunity for self-development; but at the same time it weakened the stimulus to exertion. It was based upon the assumption that opportunity alone is enough, that a man will put forth his utmost powers if he can do so in a congenial field. Yet this is by no means true, even in the case of the highest genius. Many a man of talent has worked only from the stress of poverty, groaning all the time at his hard fate. Shakespeare himself did much of his writing under the pressure of finishing plays for the stage; and the difficulty of keeping artists and literary men up to time is notorious, — a difficulty not wholly due to the fitful inspiration of the muse.

If opportunity alone were enough, hereditary wealth, which vastly enlarges opportunity, ought to increase intellectual productiveness. There ought to be no place "where wealth accumulates and men decay." But there is too much truth in the common belief that abundant means usually lessens the output of creative work; and even Shakespeare, when rich enough to retire as a country gentleman, wrote no more. The mere opportunity for self-development, and for the free exercise of one's faculties, the mere desire for self-expression, are not enough with most men to bring out all their latent powers. This is because in civilized life we are seeking to foster an activity far above the normal; we are striving to evoke a mental energy much greater than that required for a bare subsistence, and unless education can effect this it is a failure. In addition to opportunity, there must be a stimulus of some kind.

Under the old rigid curriculum the stimulus was supplied in part by competition. Since all the students were following the same course they were naturally ranked by their marks, and there was no little emulation among the more ambitious ones. Rivalry, with its component elements, the desire to win and the still stronger desire not to be beaten, is a pervasive sentiment in human nature, often most prominent when the object itself is least worth striving for. It is constantly shown in trivial things, from the school-boy who quickens his pace when a stranger walks faster than he, to the countryman who hates to have his horse passed on the road. The intensity of the emulation depends, in fact, far less upon the value of the end to be attained than upon the ease with which the chances of the contestants are compared; provided, of course, they are nearly enough matched to make the result uncertain. A race where the participants run side by side on the same track is obviously more exciting than one in which they start at considerable intervals, or run over different roads out of sight of one another. That is the chief reason why an athletic contest, or a physical struggle of any kind, is more interesting than almost any other competition. The sport is visible, its progress can be easily watched, and the varying chances of the players are readily compared. The world does not really believe that athletic success is the most desirable form of achievement on earth, and yet men tend to transfer a part of their emotions from the contest itself to its results. Thirty thousand people cannot go to a football game, and become greatly excited over it, without being convinced that the victory is in itself a highly important matter. Thus competition provokes rivalry, intense rivalry gives rise to a keen interest, and this in turn enhances the apparent value of the object for which the contest is waged. It is one of many instances where a state of mind is produced by stimulating the secondary emotions to which it naturally gives birth.

But the free elective system in college has reduced the spirit of competition in scholarship to a minimum. Perhaps no two men are taking precisely the same series of courses, and hence their achievements are incommensurate. Like the Caucus Race in *Alice in Wonderland*, every one begins and ends where he pleases, save that he must take at least a certain number of courses; and, as on that famous occasion, little interest is taken in the distribution of prizes. But it is the fashion to say that young men of college age ought not to work for prizes, or rank. This, we are told, is a low motive; and a man ought to study for the knowledge, the training, and the culture he acquires. In short, he ought not to need the spur of competition, or any other external stimulus, because it ought to be enough for him that his future welfare is in his own hands, and his own best interests ought to guide him in the way he should go. But such an assumption leads to a rather startling conclusion; for if the ordinary undergraduate can be trusted to act most wisely of his own accord, if his natural impulses are correct, then his attitude toward

his studies is what it should be. If he has less respect for
scholarship than one might wish, nevertheless under this
assumption he is right, while we who disagree with him must
be wrong.

It may be that the need of competition or other stimulus to
exertion among undergraduates depends upon the position
which the college occupies in the general scheme of education,
and upon the intricate functions of play and work in building
up the faculties of mind and body. If so, it may be worth
while to consider these questions briefly.

Of late years we have been taught much about the value of
play in the development both of animals and of man; and for
that purpose the word is commonly used to denote those acts
which are performed for mere pleasure without any other
serious motive.[1] Now I am perfectly aware of the iniquity of
employing a technical term in an unusual sense; and yet on
this occasion I propose, contrary to usage, to define play as
any action of which the physiological object is a development
of the powers of the actor, as distinguished from the accomplishment of a result in itself useful, or the acquisition of the
means for reaching such a result. This seems a more apt definition in connection with education, because thereby attention is fixed on the physiological and educational object, not
on the personal motive of the actor. To illustrate what is
meant, let us look at the case of the over-studious boy, who
is compelled to coast or ride when he does not want to do so,
and does not enjoy it. We say that he is obliged to play, but
that is a contradiction in terms if play means only things done
for pleasure. Again, if pleasure is the criterion, and a student
takes, because he enjoys it, an additional course beyond the
number required by the curriculum, it must be classed for
him as play; while for the student next him, who is taking
only the prescribed number of courses, it is not play. If, on
the other hand, he is a member of an athletic team, not for

---

[1] For example, Karl Groos's *The Play of Man*, translated by Elizabeth L.
Baldwin.

the mere fun of it, but because he thinks it good for him, or because he hopes that he can help his college to win the game, then again it is not play; and as we shall see hereafter, a large part of the physical sports of youth are in fact pursued from motives other than mere pleasure.

A pursuit, then, which is followed, whether voluntarily or by compulsion, because it tends to develop the mind or body, is play; while one that is followed for the sake of gain, or because it supplies the manual skill or technical knowledge needed to earn bread, is not play. The application of the definition to studies is clearly shown in the varying relations between general education and professional training. In American schools for engineers it has been common to intersperse a certain amount of general education among the technical courses. But in the schools of divinity, law, and medicine it has been the tradition to confine the teaching to strictly professional matters. Conversely, the American college of the older type was devoted entirely to studies that were deemed to be of general educational value, without having any direct professional bearing. So far as this object has been retained, and for the most part it still holds its ground, the college may be regarded as the last period of play. Do not misunderstand me. By play I do not mean anything trivial, unessential, or even necessarily pleasurable. I refer to pursuits which develop the mental, physical, and moral powers, as distinguished from the acquisition of directly profitable attainments. While any one may quarrel with this use of the word "play," the thing itself is intensely serious. It is the chief occupation of the most formative part of life, and should therefore be taken in a spirit of earnest determination.

For class-room purposes this is, no doubt, the well-worn distinction between liberal or cultural studies on one side, and professional or vocational ones on the other; but it is wider, inasmuch as it includes outdoor sports, and that is the reason I use it. The object, for example, of athletics in college is physical development; yet if a member of a baseball nine were paid for his services, or if he joined it in order to fit himself to become a professional hereafter, for him it would not be play. Now, I believe that there is a close analogy between outdoor sports and those indoor studies which are pursued for intellectual development, especially in regard to the question of stimulus by competition.

According to the usual definition of play, as an action in itself pleasurable and pursued from that motive alone, any other stimulus is obviously unnecessary. But after early infancy that is not quite true of what we commonly understand by play. With very young children mere delight in exercising nascent faculties may be enough to provoke all the activity needed to develop those faculties, but that condition is soon outgrown. With most animals, indeed, the struggle for existence begins so early that the development by play covers only a brief time of rapid growth in which pleasure may be a sufficient incentive. Man, however, goes through a long period of adolescence before he is self-supporting, and with the progress of civilization it seems destined to become longer and longer, at least for pursuits that require intellectual labor. During a very small part of this period can we trust to the propelling force of enjoyment alone, even for the training of the physical powers. The mere pleasure of exercise soon ceases to suffice, because muscular strength and nervous and moral force can be brought to a high point only by strenuous exertion that surpasses the bounds of strict physical enjoyment. To make the most of himself the boy must be induced to put forth an uncomfortable effort, and for this he must have an external stimulus of some kind. No one who knows much about intercollegiate football believes that most of the men are on the team chiefly because the game itself is pleasurable; and, in fact, other motives than immediate pleasure enter largely into all violent competitive sports after an early period of childhood. It is safe to assert that if young people took part in games only so far as they enjoyed the exercise, without being affected by ambition or the opinion of their fellows, a large portion of the more strenuous sports, and therewith much valuable training, physical and moral, would be lost.

The stimulus needed is usually found in competition; and, in fact, the object of throwing a boy into contact with others of his own age is not only to train his social instincts but also to bring him into rivalry with his mates, to make him play with them games which test his powers, and stimulate him to use them to the full. Within the range of their immediate interests, young people are good practical psychologists, from whom we have still much to learn by studying the way they organize their sports to provoke exertion or select superior capacity; and it may be observed that competition in sport becomes more intense as maturity is approached. No doubt competition is often carried too far, until it has the effect of eliminating from the arena all but a few champions of pre-eminent qualities. In his *Social Life in Greece*, Professor Mahaffy pointed out the advantage to the community of the field sports of Sparta, in which every one of ordinary strength could engage, as compared with the gymnastic games of Athens, where only remarkable athletes took part and the rest of the young men looked on. Athletic sports in our colleges involve the same danger, by tending to accentuate the selective principle at the expense of the physical improvement of the whole body of students. But the fact that competition may be carried farther than is wise does not prove that it is not valuable as a stimulus, that it is not indeed the main factor in the physical development of youth.

There is certainly no less need for an effective stimulus in scholarly than in physical training, but it is far more difficult to use, because we cannot at present rely on the same constant enthusiasm on the part of the young people themselves. In the professional schools this matter is in a satisfactory state today. Fifty years ago there appears to have been no little apathy about study in these schools, but they have now succeeded generally in convincing their students that excellence in the work of the school has great importance, both as an equipment for their coming career, and as an indication of future success. In some cases competition is indeed used with marked effect, but it is not indispensable, because the student has the powerful incentive of feeling that he has begun his life's work, in which his prospects depend upon his diligence. The schools for engineers where general and technical subjects are taught side by side bring into sharp contrast the strong professional motive and the feebler desire for self-improvement. It is difficult there to make the ordinary student realize the value of a cultural course. He is apt to regard it as something foreign to his regular work; something very well in its way, but not essential to success in his future career. He labors without a groan on mathematics, which most college undergraduates shun like a pestilence, while he treats English literature or the history of his country lightly, as a pleasant enough accomplishment hardly worthy of strenuous effort.

At the other end of the educational ladder, also, in the preparatory school, competition, although highly useful, is not indispensable. The boy is subject to discipline, accustomed to obey, and much influenced by the precepts and wishes of his parents and teachers. If a good boy, he tries to do well, and being under constant supervision he tends to conform to the expectations of those about him. The serious difficulty begins in college, where he is plunged into a far wider liberty — a freedom that brings vast opportunities, intellectual and moral, by which he may rise, but which on the other hand he may abuse. The old schoolboy motives for hard study he has left behind; the professional ones are not yet in sight; and it is not easy to make him appreciate the seriousness of the education within his reach. To some extent he believes that it is good for him, and he intends to obtain a real advantage from it. In most cases he is not satisfied by getting through with the least possible exertion. He means to do reasonably well, but he has no idea of the benefit to be derived from striving for excellence. In short, he has a fair but not a high standard.

Now, there is no grave difficulty in enforcing a fair amount of work; and of late years our colleges have wisely turned their attention to the matter, making the minimum requirements distinctly more severe than they were. We can, in fact, raise the minimum for a degree to any level that we may desire, provided we recognize frankly what that level implies. Suppose, for example, that the dullest tenth of the students who enter college ought not to graduate, no matter how faithfully they toil; then the line will be drawn at such a point that the dullest man above that tenth can get through if he devotes to study as many hours as a young man of ordinary health can properly spend over his books. But, in that case, a brighter man will need less effort to reach the same result; and, as differences in natural ability are very great, a student who stands in capacity among the more talented half of his class can get through with very little work. On the other hand, we could so draw the line that only the brighter half of the class could graduate at all; and in that case we should have, like the German universities, a large mass of students who had no intention of taking a degree, but who could hardly be refused the privilege of living about the college as special students so long as they were well behaved.

We can, therefore, set the minimum where we please — a minimum, however, in which the amount of work required is in inverse proportion to natural ability — but we cannot by that process compel a clever student to be industrious. We can set a minimum of capacity, and establish a ratio between brains and labor, but we cannot thereby set up a high standard for men of ability. For that purpose we need something more than a minimum requirement, and this brings us to our really difficult problem, that of applying a stimulus.

College work may affect the fortunes of a lifetime more profoundly than the studies either of boyhood or of the professional school, but the ordinary student does not know it.

The connection is too vague, too subtle, for him to see; it rests on intangible principles, the force of which he does not feel. It is in college, therefore, that an external stimulus is most needed; yet college is the very place where it is found the least. The result is that a fellow who ranks high in school, and works like a tiger when he studies his profession, is too often quite satisfied with mediocrity in college. The disintegration of the curriculum caused by the elective system in any of its common forms, the disdain of rank as a subject for ambition — encouraged by students, by the public, and sometimes even by instructors — and other forces that have crept in unawares, have brought us to a point where competition as a stimulus for scholarship has been well nigh driven from the college. Again, I must ask you not to misunderstand me when I speak of the elective system. No sane man would propose to restore anything resembling a fixed curriculum in any of our larger colleges. We must not go backward, we could not if we would; but neither must we believe that progress consists in standing still. We must go forward, and our path must be such that a choice of electives shall not lessen, among those capable of it, the stimulus to excellence.

Now, there is no reason to suppose that young men have by nature a stronger desire for physical than for intellectual power, or a greater admiration for it; yet, largely by the free use of competition, athletics, in the esteem both of undergraduates and of the community at large, has beaten scholarship out of sight. The world today has a far higher regard for Newton, Locke, and Molière than for Augustus the Strong; but in our colleges "the physically strong," as Carlyle called Augustus, would attract much more attention. I am not one of those who condemn athletic contests, for I do not think we can afford to diminish any spur to activity in college, but I am convinced that we ought to stimulate other forms of energy, and that we can get many a hint from athletic experience. The production of true scholars, or even of the scholarly tone of mind, is not the only object of the college. It aims to produce men well developed in all directions, and it has many agencies for doing so outside the class-room; but it cannot exist for these alone, and if it fails on the scholarly side it will be irrevocably doomed.

One hundred years ago the English universities awoke to behold the low state of scholarship among their students. It boots nothing to inquire how it compared with the worst that has ever existed here, but it was bad enough. They met it by a frank resort to competition. First in one subject, and then in another, they established a degree with honors awarded in several grades, and they succeeded in making the honors, not only a goal of ambition, but, what is more, an object of general respect. They gave prizes, too, still eagerly sought; and, in short, the stimulus to scholarship rests on an elaborate system of competition for prizes and honors. Of course, there are voices raised against it, protesting that the muses ought to be wooed for worthier motives; but it is our province to make the most of men as they are, not to protest that they ought to have an innate love of learning. The problem of human nature, the question whether we could have made it better if we had presided at creation, is too large to discuss here.

The fact remains that the Oxford and Cambridge men are firmly persuaded that success at the bar, in public life, and in other fields is closely connected with high honors at graduation; and the contest for them is correspondingly keen. The prizes and honors are made widely known; they are remembered throughout a man's life, referred to even in brief notices of him — much as his athletic feats are here — and they certainly do help him powerfully to get a start in his career. The result is that, by the Isis and the Cam, there is probably more hard study done in subjects not of a professional character than in any other universities in the world. What defects the system may possess, its strength and its weakness in other directions, need not detain us. The structure of English society, on which the old universities are built, is very different from ours; yet there are qualities in human nature that are common to all mankind, and without copying an institution we may, by observing it, find the secret of its success. Although we do not follow, we may learn.

Competition as an effective stimulus to scholarship in our colleges suffers today from a widespread feeling among the students that the distinctions won are a test of industry rather than of superior intellectual power. This conviction finds its expression in the term "grind," which is applied with great impartiality to all high scholars, instead of being reserved, as it seems to me it was formerly, to a certain kind of laborious mediocrity. The general use of the word is certainly unjust, for statistics show that, as compared with other men, the high scholars win a far larger share of distinction in the professional schools and in after life. But the feeling contains a grain of truth. In our desire to ensure from every student a fair amount of work, we are too apt to use tests that measure mere diligence, with the result that high rank in college is no sure measure of real ability. This has been to a great extent avoided in England by distinct honor and pass examinations, the questions in the former being of such a nature that industry alone cannot, it is believed, attain the highest grade; and this is an important matter if high rank is to command admiration. It is surely possible to devise tests which will measure any qualities that we desire to emphasize; but do we not touch here upon one of many indications that we have lost the key to the true meaning of the college? The primary object of the professional schools is knowledge, a command of the tools of the trade, and a facility in handling them; while in college the primary object is intellectual power, and a knowledge of facts or principles is the material on which the mind can exercise its force, rather than an end in itself. If we could make the world believe that high rank is a proof of intellectual power, our task in instilling among undergraduates a desire to excel would be simple.

The difficulty in stimulating scholarly ambition is enhanced by a new, and on the whole a higher, moral tone among college men. The philosophers of a century ago preached the harmony of interests both in politics and economics. They taught that, in seeking his own highest good, a man promoted that of all the world; and they looked forward to a millennium based on universal self-interest. With the waning of this creed, a more altruistic spirit has replaced the extreme individualism of our fathers; and, as usual, the new tendencies are particularly strong in the rising generation. In 'college, the upperclassmen feel a responsibility for the welfare of the younger students, and look after them, to an extent that would have been regarded as extraordinary, if not indeed meddlesome, half a century ago.

The sense of mutual obligation, and with it the corporate spirit, has grown apace. A man no longer wants to feel that he is working for himself alone; he wants to labor for the organization of which he forms a part, because that seems to him a nobler motive. This is one reason for the halo that surrounds the athlete; while the scholar seems to be striving for nothing better than personal distinction. If he is seeking a pecuniary scholarship, his aim, though needful, appears sordid; if not, it seems at best selfish, and therefore unworthy of the highest admiration. But the member of the football team who risks his limbs in a glorious cause, whose courage and devotion are placed freely at the service of his alma mater, stands out as a hero worthy of all the praise that can be lavished upon him. Many a man, deaf to all other appeals, can be induced to make a creditable record in his studies on the ground that otherwise he cannot play upon a team, and that it is his duty to do something for the honor of his college. Such sentiments deserve respect, although to a serene philosopher they may seem a substitution of coöperative for personal selfishness. But they assuredly place an obstacle in the path of any one who would try to raise the esteem for scholarly attainment. The undergraduate sees no way in which scholarship adds lustre to his college, and this complicates the problem of making it admirable in his eyes.

We have seen that the sifting out of young men capable of scholarship is receiving today less attention than it deserves; and that this applies, not only to recruiting future leaders of thought, but also to prevailing upon every young man to develop the intellectual powers he may possess. We have seen also that, while the Graduate School can train scholars, it cannot create a love of scholarship. That work must be done in undergraduate days. We have found reasons to believe that during the whole period of training, mental and physical, which reaches its culmination in college, competition is not only a proper but an essential factor; and we have observed the results achieved at Oxford and Cambridge by its use. In this country, on the other hand, several causes, foremost among them the elective system, have almost banished competition in scholarship from our colleges; while the inadequate character of our tests, and the corporate nature of self-interest in these latter times, raise serious difficulties in making it effective.

Nevertheless I have faith that these obstacles can be overcome, and that we can raise intellectual achievement in college to its rightful place in public estimation. We are told that it is idle to expect young men to do strenuous work before they feel the impending pressure of earning a livelihood; that they naturally love ease and self-indulgence, and can be aroused from lethargy only by discipline, or by contact with the hard facts of a struggle with the world. If I believed that, I would not be president of a college for a moment. It is not true. A normal young man longs for nothing so much as to devote himself to a cause that calls forth his enthusiasm, and the greater the sacrifice involved the more eagerly will he grasp it. If we were at war, and our students were told that two regiments were seeking recruits, one of which would be stationed at Fortress Monroe, well housed and fed, living in luxury, without risk of death or wounds, while the other would go to the front, be starved and harassed by fatiguing marches under a broiling sun, amid pestilence, with men falling from its ranks killed or suffering mutilation, not a single man would volunteer for the first regiment, but the second would be quickly filled. Who is it that makes football a dangerous and painful sport? Is it the faculty, or the players themselves?

A young man wants to test himself on every side, in strength, in quickness, in skill, in courage, in endurance; and he will go through much to prove his merit. He wants to test himself, provided he has faith that the test is true, and that the quality tried is one that makes for manliness; otherwise he will have none of it. Now, we have not convinced him that high scholarship is a manly thing worthy of his devotion, or that our examinations are faithful tests of intellectual power; and in so far as we have failed in this, we have come short of what we ought to do. Universities stand for the eternal worth of thought, for the preëminence of the prophet and the seer; but instead of being thrilled by the eager search for truth, our classes too often sit listless on the bench. It is not because the lecturer is dull, but because the pupils do not prize the end enough to relish the drudgery always required for skill in any great pursuit, or indeed in any sport. To make them see the greatness of that end, how fully it deserves the price that must be paid for it, how richly it rewards the man who may compete for it, we must learn — and herein lies the secret — we must learn the precious art of touching their imagination.

ADDRESS AT THE AWARD OF ACADEMIC DISTINCTIONS

HARVARD, DECEMBER 17, 1909

THIS meeting is held not merely to honor the men who have won prizes, attained high rank, or achieved distinction in studies. In a larger sense it is a tribute paid by the University to the ideals of scholarship. It is a public confession of faith in the aims for which the University was established. We may, therefore, not inappropriately consider here the nature and significance of scholarship.

Without attempting an exhaustive catalogue of the benefits of education, we may note three distinct objects of college study. The first is the development of the mental powers with a view to their use in any subsequent career. In its broadest sense this may be called training for citizenship, for we must remember that good citizenship does not consist exclusively in rendering public service in political and philanthropic matters. It includes also conducting an industrial or professional career so as not to leave the public welfare out of sight. The man who carries on his business or profession in reckless disregard of the interests of the community is not a good citizen, however zealous he may be in advocating political reforms, or in devoting his time to schools and hospitals. Efficiency, integrity, and public spirit in the occupations by which men earn their livelihood are essential to the prosperity of the community, and therefore a mighty factor in public service. Popular government is exacting. It implies that in some form every man shall voluntarily consecrate a part of his time and force to the state, and the better the citizen the greater the effort he will make. But it does not release him from the duty, incumbent in every commonwealth, to regard his whole work in life from the standpoint of the common welfare. Using the words in this broad sense, training for citizenship is certainly one of the principal objects of a college education. But if college studies are well adapted to the ends they are designed to attain, and if the making of good citizens is among the most important of those ends, then proficiency in college studies must, other things being equal, afford a better preparation for citizenship than lesser excellence.

On the function of colleges in fitting men for citizenship and for active work much emphasis has been laid of late. Yet it is not the only aim of college studies. Another object is cultivation of the mind, refinement of taste, a development of the qualities that distinguish the civilized man from the barbarian. Nor does the value of these things lie in personal satisfaction alone. There is a culture that is selfish and exclusive, that is self-centered and conceited. The intellectual snob is quite as repellent as any other. But this is true of the moral distortion of all good qualities. The culture that narrows the sympathies, instead of enlarging them, has surely missed the object that should give its chief worth and dignity. The culture that reveals beauty in all its forms, that refines the sensibilities, and expands the mental horizon, that, without a sense of superiority, desires to share these things with others, and makes the lives of all men better worth living, is like the glow of fire in a cold room. It is a form of social service of a high order.

A third benefit of college education is the contact it affords with the work of creative imagination. The highest type of scholar is the creative scholar, just as the highest type of citizen is the statesman. The greatest figures in history, as almost everyone will admit, are the thinkers and the rulers of men. People will always differ in the relative value they ascribe to these two supreme forms of human power. But if one may indulge in apocalyptic visions, I should prefer in another world to be worthy of the friendship of Aristotle rather than of Alexander, of Shakespeare or Newton than of Napoleon or Frederick the Great.

The imagination essential to productive scholarship cannot be conferred, nor can the lack of it be wholly obscured, by education; but much can be done to fan or dampen the flame. It is possible to take too seriously the advice of an American educator who exclaimed, "Wherever you find among the students a spark of intelligence, water it, water it!" Perhaps we may sometimes follow that singular injunction without knowing it; or perhaps we fail to kindle the capacity for original thought among young men by giving disproportionate attention to a single factor in the process of education — the factor of teaching.

Not least among the changes that have come over education within a generation has been the improvement in teaching. That function has received vast attention of late years. It has been studied with great care, and by the use of modern scientific methods. It has become prominent as it never was before, until in the minds of most people teaching and education have become synonymous. In fact the distinction I mean to draw between the two may not be self-evident. I will, therefore, define education as the whole process of mental development provoked by the reaction of the mind upon stimuli of all kinds from outside; while teaching may be described as the imparting of information, of ideas, of methods of thought, directly by the teacher to the pupil. Of course I am aware that the word *teaching* is commonly used with a broader meaning, and that every good teacher does more than teach in the sense in which I use the term. But the word is commonly used vaguely, and for the purpose of discussion it is well to attach a precise if unconventional meaning to a term.

To illustrate what I mean: When I was a schoolboy we were taught little. We studied by ourselves, and the recitation was mainly in the nature of a quiz, designed to ascertain whether we had done our work. Difficulties were, no doubt, explained; we were helped over hard places; but in the main we were given tasks, and worked out the problems by our own efforts. Now that has all changed. One familiar with the older methods can hardly enter an ordinary school without being impressed by the far larger part played by direct instruction, and in the main the change has been vastly for the better.

The new tendency is by no means confined to the common schools. It may be seen also in our institutions of higher learning, where the recitation has been largely replaced by the lecture, and the instructor is not unnaturally inclined to impart the results of his own careful researches rather than the commonly accepted body of learning. Some years ago a distinguished professor in one of our colleges explained that he did not want his students in an elementary course to read for themselves lest they acquire erroneous impressions. The remark provoked a smile, and probably was not meant seriously, but it gives point to Mr Dooley's description of the freshman who is asked by the authorities which of the great subjects of learning he would like the professor to study for him. We see the effect in the changed conception of a university, from a place where every possible subject can be studied, to a place where every subject is taught; and too often we strive in vain to cover the whole field of knowledge with a tessellated pavement of courses, no one of them by itself broad enough to show the pattern. We see the effect again in the tendency of the student to rely too much on his courses alone for his education, to feel that his omission to take a course on a subject is a rational excuse for ignorance of things which an educated man ought to know.

The increased prominence of teaching, and therewith the greater excellence in methods, has been an incalculable gain. It carries the ordinary youth along his path more rapidly. It guards him from pitfalls, and saves him much valuable time. It is far the shortest and safest means of travelling the long road hewn by the pioneers of knowledge through the wilderness of life; but it is not the only factor in education; and this is perhaps especially true of the college as compared with the professional schools; for in these a man must be equipped for his future career with a large amount of detailed knowledge; while the chief object of the college is more especially to develop his capacity for seeing clear and thinking straight. An excessive prominence of teaching in the educational system is not, therefore, harmless.

One of the characteristic defects of educational thought has been the habit of resorting to similes, which are sometimes misleading. George Eliot remarks that the youthful mind is often compared to a field, which must be ploughed and harrowed before the seed planted in it will germinate. But then, as she says, when the digestive simile is used, and the mind is compared to the stomach, any talk of harrowing seems out of place. The simile of nutrition sounds well, but to my mind the process of teaching, especially in the form of cramming for examinations, sometimes resembles more nearly the operation of a cook stuffing a goose with chestnuts. That is bad teaching, for teaching is both good and bad; but even the best teaching, if we use the word in the sense indicated, is insufficient.

No one would suppose that the force of a lion's cub can be fully developed by mere feeding, without the need of hunting for his prey; and in the same way teaching alone, that is the imparting of learning without strenuous effort on the part of the student, does not call out the enterprise, the aggressiveness, and the self-reliance indispensable for productive scholarship. In short, a disproportionate emphasis on teaching tends to produce mediocrity, and that is the most serious evil from which American universities suffer at the present day. To rise above mediocrity in scholarship requires not only native talent, and diligence in set tasks, but a sort of ferocious energy, an insubordinate resistance to the authority of the teacher, although he may himself have a good right to claim the freedom of a pioneer. There is ample opportunity for it here in our advanced courses; for theses or problems, and still more prize essays, afford abundant chance for independent thinking. Nor, in spite of the prevalent impression among students, does any good instructor desire a docile compliance with his views. On the contrary, where he turns over a pile of examination books, or reads thesis after thesis, he is ever hoping to catch a fresh note, and is disappointed to hear only the echo of his own remarks.

It may be that we do not strive to foster creative imagination in the wisest way. It may be that in our attention to method we check originality; that in trimming the plumage we clip the wings. Do we not fall short in two ways? First by failing to distinguish clearly between the process of conceiving ideas, and the method of ascertaining truth. These are not the same thing, and may take place in wholly different ways. By a flash of intuition a man conceives the idea, let us say, that all species of creatures are descended from a common stock, and have become distinct by natural selection. He then proceeds to ascertain whether the theory is true by a long series of observations and experiments. I do not say that this is the invariable process of reaching a new truth; but it is certainly common that the pregnant hypothesis comes near the beginning, not at the end, of a life of research. Of course the discoverer must have a considerable knowledge of the subject before ideas about it will come to him at all; but what I want to point out is that new generalizations do not come so much by induction from a vast mass of accumulated details, as through inspired guesses based on insufficient evidence; the fecundity in guesses depending mainly on the native imagination, their value chiefly on the profundity and range of the mental training. If this be true, the appropriate education for a productive scholar, whatever the field of his future study may be, should include the stimulating of imagination, and the disciplining of thought by the habit of dealing with abstract ideas and general conceptions.

Another way in which we are prone to check originality is by the idea that young men ought to restrict themselves to problems of narrow scope, and that as they grow in knowledge and wisdom they can gradually extend their vision over wider fields. But this would seem out of accord with the normal order of things, for by nature young men rush in where sages fear to tread; and it is fortunate that it is so, or there would be little rushing in at all. A young man ought, no doubt, to do several things before he presumes to try flights for himself. First, as a foundation he must get all he can from teaching, from books, and from every other source of information, or he will simply waste his time in trying to do over again what others have done better before him. Second, he must learn what it means to do a small bit of work thoroughly, for otherwise he will never do anything, great or small, well; and third, he must be fully conscious that any grand conceptions he may form of the problems of the universe are, as they stand, of no value to the world. He must not regard them as contributions to any knowledge but his own. Yet, if these things be understood, his assaults upon the great problems of life are precious things, to be by every means encouraged. They are the normal method of exercising his larger powers, and if he has any real imagination, they form the mirage upon the horizon that leads him on. In the constructive work of life man rarely builds beyond the ground-plan he has early sketched. He is fortunate if he builds solidly over a small part of it, and the completed work often departs greatly from the first crude sketch; but if that is not bold in outline the building is apt to be cramped and insignificant, useless for the successor who would enlarge it. Youth is the time for large, if crude, ideas; and if one could examine a man's whole mind at twenty-five it would be easy to prophesy whether or not he has any chance of real achievement. If at that age he has no large ideas, it is safe to say that he will never have them.

When I spoke of the benefit of college life in training for citizenship, and in imparting culture, I was obviously dealing with things which lie within the reach of every student; but in speaking of creative scholarship you may think that I am appealing only to the few men who have the rare gift of creative genius. But happily the progress of the world is not in the exclusive custody of the occasional men of genius. Great originality is, indeed, rare; but on a smaller scale it is not uncommon, and the same principles apply to the production of all creative work. The great scholar and the lesser intellectual lights differ in brilliancy, but the same process must be followed to bring them to their highest splendor. Nor is it the genius alone, or even the man of talent, who can enjoy and aid productive thought. It is not given to all men to possess creative scholarship themselves; but most men by following its footsteps can learn to respect it and feel its charm; and for any man who passes through college without doing so, college education has been in one of its most vital elements a failure. If he has not recognized the glowing imagination, the lofty ideals, the patience and the modesty that characterize the true scholar, his time here has been spent, not perhaps without profit, but without inspiration. We feel this with peculiar keenness now that there has passed out from among us one who possessed those qualities in such abundant measure as Charles Gross.

All productive work is largely dependent upon appreciation by the community. The great painters of Italy would have been sterile had not the citizens of Florence been eager to carry Cimabue's masterpiece in triumph through the streets. Kant would never have written among a people who despised philosophy; and the discoveries of our own day would have been impossible in an unscientific age. Every man who has learned to respect creative scholarship can enter into its spirit, and by respecting it he helps to foster it.

HOW TO SECURE AMONG STUDENTS A HIGHER APPRECIATION OF SCHOLARSHIP

ASSOCIATION OF AMERICAN UNIVERSITIES, 1910

THAT the appreciation of scholarship among students at the present day is very low would hardly seem to need demonstration. In the case of colleges it is notorious; and what is true there is certain in time to work down into the schools to an even greater extent than it has done already. The sayings familiar among students, such as that high scholars never amount to anything afterwards, that in later life the sports pass the grinds, are sufficient evidence of the way in which they regard rank. It requires, indeed, little familiarity with students ourselves to recognize that they not only regard the athlete, or the man of social prominence, as a far more promising personality than the high scholar, but that rank in itself is in their minds little or no indication of the qualities that make for success in life. This feeling seems to have been progressive, as is shown by the very words used to indicate the student who works hard. A generation ago he was called "grind," but now he is often referred to as a "greasy grind," the adjective, of course, being used to imply contempt. In fact it may be doubted whether the respect for scholarship has ever been so low in any institution of learning as it is in American colleges at the present day. If this be true in our colleges, which ought to be the very center of scholarly aspiration, how are we to secure a higher appreciation of scholarship? The first thing is for us, who are engaged in education, to appreciate, ourselves, that high scholarship is valuable.

[Then follows a summary of the statistics of rank in College and the School of Law and Medicine in the next paper.]

These results, covering as they do so long a period of time, and so large a number of men, would appear to be conclusive on rank in college as an indication of excellence in the subsequent professional school. Moreover, the data collected would appear to show that the same thing is true of high scholarship at school. For it appears that the men who attained a *cum laude* in the Medical School averaged in entering college only two-thirds as many conditions, and were six months younger than the men who did not get a *cum laude* in the Medical School. For the Law School again the same thing appears more markedly. The men who graduated *cum laude* there averaged on entering college only about one-third as many conditions, and were eleven months younger than the men who did not get a *cum laude*. In short, it appears that at least through the period of entering upon professional practice, on the average, the boy who is a good scholar in school is a good scholar in college, and a good scholar in the professional school afterwards, and no doubt a successful man in life. Of course it will be suggested that this means merely that a boy who is naturally bright and diligent retains these qualities throughout life, but that is the main point to be established. The essential thing is that high scholarship in school and at college does indicate that the individual is naturally bright, and possesses those moral qualities which are decisive in a man's career. It has been suggested that if scholarship is a mere test of the fact that a boy is born with these qualities it will not act as an incentive to hard work; but the answer is that the doctrine of predestination never prevented anyone from striving to prove that he was one of the elect. So much for this point that I have tried to make, — that high scholarship in school and in college is really highly valuable, and is an indication of success in life. The first thing for us to do is to admit that fact. The second is to recognize that we do not at present appreciate the importance of high scholarship. Of course we think we recognize it, and are shocked to be told that we do not; and yet it is not difficult to produce many proofs of our failure to appreciate excellence in school or college work at its true value. The community about us is constantly saying that high scholars rarely amount to much, and that it would rather employ a successful athlete than one who had taken high rank; and we who are engaged in education either share these views in a sneaking sort of way, or sit by in silence, and allow them to pass unchallenged. Even on academic occasions our recognition of excellence in the work of school or college is too often half-hearted, and therefore ineffective; and I must admit freely that in this the colleges are greater sinners than the schools. To take another piece of evidence: Let anyone compare the amount of discussion that takes place about the subjects of the school and college curriculum with the discussion which relates to the intensity of the application of students. Our teachers' meetings, our educational and non-educational magazines, are crammed today with speeches and articles about the subjects that had best be taught as a part of a liberal education, and those that are most fitted to prepare for definite careers; but very little is said about the amount of mental effort that the pupils put into their work. Again, in selecting a school or other institution, how much we hear about the subjects taught, about the methods of teaching, and how little about the standard of scholarship maintained. This is particularly true where a university has an arts and a science course. We are told much about the relative advantages of these different courses as an equipment for life, but scarcely anything about the relative severity of the standards in such courses; and yet in some cases the divergence in that respect is very great, — probably far more important in the long run than the question of the subjects pursued.

Another proof of our indifference to scholarship or rank of students is readily given. For admission to any grade of instruction we are in the habit of requiring that a boy or young man shall have completed the work of the preceding grade;

that he shall have done the minumum amount needed to secure a diploma or degree. This is very proper; but how often
do we inquire how well he did it? How much stress do we lay
upon anything above the minumum, upon the standard attained? One of the few cases where attention is given for this
purpose to the rank obtained is to be found in the case of the
Harvard Law School, — the department of the University
whose superior excellence is most universally admitted.
There it is provided that graduates of colleges of high grade
may be admitted upon producing their diploma; but graduates of other colleges only upon producing together with their
diploma a sufficient certificate that they ranked in the first
third of the class in the work of their senior year. Most
people, including those who devote their lives to education,
would probably think this rather an odd, if not pedantic,
provision. Yet it has probably contributed to the selecting
influences that have made the Law School a picked body of
men, and by so doing have helped it to maintain an unusually
high standard of work. It is far more common to require, —
as is done by many medical schools, — that the candidate for
admission shall have pursued certain courses, and received
the minimum degree of credit, no attention being paid to
anything above that degree of achievement, and no advantage being given to the man who has proved himself in his
preliminary work of more than ordinary calibre.

Still another example of failure to set a high value on rank
or unusual excellence in studies is found in the way in which
school and college catalogues publish the degrees possessed
by their instructing staffs. It is customary to insert the degrees obtained as a kind of guarantee of the standard of the
schools, and some of the smaller colleges, indeed, will not
appoint an instructor who is not a doctor of philosophy. But
do our schools or colleges ever mention in their catalogues the
honors or rank a man has achieved in college? Of course not.
But why not? The English schools do so. There you find
after a man's name a statement that he took a first-class in

classics, that he was the Ireland scholar, or the like. We do not mention such distinctions in our catalogues, because we do not really regard them as of any great importance. The English do so, because they consider them as of great significance, and hence the young men strive hard to win them. We do not think it worth while to refer to these things, and what we do not value the young men can hardly be expected to value more.

These illustrations have been given not to show that the American public does not value scholarship highly, but that the people engaged in education do not — the instructors themselves. In fact it is hardly an exaggeration to say that at the present day the public are quite as prepared to rate the value of excellence of a school or college highly as the instructors are themselves. Is it not true that the whole American people is deeply impressed with the doctrine of equality, and to some extent dislikes indications of superiority? It prefers to see all the boys and girls who have obtained diplomas, or all young people who graduated from a college, placed on a par instead of seeing some of them treated as distinguished above their fellows. But the danger is that that attitude of mind tends to foster mediocrity at the expense of excellence.

If I am right in these two points: first that high rank in scholarship at school and college is of great importance as a preparation for a career in life, and as an indication of the mental and moral qualities that spell success; and second that the men engaged in American education fail to appreciate it, — then I need hardly say more. There is little use in suggesting artificial incentives to do something that we do not ourselves think is worth doing. So long as we, the teachers, are lukewarm it boots little to whistle to keep someone else's courage up. We need first of all to educate ourselves; to learn that all holders of a diploma or degree are not equal in natural gifts or training; that there are vast differences between people who have passed through the same course with at least minimum credit, differences deeply significant and quite as vital to education as the subjects that lead to a degree. If, on the other hand, we recognize at its true value the significance of superiority in school or college work, the forms of expressing it would be easy enough to invent; they would almost come of themselves.

Of course I shall be met at this point with the objection that neither school boys nor young men ought to be encouraged to study for rank; and to a certain extent that is a very proper feeling; but if we analyze it closely it means two distinct things according as we regard the object or the motive. People often speak of studying for marks as against studying for knowledge or power, implying that the two things are not identical, if not indeed inconsistent. Where that is true the marks are badly given. If a pupil can win marks without getting knowledge, or win marks out of proportion to the knowledge and grasp of the subject attained, then the marks are a bad measure of his attainment; and that, I am sorry to say, is far too often true. We give our marks on memory or on a certain superficial skill in displaying information, instead of giving them on tests that really measure the qualities and attainments that we think admirable. So far then as the object is concerned, if our marks are not a good measure of true scholarship, then the fault lies not with the pupil's effort of attempting to attain marks, but with the system by which the marks are given. It lies not with the pupil but wholly with the teacher. The question of motive introduces another consideration. We speak as if there were something unworthy in studying for marks. Let us free our minds from cant. Is there anything unworthy in a boy's running a race to win, or playing a game for victory? Or ought he during the contest to leave the goal out of sight, and think only of perfecting his muscles? The wreath of olive or of laurel is not prized or striven for for any intrinsic value, but because it symbolizes the successful forthputting of an effort that is worth while. And in the same way, if marks really measure excellence, as the results would seem to show, then it is certainly proper to strive for the excellence which they indicate.

When we say that there is little use in suggesting artificial incentives to scholarship unless we think ourselves that high rank is worth attaining, let us remember to put the accent upon this last proviso. The mere public recognition of scholarship has a certain importance. It is one of many cases where the forms themselves are not without effect, for we know that every emotion is stimulated by exercising the forms of its own expression. Solemn ceremonies help a belief in the solemnity of the thing celebrated. Singing patriotic songs does inspire some patriotism; and no doubt in savage communities barbarous executions do produce some horror of crime, and so on throughout the whole gamut of human feeling. And, conversely, the absence of the forms tends to an atrophy of the emotion itself. If we go on year after year saying that scholarship ought to be its own reward, or that it is unworthy or undignified or childish to give it any public recognition, can we be surprised that the thing itself falls out of notice and ceases to be admired?

Let us, therefore, give expression to our respect for rank in school and college by all appropriate methods, but let us do so with a firm conviction that in doing it we are recognizing real merit and not going through a perfunctory ritual that has lost its essential meaning. The exact forms that we adopt are unimportant. The more natural they are the better adapted for their purpose. The vital thing is that they should be a genuine expression of opinion. And in selecting graduates of colleges for employment of any kind, let us pay attention not only to the fact that they have obtained a degree, but to the probable qualities of the possessor as indicated by the excellence of his work in winning that degree. Let us make the student feel that the distinction bestowed upon him in achieving rank is not merely a school-boy prize for good conduct, but an earnest of future achievement. Above all let us have the courage of our convictions. In all our educational organizations let us remember that high excellence means ten times the qualifications of the mediocrity that is good enough to pass.

After giving this address I received the following letter, which throws light on the situation and its difficulties:

Oct. 29, 1910.

PRESIDENT LOWELL
HARVARD UNIVERSITY.

Respected Sir: —

I have read with great interest extracts from the public press containing your alleged views on scholarship before the university convocacation. Although I suppose my inquiry will present nothing new to you I cannot help but ask with deepest feeling, "Who is to blame?" I sent my son to the University of —— and soon began to note that he was in my opinion devoting more attention to the social side than to the intellectual, or to meeting the problems of life as I saw them. At last I went to the University and interviewed the dean of his department. He said practically that times had changed since he and I had received training; that the demands of modern life required that one's address and social advantages count for more than high scholarship, and wound up by saying that "every student hated to be called a grind," and I returned silenced in argument but not convinced. As to its extension to lower schools I will only say I am at present struggling with the same problem. My youngest son who has averaged from 95 to 100 in his grammar grades recently entered the High School. I can see that the fraternity and the football question are beginning to absorb his attention. His first and only mark there shows only the average but to my objection he states that he has made the necessary marks showing to me that he has or is adopting a new view point. Having had the run of a fairly good library (private) it has been a matter of pride to me that he had remembered as well as read a great deal of literature that ordinarily one of his years does not meet, and consequently his use of English was above the average. Now he has no time for much more than the newspaper (which I encourage) and the magazines. I believe his intellectual atmosphere has changed. How much this is due to the High School's affiliation with the University and training for that instead of life I will leave to you. While I do not believe the school can ever supplant the home training I do believe that the former often antagonizes the latter, and that parents having old-fashioned views are unable to cope with the influences so prevalent in the environment. So far has this influenced my views that I have seriously questioned whether it pays to send a boy to a University unless he has pronounced views differing from the majority, and more backbone than the majority of young boys.

I think in the West we do not have to contend as yet with the idea prevailing in the East from my observation that a University training is almost essential to marked success in almost any walk of life. I certainly do not go as far as Joseph G. Cannon when he says that "college training does not of necessity do a young man harm" but I sincerely believe its influence is decidedly to give wrong ideals and lessen in great measure his capability for good as a citizen. Perhaps I am wrong and many of my friends oppose my ideas but I have for years felt so deeply on this subject that when I read your alleged remarks I could not but pray that other men of your prominence in educational circles might consider this problem seriously. You must excuse my intrusion on your valuable time.

I only desire to add a little testimony to the truth of your position. I am, sir, with great respect,

                                    Very truly yours,

COLLEGE STUDIES AND PROFESSIONAL TRAINING

A Statistical Study in Harvard University

The Educational Review, New York, October, 1911

Educators are proverbially conservative, and it is only in comparatively recent times they have turned to the experimental methods of science as a substitute for deductive reasoning based upon hypotheses. The experiments have dealt in great part with the most pregnant of all educational problems — the question how far an aptitude acquired in one field can be transferred to another. The upshot of many experiments made of late years by a number of independent observers would appear to be: that, in so far as the acquired aptitude depends upon familiarity with the subject-matter, it can be transferred little, if at all; that, in so far as it rests upon methods of thought, in other words, upon mental processes, it can be transferred to a considerable extent wherever the same methods are applicable; and finally that, in so far as it is based upon general principles of work, or what is perhaps the same thing, upon a general moral attitude, upon such qualities as diligence, persistence, and intensity of effort, it can be transferred almost indefinitely.

Now we do not know to what extent each of these three elements enters as a factor in any continuous course of study, or in what way their relative importance may vary at different stages of maturity. The experiments have been made, for the most part, with school children, and it may be that young men and women are more capable than children of applying in a new field methods of thought acquired in an old one. The experiments have been made also — and very properly — with a view of isolating particular aptitudes, and it may be that in the more complex pursuits of higher education, where many methods of thought are employed, and perhaps a number of aptitudes developed, the transferability becomes greater. This is, indeed, what we call resourcefulness, and has been supposed to be one of the chief benefits of a broad education.

Moreover, the experiments have covered very brief periods, often not more than a couple of weeks, and it may well be that in so short a time methods of thought are acquired little, and a general moral attitude still less, as compared with a familiarity with the subject-matter. If so, the last of those elements would be given an exaggerated prominence. If experiment should show that a boy who played baseball or tennis for a fortnight gained nothing in ability to row a boat, it would not follow that the general dexterity and the physical and nervous vigor he would acquire by playing those games for several years would not give him a vast advantage in rowing over a boy who, during all that time, had taken no strenuous exercise at all. Nor does it follow that, although when first placed in a boat he might be very inferior to a trained oarsman, he might not with a little practise improve rapidly until the difference had almost, if not quite, disappeared. Education can never be made fully an experimental science, for highly instructive as the experiments are, they cannot be continued long enough to test thoroughly the results of different curricula. We cannot, merely in order to see what the consequences will be, subject boys to a course of study covering several years, unless we believe that it is the best for them. Except for experiments, therefore, too brief to have a lasting effect upon the pupil, we are confined to observing the results of various types of education adopted, not for experimental objects, but because they are supposed to be good for the student.

Fortunately, in the case of our colleges we have in America a great variety of curricula chosen by the students themselves, and it would seem that some light may be thrown upon these problems by a careful examination of the different courses pursued by undergraduates. A difficulty presents itself, however, in measuring the results. Archimedes declared that if he had a lever long enough, and a fixed point to rest it on, he could move the world. In this case it is not easy to find the fixed point. Statistics have been compiled on several occasions to show the relation between rank in college and success in life, the success in life being usually measured either by the appearance of the names of the graduates in *Who's Who in America*, or by the estimates of classmates and others. But the first of these tests gives too much weight to purely literary or scholastic qualities, the latter to a prominence often due in great part to wealth acquired by inheritance or marriage. Neither of them is, therefore, an accurate criterion of personal achievement. For this purpose the rank attained in a professional school after graduating from college has great value. It is not, indeed, a measure of ultimate success in life. It is by no means remote enough from college for that; but it has, at least, the merit of being a fairly accurate test of capacity so far as it goes.

In applying, however, any method of determining the relation between elective college studies and subsequent achievement, we must beware of assuming that the results are necessarily a consequence of the college work, for there are two factors in the problem, two independent variables in the equation; one of them the value of the college work in training the mind, the other the selective process whereby men of different tastes and abilities are drawn to elect the subjects for which they have a natural aptitude. If, therefore, the men who pursue certain subjects, or who attain high marks in them, have a better rank in the professional school than their comrades, it may be because the study of those subjects, or the effort put forth to obtain the marks, has fitted them in a peculiar degree for the professional work; or it may be that the men are impelled to choose those subjects, or to work hard, by the very qualities which would insure proficiency in the professional school whatever their college training had been; or again these two factors may be combined in unknown proportions. Now it is clearly important to separate the effects of the two factors, if possible, so that one of them can be measured by itself; and this is in fact done where the result is negative. If the men, for example, who have pursued quite different subjects in college do equally well in the professional school, it proves that the training given by one of those subjects is not distinctively superior to that given by another, for there is obviously no selective factor at work which would counterbalance any such superiority. This is one of the cases where a negative result is more decisive than a positive one. If, on the other hand, the result is positive, and college work in any subject, or of any grade, is followed by a peculiarly high average rank in the professional school, we must have the presence of these two factors constantly in mind, and try to contrive some other test which will eliminate or reduce the effect of one of them; we must seek another equation between the two independent variables.

Harvard University is singularly rich in material for determining the relation of college studies to the work of the professional schools, because nowhere in the world have so large a body of undergraduates been so free, for so long a period, as in Harvard College to study whatever they chose, and to make any combination of courses they pleased. With the exception of one required course in English, and sometimes one in another modern language, the election of courses has been almost wholly free for a quarter of a century, and in fact the variety of combinations made has been almost limitless. Moreover, the law and medical schools have contained a large number of graduates of Harvard College, and this is essential for a fair comparison of the results, because there is little use in comparing men who have studied, let us say, history in our college with those who have studied science in another, unless we can assume, what is rarely true, that the quality of students and the standards of scholarship in the two colleges are the same. The necessity for such a limitation upon the field of inquiry is brought out clearly by a fact which appeared in compiling these statistics. There existed at one time in the Lawrence Scientific School of Harvard University a course in anatomy and physiology, supposed to be a good preparation for the study of medicine; but the few bachelors of science in this course who entered the medical school did so much less well than the bachelors of arts from the college that in the following computations they have been omitted entirely. To have included them would have reduced the average grade in the school of men who had taken scientific courses in their undergraduate days, and thus tended to ascribe to that subject an inferiority due in reality to other causes.

The statistics here presented cover, therefore, only bachelors of arts of Harvard College who graduated afterwards from the Harvard Law and Medical Schools, and they comprise only men who took twelve courses, or nearly three years' work, in the college.[1] Both of the professional schools confer ordinary and *cum laude* degrees, and these have been used as the test of excellence, although, as we shall see, the standard of the *cum laude* differs greatly in the two schools. The statistics for the law school cover the twenty years from 1891 to 1910 inclusive, and as the course in the school was three years, and in the college four, this goes back to the men entering the latter in 1884, about the time that the elective system bore

[1] To include men spending only a year or two in the college would vitiate the basis of comparison as regards both the subjects pursued and the rank attained. Six courses in one field out of eight or ten are a very different thing from six courses out of sixteen or seventeen. Moreover the *cum laude* in college was given in part upon the number of high marks in courses, and hence a student who spent only a short time there, although an excellent scholar, could rarely win it.

The figures given in this paper differ slightly from those in the *Harvard Graduates' Magazine* for December, 1910, partly on account of the correction of errors, but chiefly because of degrees in the professional schools granted after the normal year of graduation by reason of a failure to complete the work, or pay the fees, at the proper time. The figures given here accord with the last quinquennial catalogue.

full fruit. For the medical school, the figures cover the six-teen years from 1895 onward, because for several years be-fore that time the *cum laude* was given only to men who remained in the school four years, those who graduated in three years receiving a plain degree no matter how high their grade.

It may be well to add that the subjects pursued in college are divided, for the purpose of this study, into the four groups established for the new regulations on the choice of electives: the first group containing language, literature, fine arts, and music; the second, the natural sciences; the third, history, economics, and government; the fourth, philosophy and mathematics. Statistics have been compiled of the students who took in college six or more full courses in any one of these groups, and the proportion in each case who achieved a *cum laude* in the professional schools.[1]

But before examining them, it is well to consider the aver-age choice of subjects in college by the men who afterwards graduated from those schools. They are shown in diagrams 1 and 2.[2] The chief differences to be noted between the future lawyers and physicians are that the former took on the aver-age a little more classics, much more history, government, and economics, less German, and far less natural science. These differences are almost equally marked among the men who obtained a high rank in the professonal schools, and those who did not; for in the diagrams the elections of the men who won a *cum laude* in the school are indicated by dotted lines, the elections of the rest being shown by plain lines, and it will be observed the two kind of lines are remark-ably close together. The most notable departures are the

---

[1] The tables give the number of cases of election of six or more courses in one group, not the number of men who elected them. One man may not have taken six courses in any group, while others may have taken six courses in more than one group, so that the number of cases and the number of men are not identical.

[2] Subjects in which the average was less than three-tenths of a course are omitted altogether. These diagrams are on page 88.

slightly larger amount of classics and mathematics taken by the future *cum laude* men, and in fact the other men showed, as might be expected, a trifle more tendency throughout to select the subjects reputed less difficult.

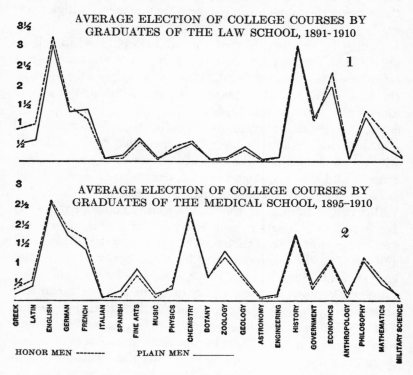

AVERAGE ELECTION OF COLLEGE COURSES BY
GRADUATES OF THE LAW SCHOOL, 1891-1910

1

AVERAGE ELECTION OF COLLEGE COURSES BY
GRADUATES OF THE MEDICAL SCHOOL, 1895–1910

2

HONOR MEN ---------- PLAIN MEN _____

To return to the statistics of the students who took in college six or more courses in any one of the four groups of studies. These are displayed graphically in diagrams 3 and 4. The first column at the left of diagram 3 indicates, for each of the four groups, the number of cases where a man took six or more courses in one group, and did not win a *cum laude* in the law school. The lowest division, with the vertical lines, represents literature and language; the second, which is white, natural science; the next above, with horizontal lines,

3

DEGREES IN THE LAW SCHOOL, 1891–1910

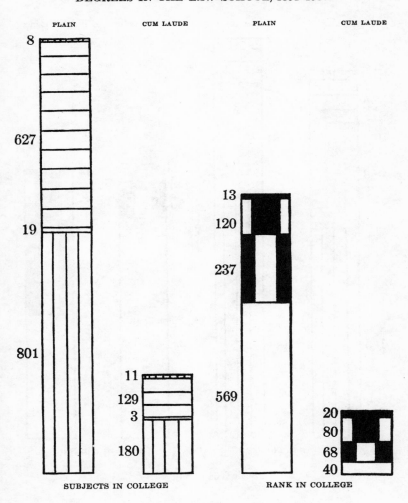

Scale = 320 to an inch

4

DEGREES IN THE MEDICAL SCHOOL, 1895–1910

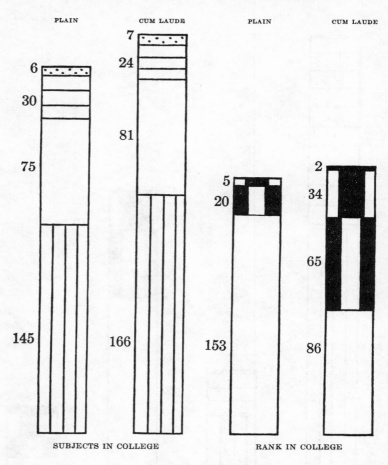

PLAIN   CUM LAUDE   PLAIN   CUM LAUDE

SUBJECTS IN COLLEGE   RANK IN COLLEGE

Scale = 64 to an inch

history and political science; the uppermost division, with dots, philosophy and mathematics. The second column indicates in the same way the number of cases where a man took six or more courses in one group, and obtained a *cum laude* in the law school. An inspection of these two columns shows at a glance that a little less than one-fifth of the graduates of Harvard College who entered the law school won a *cum laude* there, and that this proportion is nearly the same for each group where the numbers are large enough to be decisive, the figures for the four groups being as follows:

		Plain	Cum laude	
I	(Literature and language)	801	180 or	18.4%
II	(Natural science)	19	3	13.6%
III	(History, political science)	627	129	17.1%
IV	(Philosophy, mathematics)	8	11	57.9%

The only notable departure from the normal is in the small fourth group, and this is due to the students of mathematics — a fact to which we shall return later. But for the moment the thing to be observed is that, save in the case of mathematics, the second column is an almost exact miniature of the first; or in other words, that one subject does not seem to be a markedly better preparation for the study of law than another.

Contrary to current opinion, the same fact appears not less clearly from the statistics for the medical school. The comparison in that case is, indeed, more striking, both because the selection of studies in college was more evenly distributed among the four groups, and because the *cum laude* is given more freely so that the two columns are nearly of the same size. The first two columns in diagram 4 are, indeed, almost counterparts of each other, the figures for the four groups being as follows:

		Plain	Cum laude	
I	(Literature, language)	145	166 or	53.4%
II	(Natural science)	75	81	51.9%
III	(History, political science)	30	20	44.4%
IV	(Philosophy, mathematics)	6	7	53.8%

The proportions are, on the whole, singularly even in all the groups, and the numbers would seem large enough to prove that natural science in college is certainly not a markedly better preparation for the study of medicine than other subjects. This is not, of course, the common view of medical professors, but the reason for that may not be far to seek. The young man who has acquired some familiarity with natural science and the use of instruments has, no doubt, an initial advantage in the study of medicine, and is much easier to teach at the outset. Figures compiled for a single class at the Harvard Medical School three years ago showed that excellence in the first year courses in anatomy and histology was in proportion to the amount of biology studied in college; and this is confirmed by more extensive statistics covering the whole period of sixteen years. It appears that the men who had taken in college ten or more courses in natural science had a better average rank in the first year at the medical school than those who had taken six or more, and less than ten, such courses, while these in turn stood better than the men who had taken less than three such courses.[1] But that the initial advantage was soon overcome in the course of professional study is shown, not only by the fact that the men who had devoted themselves to other subjects in college had, at the end of the four years in the school, as large a proportion of degrees *cum laude* as those who had pursued natural science, but also by the fact that whereas of the men who had taken in college six or more, and less than ten, courses in that subject, 54.1 per cent obtained a *cum laude*, of the twenty-three men who had taken ten or more such courses only nine, or 39.1 per cent, did so, and of the forty-six men who had taken less than three such courses, twenty-eight, or 60.9 per cent, won a *cum laude*. From figures so small as these, it would be absurd to conclude that the study of natural science

[1] Before entering the school, a student must have taken two courses in chemistry or their equivalent.

in college is a detriment to a medical education, but they tend to show that exclusive pursuit of natural science is not always a conspicuous benefit, and that a man who has neglected that field is not necessarily at a disadvantage. So far as they go, they appear to reinforce the conclusion that one subject is not distinctly better than another as a preparation for professional education.

Let us turn from the question of the subject studied to that of the proficiency achieved in it. The second pair of columns in diagrams 3 shows the numbers of men attaining certain grades in college who won, and failed to win, a *cum laude* in the law school. The first of the two columns depicts the men who failed to achieve that distinction in the school; the second, those who won it.[1] The white spaces at the base of each column indicate the men who graduated from college with a plain degree; the spaces next above, with two narrow black lines, the men who graduated from college with a *cum laude*; the next spaces, with a broad black line in the center, the men who graduated with a *magna cum laude*; and finally, the wholly black spaces at the top the men who graduated with a *summa cum laude*. Comparing these with the first pair of columns at their left, the shorter column of the second pair is by no means a miniature of the taller one, as in the first case. On the contrary, the proportion of white is much larger in the tall column, and the darker the space, the less its proportion in that column. In other words, the higher men's rank in college, the better their chance of winning a *cum laude* in the law school, and the chance increases rapidly with the excellence of the college rank. Of the six hundred and nine men who graduated from college with a plain degree, only forty, or 6.6 per cent, obtained a *cum laude* in the law school; of the three hundred and five who graduated from college with a *cum laude*, sixty-eight, or 22.3 per cent, won a *cum*

---

[1] The difference in size of the two pairs of columns is due to the fact that the first pair represents the number of cases of six courses in a subject; the second pair the number of men. Cf. note 1, p. 87.

laude in the law school; of the two hundred with a *magna cum laude*, eighty, or 40 per cent, did so; and of the thirty-three with a *summa cum laude*, twenty, or 60.6 per cent. Thus the chance of winning that distinction in the school was more than three times as great for the man who left college with a *cum laude* as for the man with a plain degree; six times as great for the man with a *magna cum laude*; and nine times as great for the *summa cum laude*.

The two pairs of columns in the diagram for the medical school show the same contrast, and the figures tell the same story, although in different proportions, because the honor degree in that school is awarded on a standard less severe. Of the two hundred and thirty-nine men who graduated from college with a plain degree, eighty-six, or 36 per cent, won a *cum laude* in the school; of the eighty-five with a *cum laude*, sixty-five, or 76.5 per cent; of the thirty-nine with a *magna cum laude*, thirty-four, or 87.2 per cent; and both of those with a *summa cum laude*, or 100 per cent.

Now these results, being positive, and involving the two factors of selection and training, give us no means of distinguishing the effects of each of those factors. They do not tell us whether the success in the professional school of the higher scholars in college is due to the work they do as undergraduates, or to the fact they possess by nature qualities which lead to high rank in both places. We must, therefore, seek some other test that will eliminate, or reduce in importance, one of the factors, in order to ascertain the effect of the other. For this purpose, we may take the passing of the entrance examinations to college, which may be regarded as a rough measure of natural ability and industry.[1] If the students entering Harvard College came from a great variety of schools differing much in educational standards, the entrance examinations would be at least as much a test of the excellence of the schools as of the capacity of the candidates; but hitherto that has not been the case. The last report of

---

[1] Or more strictly of intellectual state when admitted.

the chairman of the committee on admission shows that at least two-thirds of the boys admitted are prepared in a comparatively small number of schools that undertake regularly to fit for the college. Under these conditions, it is reasonable to suppose that the passing of the examinations is mainly a measure of the scholarly qualities of the candidates. Again, if all students after entering college were studious, the difference between their standing at the entrance examinations and their rank in college might be attributed to their progressive intellectual development. But every one familiar with student life knows that this also is not the case; that low rank on the part of men who entered well is commonly due not to lack of ability, but to absorption in other college activities, or to indolence bred in the new environment. We may assume, therefore, that excellence in passing the entrance examinations is a rough test of natural scholarly qualities; and that if, among the men thus shown to possess these qualities, there is any substantial divergence in the professional school between those who have ranked well in college and those who have not, the difference must be attributed in large part to the effects of the training so obtained.

The relative rank in the college and in the law school of the men who entered college with and without conditions is shown in the following table:

HARVARD LAW SCHOOL, 1891–1910

TOTALS	ENTERED COLLEGE CLEAR						ENTERED WITH CONDITIONS						PER CENT OF C. L. in Law School of men entering college		
	Rank in College			Rank in Law School			Rank in College			Rank in Law School					
	PLAIN	C. L.	M. C. L.	S. C. L.	PLAIN	C. L.	PLAIN	C. L.	M. C. L.	S. C. L.	PLAIN	C. L.	CLEAR	COND.	BLOB
609	269				239	30	340				330	10	11.1	2.9	6.5
305		179			126	53		126			111	15	29.1	11.9	22.3
200			148		83	65			52		37	15	43.9	28.8	40.
33				29	12	17				4	1	3	58.6	75.	60.6
1147				625	460	165				522	479	43	26.4	9.	18.1

(Braced values in the per cent columns: 37.6 for CLEAR rows 2–4; 18.1 for COND. rows 2–4; 31.2 for BLOB rows 2–4.)

It will be observed that the men who entered college clear, and those who entered with conditions, form two groups not very unequal in size, the former numbering six hundred and twenty-five and the latter five hundred and twenty-two. The men who graduated from college with distinction, and those who graduated with a plain degree, form two other groups even more nearly equal, the former being five hundred and thirty-eight and the latter six hundred and nine. Now, if we compare the achievements of these groups in the law school, we find that of the men who entered college clear 26.4 per cent, and of those who entered with conditions only 9 per cent, won a *cum laude* in the law school; while of the men who graduated from college with distinction 31.2 per cent, and of those who graduated without distinction 6.5 per cent attained a *cum laude* in the school. These figures indicate that both natural aptitude, as shown by the entrance examinations to college, and the training acquired by hard work there, as shown by college rank, are substantial factors in attaining a high grade in the law school. If the entrance examinations were an exact test of natural ability, so that we had eliminated one of the factors entirely, instead of merely reducing its importance, we should be able to go farther and say that the two factors are not very unequal in force, the greater importance, if there be a difference, attaching to hard work in college.

The same result is obtained if, by means of these two factors, we make a cross division into four groups; for of the three hundred and fifty-six men who entered college clear and graduated with distinction, 37.9 per cent won a *cum laude* in the law school; of the one hundred and eighty-two who entered with conditions and graduated with distinction, 18.1 per cent; of the two hundred and sixty-nine who entered clear and graduated without distinction, 11.1 per cent; and of the three hundred and forty who entered with conditions and graduated without distinction, only 2.9 per cent. Clearly the man who has never been a scholar before he entered the law school has a very minute chance of distinguishing himself there.

Curiously enough the chance of a *cum laude* in the law school is nearly the same for the man who enters college clear and does not graduate with a *cum laude* as it is for the man who enters conditioned and graduates with a *cum laude*; and it is the same for the man who enters clear and graduates *cum laude* as it is for the conditioned man who graduates with a *magna cum laude*. When we come to the *summa cum laude*, the numbers are too small to be of value, and it may be assumed that entrance with conditions followed by so high a grade in college means defective preparation at school.

The statistics for the medical school tell the same story with a greater emphasis upon the importance of rank in college, although the number of men who obtained more than a *cum laude* there is too small to justify comparisons in detail. The figures are as follows:

HARVARD MEDICAL SCHOOL, 1895–1910

| TOTALS | ENTERED COLLEGE CLEAR | | | | | | ENTERED WITH CONDITIONS | | | | | | PER CENT OF C.L. in Medical School of men entering college | | |
| | Rank in College | | | | Rank in Med. School | | Rank in College | | | | Rank in Med. School | | | | |
	PLAIN	C. L.	M. C. L.	S. C. L.	PLAIN	C. L.	PLAIN	C. L.	M. C. L.	C. L.	PLAIN	CT L.	CLEAR	COND.	BOTH
239	99				57	42	140				96	44	42.4	31.4	36.
85		57			15	42		28			5	23	73.6	82.1	76.5
39			28		4	24			11		1	10	85.7 (78.1)	90.9 (84.6)	87.2 (80.1)
2				2	0	2				0	0	0	100.		100
365				186	76	110				179	102	77	59.1	43.0	

We are now in a position to consider the one apparently positive result of the pursuit of different subjects in college, that is the superiority in the law school of the men who took six or more courses in the group of philosophy and mathematics. This, as already pointed out, is in fact due to those who elected mathematics; but the number of men who took six courses in the subject is so small that it seemed well to enlarge the class by including all those who took four or more courses. There were only sixteen such men in all during the twenty years, of whom ten won a degree *cum laude* in the law school, whereas at the average rate only three would be expected to do so. But if we examine the grades of these men in college, we find that they were far above the ordinary rank, three of them having graduated *cum laude*, eight *magna cum laude*, and two *summa cum laude*. Calculating the chances for men of that rank, it appears that 5.28 of them would be expected to attain a *cum laude* in the law school. This is nearer, but still far below, the actual result.

It is interesting to compare with the mathematicians the men who took four or more courses in the classics. They numbered one hundred and fifteen, being decidedly more frequent in the earlier years. At the average rate for the whole class, twenty-one of them would have obtained a *cum laude* in the law school, whereas in fact thirty-one achieved it. But the men who elect classics are also better scholars than the average, and calculating their chances according to their rank in college, we should expect to find twenty-seven of them in the *cum laude* list of the law school, a number not very far from the actual result. If, therefore, one can draw any inference from figures so small, the case of mathematics is singular. Unless some other element enters into the problem, such as an unusually high standard in the department, or an unusually vigorous intellectual appetite on the part of students who elect the subject, the result may be supposed to indicate, so far as it goes, that mathematics, although rarely selected for the purpose, is a particularly good preparation for the study of law; perhaps because the methods of thought in the two subjects are more nearly akin than is commonly supposed.

Leaving aside this possibly exceptional case, the conclusions to be derived from the facts presented in this paper would seem to be that, as a preparation for the study of law or medicine, it makes comparatively little difference what subject is mainly pursued in college, but that it makes a great difference with what intensity the subject is pursued — or, to put the same proposition in a more technical form, familiarity with the subject-matter, which can be transferred little if at all, is of small importance in a college education, as compared with mental processes that are capable of being transferred widely, or with the moral qualities of diligence, perseverance, and intensity of application which can be transferred indefinitely. The practical deduction is that in the administration of our colleges, and, indeed, in all our general education, as distinguished from direct vocational or professional training, we have laid too much stress on the subject, too little on the excellence of the work and on the rank attained.

THE DUTY OF SCHOLARSHIP

ADDRESS AT THE INAUGURATION OF PRESIDENT MEIKLEJOHN, AT
AMHERST, OCTOBER 16, 1912

IN MATTERS unessential to the public welfare, or of doubtful import, diversity is highly beneficial. It is the very seed of progress. But in matters that affect the community either directly or indirectly by setting an example, by raising or lowering the standards of conduct, the public is justified in exerting pressure by expressing approbation or disapproval. It is, indeed, bound to do so because public esteem and criticism are potent forces in the maintenance of moral principles, and their absence is a source of moral laxity. Legislation against abuses has usually been less effective through the penalties it has imposed than through creating a fresh sense of right and wrong; and where it fails to do this the law is usually not enforced or is evaded. Great reforms derive their momentum from awakening the public conscience, so that men become aware of new duties, and, what is not less important, judge their neighbors by a new standard.

One of the new duties to which our prolific age has given birth is that of education. It is our pride, our spoiled child. Upon it we lavish, from public treasuries and private benefactions, sums that would have been thought incredible a hundred years ago. We offer opportunities of study unequalled hitherto; but opportunity is valuable only so far as it is turned to good account, and that can be done only by the pupil. If he is neglectful or reluctant the opportunity, however great, procured at whatever cost, becomes unfruitful. Dante in despair cried out that it was useless for Justinian to mend the bridle if the saddle were empty; and in this case the student is in the saddle. Similes have been the snares of educational discussion; but since they are habitual I will use an-

other. We have long done away with the idea of treating the
student as a creature to be fattened by force, of stuffing the
goose with chestnuts. We try to induce the youth to take intellectual nourishment by tempting his appetite. We offer
him an elaborate bill of fare composed of viands, chopped
fine to save him trouble in eating. Nay, we go farther, and
bettering in practice certain imported theories, not much followed in their native land, we proclaim that education ought
to be a wholly pleasurable exercise, without conscious, or at
least painful, effort; as if with an ordinary man the development of any power, physical or mental, could be brought
anywhere near its highest point without strenuous exertion
carried by moral force beyond the limit of mere enjoyment.

Where we have appealed to the student to exert his will
power in his work we have done so almost wholly on the
ground of personal interest. We have told him that he will
succeed better in after life. We have pointed out to him that
the study of this or that subject, or at best that excellence at
his tasks, will give him an advantage in the pursuit of his
profession. So far as it goes this is good, for anything that
tends to make him take his work more seriously is in the
right direction. But in college, where he is not directly preparing for his distinct career in life, it is hard to make him see
it. We are a people so practical, so much in the habit of looking for immediate results, that we do not readily perceive the
connection of the more remote causes and effects. The student asks how excellence in a subject that he will not use
directly can benefit him, and fails to grasp the bearing of
early mental habits on his whole subsequent activity, whatever that may be. He has not the blind faith in the educational process that comes from generations of experience.
Cannot we appeal to a higher motive also, and appeal not in
vain?

If our people are willing to make large sacrifices for education, and are right in doing so, it is because education is
good for the community; and if so the welfare of the com-

munity demands that the opportunities offered shall be used to the fullest extent. It is, therefore, the duty of the student so to use them. His attitude towards his instructor as described by President Patton, "You are the educator, I am the educatee; educate me if you can," is not only foolish, it is immoral. It is a waste of public resources, worse than that of coal or water power, because it is a waste of human resources, of the life blood of the nation. On the other hand, the student who makes full use of the opportunities offered, who is industrious and becomes proficient, merits commendation and esteem, not merely because he has been wise in his own behalf, but still more because he has helped to carry out the object for which the education is provided. As a good citizen he has done his duty by the community. If people believe this, not as an abstract proposition, but with the same fervor as other moral convictions, with half the intensity that they put into our general faith in education, it could be impressed upon youth at the most impressionable age, and the response would be great.

Japan has astonished the world by her feats in arms and in civilization. Is it unreasonable to attribute her achievements in large measure to the fact that some three hundred years ago her Samurai adopted, and have ever since retained, the habit of earnest study? In the course of a century these feudal knights acquired the conviction that an obligation lay upon every member of their class to be not only a warrior and a gentleman but also a scholar. They trained their bodies, their minds, their capacity for endurance, and when the hour sounded for the opening of their land to European ideas they were ready to go forward on the new path with the vigor of stored-up energy. Theirs was the sense of duty of a privileged caste, and strong traditions for good or for evil are more easily formed among a distinct class than in a nation. But democracy assumes that the whole people are capable of a deep sense of public duty, and that if the obligation is recognized it will be fulfilled.

If then it is the duty of youth in our land to use to the full the opportunities offered by the education which the nation has provided for the public good, they are, like the Samurai of Japan, under an obligation to become scholars. Scholarship involves hard work, self-sacrifice, renunciation of facile indolence and of many a fleeting pleasure. Can we expect that of our young men? We can expect nothing else if we convince them that the demand is serious. Anyone who thinks that the ambition of youth is to be carried to the skies on flowery beds of ease is out of place in a college. The attempt of such a man to temper natural idleness by discipline would make the college a combination of a health resort and a penitentiary. Discipline is a necessity for those whom higher motives do not stir. It must be used to drive the laggard and eliminate the unfit; but the normal young man, the man worthy of college life, craves — even if not himself aware of it — a chance to use his power for a noble end; and if the end fires his imagination, he is not deterred by the discomforts in the path. If it were not so we should be of all men most miserable, or we should not stand where we are. The difficulty lies less in the student's reluctance to heed the call than in his failure to hear it. If we could convince him that he renders a true service to the country in his undergraduate days by training his own mind in thorough scholarship, we should have less cause to lament his intellectual apathy or his indifference to the studies that colleges are founded to promote.

THE SELECTIVE FUNCTION OF EDUCATION

PART OF AN ADDRESS AT THE UNIVERSITY OF MISSOURI, 1914

EDUCATION ought to be adapted to environment, and therefore we hear much discussion today about the kind of training appropriate to a democracy. Yet we may well ask whether the true object of education really varies with the kind of government or the political center of gravity. Both for the individual and for the community the aim surely ought to be to develop in each man the fullest possible use of his natural faculties, for work, for serving the public, and for the higher forms of enjoyment. Pasteur remarked that democracy enabled every man to put forth his utmost effort; and no nation, whatever its civil polity, can approach perfection if it does not strive for that result. No doubt the aim is often perverted. The characteristic defect of an aristocracy is dread of equality, and a tendency in practice to confine the advantages of higher education to the privileged classes; and, on the other hand, it is often said that democracy dislikes inequality and tends to limit the scope of education to persons not much above the average level of ability. But these are distortions of the true object demanded by the welfare of any commonwelath, which, I may repeat, is to develop in each man the fullest possible use of his natural faculties.

If, indeed, there is any difference between the kind of schooling appropriate to democratic and to other communities, it would seem that democracies have the greater need of widely diffused general education, as compared with special training for particular occupations. An aristocracy may prepare the rank and file of men to be efficient; and, in the words of the English catechism, to order themselves lowly and reverently to all their betters and to do their duty in that state of life unto which it shall please God to call them. But in a democracy where all men partake of the character of rulers, they ought to be trained in some measure for that duty. In order to promote the solidarity of thought essential for the maintenance and progress of popular government, it is important to diffuse among the citizens familiarity with the history and traditions of the race, the acquired knowledge and wisdom on which our civilization is based. To be fruitful a democracy ought to move forward, not sidewise, nor backward, nor in a circle; and hence it must learn why it is not true, as a clever lawyer once asserted, that all propositions are born free and equal and equally likely to be right. In a democracy the whole people need the education that rulers need everywhere, an acquaintance with what are, not pedantically but correctly, termed the humanities, with what man has done, with the fabric of civilization.

If a democracy needs a widely diffused general education at least as much as other forms of government, it has certainly no smaller need of highly trained skill and of leading minds, few and costly though they be. It would certainly be irrational to claim that democracy has no use for skilful physicians or medical pioneers on the ground that the average man cannot attain thereto; to assert that democracy can forego the rare types of trained mind in every field of thought, is to deny to it the highest stages of civilization.

Granting that the object of education in a democracy ought to be to develop in each man the fullest possible use of his natural faculties, three principles seem to require special emphasis. The first is the need of a variety of institutions to serve the wants of different individuals and prepare them for different careers. All schools cannot be maintained for producing the highly trained specialist, or for developing the men of rare mental gifts. To use them for that purpose would inevitably make them less fit for teaching the ordinary person. It would result in sacrificing the many pupils to the few. Nor, on the other hand, can all schools and colleges be adapted to one type of mind, — in other words, to the most numerous class, made up of the average pupils, — without sacrificing the rarer types, to the lasting injury of the community as a whole. If, therefore, the aim of democracy is to develop in each man the fullest possible use of his natural faculties, there must be, not a uniformity in educational methods, but on the contrary a variety of institutions, at least above the elementary grade; a variety such that everyone who seeks an education desirable in his interest and that of the community may find it somewhere, in accordance with his natural capacity and his aim in life.

The second principle is that schools should not only educate children, but also direct them toward the careers in which their faculties will have the largest scope by bringing to light their natural capacities, and thus select those who will benefit most by carrying their education farther than the rest.

The third principle is that children should be guarded against entering on pursuits for which they are not well fitted, as a result of making their choice of occupations prematurely, that is, before they have had a fair chance to know their true bent and show their real power.

These three principles can be illustrated by considering the problem of vocational training. From a variety of causes this subject has assumed of late years a prominence not forced upon us in the past. America has been the land of immigration, and for nearly a century the rougher kinds of work have been done in large part by the foreign-born. American children, educated in the public schools and imbued with a spirit of enterprise, have commonly risen to positions requiring more intelligence than those filled by the ordinary full-grown immigrant. Anyone who has observed the nationality of labor, and oversight, in public works and factories for two-score years cannot fail to have observed this. The sons of men who did the unskilled, or little skilled, labor in one generation have been the foremen in the next. Hence our public schools, largely unconsciously, have been fitting people to rise upon the flood of fresh immigration, and have been giving them more general education, and therewith more resourcefulness, than would under different conditions have been the case. This has been especially true on the Atlantic seaboard, where the influx of newcomers has been most distinctly felt. But we cannot expect such a condition to last indefinitely. We must be prepared to educate the children for the whole work of a modern community.

Another cause of the growing need for vocational training is to be found in the economic changes that have taken place. Not least among them is the growth of large cities. The boy on a farm learns much about agriculture out of school, and what is more, he learns the rudiments of many trades. He acquires no small skill in the use of his hands in a variety of ways which he can turn to account later whatever occupation he may pursue. But the city boy has no such advantages. He has to be taught at school what the country boy gets from his normal life; and this ought, of course, to be given him in addition to, not in place of, his regular schooling.

Another economic change that calls for vocational training comes from the rapid progress of invention and of control over the forces of nature, involving greater skill and intelligence on the part of the workman. The Greeks demonstrated the necessity of slavery by the need of brute human strength to do the work of the world; but coal has supplied the place of this, and man has now become more than ever before a director of natural forces, with the result that the workingman requires more training for his task. Yet for that very reason he ought to be given an education that will fit him not too narrowly for a single function. The progress of invention may render his skill useless, and leave him helpless by the roadside, unless he has acquired resourcefulness enough to adapt himself to new devices.

Vocational training and vocational guidance have come to stay and ought to be heartily encouraged by everyone. But their object, nature, and limitations ought also to be clearly understood, for if not, we are in danger of defeating our own end by a confusion of aims which has in the past injured more than one excellent plan of education. In the first place, let us recognize that vocational training must be vocational; that is, it must tend to fit for a definite occupation, not equally well for any career that may afterwards be preferred. If a school is established to prepare boys for clerical situations in business, it does not fit them equally well to be carpenters, school-teachers, physicians or lawyers, and *vice versa*. The *vice versa* is generally understood today, at least by the advocates of vocational training. The schooling up to the age of, let us say sixteen or eighteen, which is appropriate to the future physician or lawyer seems to be ill adapted for the boy who is to follow a trade; and it is indeed the recognition of this fact that has caused the demand for vocational training. But there is a prevalent sentiment that the training in a commercial school, for example, ought not to be an impediment to the boy who changes his mind and decides to enter a learned profession. The partizans of the older theories of education, of what is called the doctrine of formal discipline, maintained that Latin, Greek, and Mathematics offered the best foundation for any subsequent pursuit; but now the advocates of vocational training, while rejecting with scorn the doctrine so far as these particular subjects are concerned, often seem inclined to apply it to the subjects in which they are interested. Is not, they say, bookkeeping or mechanical drawing, or anything else that requires strenuous attention, as good a mental and moral discipline as any other subject of study? They forget that discipline, although an essential foundation for all good work in life, is not the only thing in education; that the member of a learned profession, and in fact any man who is to touch the world on many sides, or touch it strongly, must have at his command as large a stock as possible of the world's store of knowledge and experience; and that bookkeeping does not furnish this in the same measure as literature, history, and science. Some occupations, therefore, require a larger study than others of the more general subjects of human thought and civilization, more of what is commonly termed liberal or general education; and the more a man can get of this, consistently with his special training and with beginning his career in life young, the better for him and for the community in which his work is done.

If all this is true, we ought to guard against the danger of beginning vocational training too soon, for a change of aim after the specialized study has begun must involve a loss of time and hence of opportunity. Observe that I referred to a feeling that vocational training ought not to be an impediment to the boy who changes his mind about his career. I said impediment, not barrier. It certainly ought not to debar him; but an impediment, a delay, it cannot fail to be, and hence a loss of the full opportunity he would have possessed of preparing for some other career had he chosen right at first. A boy who has spent a year in a commercial school must lose time if he changes his mind and goes to a trade school, just as a young man who spends a year in a law school and then decides to be a physician inevitably loses time. In the same way a boy is at a disadvantage who leaves a vocational school and tries to catch up with those who have been taking a general education with a view to a learned profession. If this were not so, it would be better to have only vocational schools, and make every boy go through one of them; but every one sees that this would not be a wise plan for the pupils who have determined to carry their education farther.

The claims of those people who feel that a change of plan ought to be made at any point without loss of time suggest a demand on the railroads that a man who has taken a train from Columbia to Kansas City should be entitled to change his mind on the way, asking to be taken to Chicago; and what is more, require that he should reach there as soon as if he had taken the train for that place. If I am right, this is not only an unreasonable demand, but one that is absolutely impossible to fulfil.

The claim that a boy be placed at no serious disadvantage on the road to higher education by entering a vocational school is not only a snare to him, but is liable to affect the nature of the school itself. Teachers in schools, and for that matter in colleges, are apt to take a disproportionate interest in those pupils who intend to go farther. The schoolmaster is inclined to take pride in having his boys go to college; and if some one subject, not normally taught in the school, is required for the purpose, he is tempted to introduce it. Without deliberate intention, perhaps, he magnifies that side of his work, and talks about it until the school comes to be so popularly known as an avenue to higher education that a cry arises in the community for a vocational school distinct from this one which prepares for college. Such a fear may seem chimerical, but that very process has taken place in more than one of the public schools I have known, and doubtless any man familiar with the educational history of our older cities could point to others. We shall never succeed in maintaining thoroughly successful vocational schools until we realize that they must be strictly vocational; that the special training needed for different occupations branches off from the main trunk of general education at different points, which are not by any means absolutely fixed, but are still markedly different from one another and in some cases far apart.

Now, if it be true that a change of aim after vocational training has begun entails a loss of time and of opportunity, it would seem to follow that the moment of choice ought to be postponed as long as is consistent with a thorough preparation for the special work of life. Intelligent vocational guidance may save many mistakes in selecting a career; but mistakes will be made, and the younger the age of choice the more numerous they will be and the greater the loss involved in a change. In other words the special training should branch off from the main trunk of general education no lower down than is necessary; and this for the sake of postponing the moment of choice — quite apart from any question of the intrinsic value of the general education.

The relative proportion of general and special training may, indeed, be the same under two plans, although the time of choice is very different. In a vocational school, for example, the pupils might begin at the age of fourteen on a three years' course which contained general subjects scattered through it, equal in the aggregate to about one year of work; or those subjects might be studied before entering the vocational school, which would then have a curriculum of two years devoted wholly to special training. In each case the pupils would have precisely the same studies, but in one case they would choose their vocation definitely at fourteen, and in the other at fifteen, thereby diminishing the number and seriousness of mistakes. I am fully aware that this is not the only consideration to be taken into account in determining the arrangement of general and special studies; the general subjects may be appreciated better at a maturer age, or they may be so taught in the special school as to have a more obvious bearing on the vocation. In short, there are many reasons for and against a separation of general from special studies; and in this instance, as in many others, it may be wise to compromise between contradictory objects; but let it be a conscious compromise, not a blind attempt to attain both ends.   Certainly the advantage of postponing the moment for choosing a career weighs heavily in favor of finishing general education so far as possible before taking up specialized studies — at least in the case of vocational schools that must be entered in boyhood.

To postpone the time for the choice of a vocation not only gives the pupil a better chance of choosing his career wisely, but also gives the school a better chance of selection among the pupils, for every public school that does not prepare for a particular occupation has this double function. It ought to educate, and it ought to reveal the natural capacity of every boy or girl. It ought to give them a chance to develop their powers without being sidetracked by a precocious attraction for something below their real power; and this is the more difficult the earlier the choice of a vocation is made. The boy with a little manual dexterity, or a superficial mechanical taste, may be prematurely led into a trade when in fact he has the ability, yet unknown, to distinguish himself as an engineer, a lawyer, or a man of science; and one of the prime objects of education, above all in the fluid opportunities of a democracy, ought to be to discover, not merely the inclination of the boy, but far more his inherent capacity. Owing to the fashionable popular disrespect for "merely high scholars" we pay less attention to this function of public schools than we ought. Popular education should be, not a training alone, but also a process of sifting.

Standards in education we want, but uniformity we do not want; for the creation of a standard means raising the minimum, while uniformity means lowering that which is above the average. Therefore standards without uniformity mean requiring that all shall reach at least a certain plane, and that there may be variety above that plane. The object of variety is to provide for every boy the education which will develop him most. This rests on the assumption that unusual capacity is relatively rare and that the community must make great sacrifices to find and develop it — sacrifices, however, which in the interest of the community itself are well repaid. The sacrifice is great because the expense of educating a few is inevitably larger for each man taught than that of educating many, and because the farther education is carried the more expensive it becomes. For the present such work in America must probably be provided in large part, although by no means exclusively, by endowment, rather than by taxation. Certainly it ought not to be done at any loss or detriment to the great mass of young men who must take a shorter path to the active practice of their professions.

Let us not forget that both the educational institutions directed by the state and supported by taxation, and those maintained by endowment, form parts of a national system of public education. They ought to be so regarded by those who are responsible for them, and by everyone else; and both should be conducted with a single eye to the welfare of the community.

Now in order that a national system of education, comprising a variety of institutions of all grades, may attain the ends for which it exists, the schools must exercise freely a selective function. They must sift their pupils, measuring them, and leading them toward the kind and extent of training most fitted for their capacity. Naturally the process of sifting is not the only factor determining the point to which education shall be carried. The private and endowed schools strive to bring forward all their pupils, because parents who have the means want their children to have the benefit of higher education, whether they possess the intellectual qualities to make the best use of it or not. Nor is this a source of regret. Of all the forms of luxury the most pardonable, nay one wholly laudable, is the luxury of education. The rich man who gives his son an automobile or a yacht is not to be compared with the parent who gives him the best education to be had; and the poor father and mother who pinch themselves to send their children to college are worthy of honor from all good citizens. Fortunately, such a spirit is widespread in America, and not least strong among the descendants of the foreign-born.

But for the great mass of boys and girls higher education must be confined to those who will profit by it most, and they ought to receive it in full measure. Of all the progressive countries of the world the United States is probably the one where the school system is used least to sift out the pupils of unusual natural powers, and urge them onward to their utmost capacity. Democracy stands for many things, some of them not entirely consistent with one another. It stands for equality and for personal opportunity, and in education we are a little apt to think more of the former. Opportunity we furnish, no doubt, to all alike, and the youth who has ambition, self-confidence, and force of character finds an opening through which he may push himself to the front, but superior talent is not sought out as it is in some countries. In education we tend to travel on a minimum of requirement, to regard the ordinary diploma or degree as the goal of achievement. Excellence in school or college work is not commonly regarded as a measure of power to the extent that it is in Europe; and perhaps it is not in fact so good a measure of capacity as it ought to be for the very reason that we do not use it as such. Owing partly to working for a minimum, partly to a theory of the doctors that much study is a dangerous weariness to the flesh, we force the pace less than other nations. This is particularly true in the elementary stages, far less in the high school, but again is unfortunately too true in college.

Democracy, in one aspect at least, ought to strive in a peculiar degree to develop the individual, to bring out the many diverse qualities of its citizens. To that end it is an advantage to possess different kinds of schools, colleges, and universities; and each school, elementary and high, and each college, should be an instrument for selecting the pupils capable of still higher education. In this way alone can the community obtain the benefit of its largest resource of wealth, progress, and greatness, the capacity of its own people. Only in this way can it approach the aim of education, to develop in each man the fullest possible use of his natural faculties.

CULTURE

An Address Prepared for an Inauguration at the University of North Carolina, April 28, 1915, but not Delivered at that Time

Among those who have met to celebrate this day, I have been entrusted with the difficult task of speaking about culture. But there is nothing in the world more elusive. One cannot define or circumscribe it, for it has no precise bounds. One cannot analyse it, for its components are infinite. One cannot describe it, for it is protean in shape. An attempt to encompass its meaning in words is like trying to seize the air in the hand, when one finds it is everywhere except within one's grasp. Culture is like what the ancient Hebrews called wisdom in that it has no fixed habitation, but is all-pervading and imponderable in its essence. Everyone who has experienced it knows something of it; no one knows it all; to no two people does it wear exactly the same aspect; and yet to all who have in it any share it appears real, substantial, and of measureless worth.

In general, the term is used to denote something distinct from a command of the tools of one's trade. The lawyer, for example, or the physician, or the engineer, may have a complete mastery of all the technical learning of his profession without possessing culture. This is evident at once when he comes into contact with men of other professions. He may talk profoundly about his own subject, but have nothing intellectual in common with the other men if he lives within the four walls of his own occupation and his vision is strictly limited thereby.

That so large a part of general conversation in America relates to the weather, to politics, and to sport is not so much because these things are intrinsically more interesting or variable than in other countries, as because they are among the few subjects that everyone is familiar with and can talk about. Professional learning is, no doubt, cultivating, but standing alone it is not culture, for the reason that it is circumscribed and includes only a narrow part of the stream of human thought. For a lawyer to look through the microscope of a man of science increases his means of culture, for it broadens his ideas by revealing to his sight things before unknown. But the scientific man who can see only through his microscope has a very restricted vision of the world; and the same thing is true of every pursuit when restricted to its own limited field. When Charles Darwin said that in his later life he lost interest in almost everything except the pursuit of his own scientific studies, he stated that he was losing his sense of culture; and unless the loss promoted in some way his great work it was a misfortune.

At one time, not yet very remote, culture denoted a definite body of knowledge, the common possession of all educated men, the boundaries of which were fairly well defined by the curriculum of what was called a liberal education. The conception of such a distinction between liberal or polite learning and other information underlay the squib current at Oxford about Jowett.

> My name is Benjamin Jowett,
> I'm the Master of Balliol College,
> Whate'er can be known, I know it,
> And what I don't know is not knowledge.

But with the rapid growth of human knowledge, with the rise in rank of new professions to the same level as the older ones, with the extension of the subjects taught in a scholarly way in the institutions of higher learning, it has become obviously impossible for anyone to know more than a small part of the things that are properly termed liberal or polite. There has wholly ceased to be any fixed body of knowledge that every well educated man can be expected to possess. Nor, save the great monuments of literature, especially in one's own tongue, can any subject be said to be absolutely essential to the equipment of a well educated man, none that can be labelled indispensable for culture, — certainly none with which a man must be thoroughly familiar. Of no subject, on the other hand, can we say that it forms no part of a liberal education; of none, also, that its most complete mastery will alone deserve the name. A scholar may conceivably have a most minute and comprehensive knowledge of history, or of philosophy, or of classical literature and philology, and yet, if he has strictly nothing more, not merit the title of a man of culture.

Culture, therefore, does not mean the possession of a body of knowledge common to all educated men, for there is no such thing today. It denotes rather an attitude of mind than a specific amount of information. It implies enjoyment of things the world has agreed are beautiful; interest in the knowledge that mankind has found valuable; comprehension of the principles that the race has accepted as true. All this involves a desire to know coupled with a capacity to acquire and appreciate. No doubt men differ very much in their natural power of acquiring such a culture. Some people are born with little or no aptitude for it, others with a strong impulse for it, but no one is born possessed of it. No one can attain it without long continued toil, and an effort that may be pleasant or irksome, that may seem easy or laborious according to personal temperament and energy, but is always strenuous.

If there is no royal road to learning or to culture, no broad highway that one can traverse in rapid indolence in an expensive motor car, or cheaply for a five-cent fare, there are, on the other hand, many different paths leading to the goal — some of them well-beaten by the footsteps of those who have passed, and are yearly passing, over them; some less frequented, and trodden only by earnest men who have the intelligence and persistence to find the way. It is with the former that our colleges are chiefly concerned because it is their duty to guide students through the most certain and quickest roads to the end they seek.

But if culture itself is elusive, the roads thereto are not fixed by authoritative signboards, nor mapped out by universal agreement; and if culture no longer implies a recognized body of knowledge, there is no regular curriculum of studies leading to it. An attitude of mind is a much more subtle thing to produce, and many are the differences of opinion about the way to set about the task. One cannot speak, therefore, dogmatically as of generally accepted doctrines, but only from the standpoint of personal conviction.

Certain principles, it seems to me, may be clearly seen, or deduced from the nature of the object in view. If for culture one must have learned to enjoy as many as possible of the things the world deems beautiful; to know enough to take an interest in all knowledge that mankind has found valuable; and to have pondered enough to comprehend the ideas that the race has accepted as true, then it is obvious that to be cultivated a man must at some time have had some acquaintance with a good many subjects. The number of these, however, is not so large as one might suppose, because entrance into one field often opens the gateway to others. Appreciation of good literature in one language provides the basis for appreciating it in another, and to a less extent this is true between any two different arts. The same thing may be said of the various branches of science. Each subject has many points of contact to which any new kindred thing will adhere, so that, unless it withers away by disuse, knowledge tends to roll up like a snowball. Similes are the bane of educational reasoning, and perhaps in this case it would be better to use the language in which I have already spoken of culture, and say that an attitude of intellectual attention and appreciation having been acquired in any subject, it tends to increase and to bring fresh knowledge of things similar to those in which interest has been awakened.

The moral to be drawn is that which the late William James laid down in his *Talk to Teachers*: All thought springs from a cue; therefore increase the number of cues as much as you can. The man or woman who desires to be cultivated should strive to have at least a little familiarity with as many diverse fields of human thought as possible. No great region should be wholly a strange, unexplored wilderness, traversed only by people who utter dark sentences in an unknown tongue.

A second moral may also be taken from William James. He used to insist that no one learns a new subject after twenty-nine, and the saying sometimes hurt the feelings of people who had passed that age. Nevertheless, it is in the main true, not only because after maturity the mind is normally less receptive, but also because modern life is so full of activity, even for those who have nothing useful to do, that it is hard to find time for the heavy work of studying the elements of a new subject.

But there is another side to all this. A mere smattering of many things may give a facility in conversation, an appearance of education, a superficial aspect of culture, while the substance is hopelessly lacking.

I remember a young friend of mine of whom it was said that he was striving to acquire many accomplishments but no education. It is not enough to stake out a claim to knowledge, and run the bounds. That may be of some use against outsiders, but it yields little profit to oneself. The possessor may claim the territory, but he cannot live on it. Everyone is aware of the difference between two people in their intellectual approach to a subject with which they have only a slight acquaintance when one of them has a smattering of many things without a real mastery of any, and the other has a firm grasp of the principles in some branch of knowledge. We say that the latter has a trained mind while the smatterer has not. The trained mind recognizes quickly the distinction between superficial phenomena and the underlying causes that produce them. Such a mind goes, we say, easily to the root of the matter. This is an art that can be learned, but like other arts it can be learned only by practice, that is by getting at the root of something.

The art, or the habit, of getting at the root of things is essentially an attitude of mind. So far as the subject matter is concerned over which a mastery is acquired it may be called knowledge, but as regards other subjects it is certainly an attitude of mind, and this is the more enduring. The special knowledge may pass away, but the habit of thought does not. Let me take an example from science, for the laws of nature are as fully a branch of modern culture as anything else. If one learns by the study of geology to observe natural objects, not merely to see what is obvious to the untrained eye, but to notice those things that are related to geologic forces, he may find after a time that the names and characteristics of the different rocks, the detail in the succession of the different strata, are in great part forgotten through disuse, but the habit of observation will remain and can be applied to other natural objects. In fact, such a habit will almost certainly be kept from decay by constant use in many things. This is true of all study, no matter what the subject may be; and if so, a penetrating, thorough, and profound attitude of mind is one of the most important arts that can be acquired.

This address deals not so much with culture as with the basis for culture that can be laid by a college or university, since culture, like all education, must continue through life. All we can do as teachers is to lay the best foundation for it that we can, and the upshot of the argument here presented is comprised in the old adage that the true basis for culture is to know a little of everything and everything of something. While we may admit that this is the object to be sought, sharp differences of opinion exist, and will long remain, in regard to the means of attaining it. One question thrusts itself prominently forward. Every man who is to study a profession must, if he is serious, master that subject well; why then, it may be asked, should he not devote his previous college course wholly to getting a wide acquaintance with as many subjects as possible, and leave his thorough knowledge of one field to his professional training? The answer is obvious to anyone who has had practical experience. The mind that deals only with elementary work in many subjects rarely gets the vigorous training needed to acquire a firm grasp of any of them. The smatterer on leaving college is a smatterer. He has never learned anything thoroughly, and although he may do so later, his subsequent training will hardly relate backwards to illumine and deepen his knowledge of subjects that was superficial when he acquired it. If the best result is to be obtained, the thorough study of one subject must be contemporaneous with the diversified study of others and radiate light into them.

Another question of a diametrically opposite tendency presents itself no less forcibly. Why should not the professional study accompany the getting of an acquaintance with many other subjects, so that both go along together, the professional training supplying the backbone of the college curriculum? This a much more subtle, if not a more difficult, question, and it is one that we must actually face, because it involves a strong existing tendency among American colleges. Again the answer to it is found only in practical experience. Professional study leading to a man's career in life is, and ought to be, almost passionately absorbing in comparison with other subjects pursued at the same time. These are apt to be regarded as of lesser importance as outlying parts of the curriculum of the school somewhat arbitrarily forced upon the student, and not of direct value commensurate with the things needed in professional life. It is well-nigh impossible, for example, to persuade a student of law, medicine, or engineering that literature is for him a serious matter, on a par with his technical work. General subjects are, therefore, likely to be neglected or treated lightly when studied in a school primarily professional. When, on the other hand, professional courses are introduced into a college curriculum they are apt to suffer, not, indeed, as compared with the general subjects, but as compared with what can be accomplished in a school wholly devoted to preparation for a career. It is difficult in a college, with its alluring extra-curricular activities, to create the strong professional atmosphere that promotes the best technical training.

For men therefore who can give the time, there is a distinct advantage in pursuing their general studies before the professional ones. In short, there is much to be said for separating the work of college and professional schools. It follows also that the course in the college ought to cover a number of different subjects, together with a somewhat thorough study of one among them. What that one should be will vary with the personal aptitude of the student. In my own opinion it is better, as a general rule, that it should not be too closely akin to the subject which will engross attention in the chief occupation of life; because any direct professional knowledge that can be obtained in college is trifling compared with what can be acquired in a far shorter period in a professional school, and the attempt to obtain it crowds out some other subject that will probably never be studied at a later time.

This not the time to review the methods of education in foreign countries. To be successful, any system must be consistent with itself, and it is unsafe to graft a foreign limb onto a root unadapted to sustain it. So far as culture is concerned, our problem is to develop in harmony with our own institutions a type of education that will cause young people to enjoy the things the world has agreed are beautiful, to be interested in the knowledge mankind has found valuable, and to comprehend the principles the race has accepted as true. This is culture, and to impart it is a function of the American college.

We are sometimes told that after youths are emancipated from the rigid discipline of the schoolmaster they cannot be made to take very seriously any studies which do not have a manifest bearing on their career in life. But if it be true that they cannot be led to work hard in an earnest effort to understand the knowledge slowly wrought out, and the civilization painfully achieved by man upon this planet, then our colleges do not deserve to survive and will certainly die.

THE DUTY OF ADDING TO KNOWLEDGE

Part of Remarks Originally Made at the Boston Harvard Club
in or near 1916

The usefulness of a great university is by no means exhausted by its teaching. It has two functions, both so essential that neither can be said to be more important than the other. One is that of preserving and imparting the knowledge slowly acquired in the past, the other is that of adding to it. The question a university should ask is not whether an idea is old or new, but only whether it is true, and the universities have shown that there is no difficulty in combining the retention of what is good in the old with the strenuous search for new truth. Hitherto, America has not done its share in adding to knowledge, but has depended too much upon Europe. This is particularly true in the case of Chemistry, which has been left far too much in the hands of Germany, both on the side of pure science and in its application to industry. It is the more unfortunate because the greatest advance during the next generation in scientific discovery, in medicine, and in the arts appears to lie in the field of Chemistry. In this country we certainly need to develop its study far more than in the past, to train men as experts in the many industries in which it is essential; and we must not forget that research in pure science and in its application go hand in hand. The discoveries made in university laboratories have almost always a direct or indirect application in the life of man, and the expert in the laboratory of a manufacturing concern not only puts into practice discoveries made by the university professor, but makes new investigations of his own in the chemical principles that affect his industry. For Chemistry, our universities must have far better laboratories and a much larger number of skilled investigators.

It is a constant grief to see men who could add largely to knowledge expend themselves without doing so on account of the pressure of teaching, and of administrative work which fills their time and exhausts their strength. In many fields, in every field, we must seek to stimulate and provide opportunities for those rare spirits that are capable of productive work. In the past the attention of America has been engrossed by opening a continent and subduing a wilderness, by cultivating vast new lands, building railroads, working mines, creating factories, and turning a huge region unoccupied by civilized people into a teaming hive of industry. It has been content to receive most of its intellectual conceptions at second hand. It has not contributed to the advance of thought of which we believe it to be abundantly capable. We long to have our country great in other than material things. Carthage, mistress of commerce in the ancient world, has left no trace on human thought, while Athens, also a maritime metropolis, created the mould of thought that has dominated the modern world.

This war has cast new duties upon the new world; and they are not only financial, commercial, and political, but also intellectual and spiritual. How many young men who would have added to the scholarship of the world, how many potential philosophers, artists, and men of science have met an untimely death in Flanders, Picardy, Champagne, or around Verdun we shall never know. But we do know that among the millions who have fallen Europe has been bereft of much of the flower of its youth, and among them of many men who if they had been spared would have been the chief contributors to the sum of human knowledge, to the progress of thought and civilization. That loss we must strive to repair, and it is to our universities and colleges that we must turn.

SCIENTIFIC STUDY OF EDUCATION

An Address at the Semi-Centennial of Carleton College,
Northfield, Minnesota, October 13, 1916

Reprinted from the Harvard Alumni Bulletin of October 19

We are told in the book of Daniel, "They that be wise, shall shine as the brightness of the firmament; and they that turn many to righteousness, as the stars for ever and ever." Our country is studded with colleges to teach wisdom and righteousness; and we have met today to commemorate the fiftieth anniversary of one of those colleges. Save for the variable stars that revolve around a dark companion, the celestial bodies do not change in brightness;[1] but this is not true of institutions that teach wisdom, and Carleton College has become more luminous with the passing years. Her light is stronger now than it ever was before; and yet I suspect that even on this day of retrospect, of thankfulness for the achievements of the past, her officers of instruction and government are thinking less of what has been accomplished in the half-century since her foundation than of what will be done in the years to come; of the trimming of the lamp to make it glow with a still brighter and steadier light.

Education is the last of man's creations to follow the current of the age. At present we know less about it scientifically than about almost any other subject. Much scientific work has been done in primary education, in measuring, for example, the teaching of reading, writing, and arithmetic; but we are almost without scientific study of college education. Our methods there are partly traditional, partly empirical. It is commonly said that American universities are a combination of English and German models; that upon a college copied from England we have superimposed a German university; that the great English universities have aimed to

[1] Now scientifically disproved.

train men for citizenship, the German to train them for professions. No doubt the statement is in large part true, but we need not examine now the character of foreign institutions of learning, or strive to compute our debt to each of them. It is enough that we have both colleges and professional schools, the former having as their primary object education for citizenship, the latter training for a specific career.

Our schooling for the professions is on the whole very good; but about college education we are still much at sea. There are two reasons for this. In the first place, we are a practical people, attracted by immediate visible results. Intangible good of a general character seems to us vague, nebulous, if not unreal. We like to know the definite object of a curriculum, what in particular it is fitting a student to do. In the second place, it is comparatively easy to adjust a curriculum to a profession. The object is clear, precise, and of limited scope. A great array of subjects highly valuable in general education is discarded at the outset as irrelevant, and the bearing of the rest is ascertained without great difficulty. Education for citizenship is a far more complicated matter, because the best type of citizen is not merely the man who is familiar with his ordinary civic duties, but one who can form correct opinions, who in thought is courageous and open-minded, whose influence raises the moral and intellectual level of the community, and whose faculties have been developed as highly as possible.

The old college curriculum was based mainly on Latin, Greek, and mathematics, but with the vast growth of knowledge in these and other fields such a requirement was found to be no longer possible as the universal basis of higher education. Nor could any list of studies for a four years' college course be prescribed that was both essential and sufficient for everybody, because there is at the present stage of the world no body of knowledge which all cultivated men or women may be satisfied to possess and without which they can be considered uneducated. Since the abandonment of the old fixed curriculum we have been offered theories in abundance, but little positive, ascertained fact.

We hear much about discipline, but the word, which had a somewhat definite scholastic meaning and has been the subject of much controversy among students of pedagogy, has come to be employed popularly in a highly ambiguous sense. It is commonly used in the sense of moral discipline, rather than mental discipline or training in the use of the intellectual faculties. We are told that stenography, work at a forge or in a factory, drill in camp, and playing on a football team involve as much discipline as the ordinary college studies and merit therefore an academic credit. Clearly the discipline here referred to is moral discipline. No one would seriously contend that these subjects involved such exercise, and therefore such training, of the purely intellectual faculties as can be derived from the classics, mathematics, physics, economics, and other studies of a scholastic character. We are fully aware that in our colleges we have paid too little attention to moral discipline; that we have suffered a slothfulness, slackness, and lack of precision which are a bad preparation for any useful or happy life. We are striving, not without some success, to remedy this defect; but that is quite a different matter from the question what subjects of study will most help to develop a student's mind. The difference explains the reason for rejecting arguments to include certain subjects in the list for admission to college, on the ground that they involve as much discipline as others already included.

Of mental discipline it is unwise to speak, — I mean it is unwise to use that term. One is likely to find oneself accused of believing that the mind is divided into faculties, thought-tight comparments, each penetrable only by means of a certain subject of study taught in a certain way; or on the other hand to be charged with supposing that the mind has no faculties at all, but only an appreciation of subject matter, so that practice in adding, subtracting, and multiplying apples gives no facility in performing the same operations with shares of stock. It is well to avoid the region of these controversies, for fear of finding oneself under shell fire, with mines exploding below and bombs dropped from above.

Perhaps it is inoffensive to assume that in educating their students for citizenship the colleges ought to give them some familiarity with our civilization, ought to enable them to think clearly, to discriminate accurately and to deal with complex facts, and ought to stimulate their capacity for imagination. Let me illustrate what is meant. A man or woman who has no comprehension of Athens, of the Roman Empire, the Feudal System, Magna Carta, the French Revolution, and the history of his own race and country; who has no acquaintance with the great monuments of literature, art, and music, or with philosophic and religious thought; who knows nothing of the fundamental principles of science, such as the conservation of energy, the parallelogram of forces, the biological curve: such a one is not familiar with our civilization. No one at the present day can know all about all of these things; and yet it is not enough that one man should know one of them well, and the next man all about another, each being in profound, somnolent ignorance of everything outside his chosen field. We should be like a village in which each inhabitant had a thorough scholarly knowledge of a different vocabulary of just one hundred words, while no one knew the auxiliary verbs. In Germany there is something like a common foundation for the higher education because the university is preceded by the rigorous curriculum of the Gymnasium or the Realschule; but there is nothing fully corresponding to these institutions here, and in·our colleges we make little systematic effort to supply the deficiency. It would be well if someone would make a comprehensive investigation of the varying practice in our many colleges, with a comparative study of the results as shown in the subsequent work of the students in professional and graduate schools. Something valuable would be, and much might be, learned thereby.

To develop the ability to think aright — the habit of correct abstract reasoning and of weighing evidence — is even a more difficult problem in education than the imparting of some familiarity with our civilization. It is nevertheless essential, both for the individual that he should possess it for his work in life, and for the community that it should be possessed by its citizens. Defective reasoning in matters affecting the public may be very dangerous. We have suffered from it in the past and may still more in the future, for there seems to be a growing disregard of accuracy in thought when opposed to sentiment, emotion, or plausible theory.

Defective reasoning is exceedingly common. Many people, even educated people, do not understand why, if they observe on one occasion that a storm has cleared up at the new moon, it is no evidence at all that the moon affects the weather; or why, if they sit down thirteen at table and one dies within the year, it has no tendency whatever to prove that the dinner had any connection with the death; whereas, if, after a child with infantile paralysis is brought into a town, other cases break out, it has a tendency to prove, but gives no conclusive proof, that the disease is directly contagious; or why, if one rubs poisonous ivy on his hand and is poisoned it proves conclusively that he is susceptible to that poison. A man with a thoroughly trained mind will recognize all this at once, not because he has taken a course in formal logic or in the doctrine of chances, but because he has been in the habit of thinking clearly and weighing evidence. He has also a background of knowledge, a familiarity with many problems involving diverse factors. He sees almost instinctively that, as the weather changes constantly, coincidences with the changes of the moon must be so frequent that a single instance proves nothing; and that the only evidence of any value is a tabulation of the weather and the positions of the moon for a long period of time. He knows that people apparently in good health often die unexpectedly within the year, and that a single coincidence with thirteen at table is therefore meaningless. On the other hand he is aware that an epidemic disease must be communicated by one of a very few methods, of which direct contagion is among the most common, and therefore an outbreak of the malady after the coming of the infected person is likely to be more than a mere coincidence. Finally he knows that ivy poison is given only by poisonous ivy (and a few other plants which are rare and whose absence he can be sure of), and hence if he is poisoned it must be by ivy.

We have all met with similar instances of fallacy in reasoning. Some men think that because they have known one or two inferior scholars who have had a great success in life it shows that poor scholars do better than good ones afterwards, or at least that scholarship has no connection with success; whereas they are fully aware that if they have known one or two slow-witted boys who have succeeded it does not prove that a quick mind is not an advantage, but only that the dull minds are not wholly barred out. The winning of the race by the tortoise was an exception. No one would have staked a bet on him either before or after his victory. Everybody's logical powers and background of knowledge include hares and tortoises. We do not need, as in some other cases, elaborate statistics to ascertain and demonstrate the facts.

Almost any subject thoroughly studied under a good teacher will, no doubt, confer some power of correct reasoning and of weighing evidence; but what the relative value of different subjects may be for each of these objects we do not know. In some extreme instances we can make a shrewd guess. That pure mathematics, for example, has more effect than history in training abstract reasoning, and that history has an advantage over mathematics in teaching the use of evidence, is, perhaps, obvious. But in general we are very much in the dark, and we ought not to be if it is possible to get light.

In regard to stimulating the imagination, we are still more ignorant; and by imagination I mean not merely the preposterous creations of fancy, but the constructing of any idea not apparent — the stuff of which all resourcefulness is made. Is imagination in this larger sense stimulated best by inductive work like that of the laboratory, or by the more abstract process of deduction, or by a combination of the two, and if so in what order and proportion? Does a study of other subjects far removed from the special field assist or impede it? Is a man of science stimulated or diverted by philosophy, literature, and history; and is a man of letters aided or hindered by a study of science? In this case again single instances or a small number of cases are of little value. Personal surmises by anyone of how much more he might have achieved had his education been different are practically useless. Personal impressions of the amount of benefit a man has actually derived from certain studies are worth more. Probably something could be learned by examining the careers of large numbers of men educated by different methods but working in the same field; although we are dealing here with a subject in which personality is a peculiarly large factor.

A comparison of the progress of knowledge in medicine and in education is interesting and instructive. A century and more ago medicine was still a battleground for theories, the Brunonian theory, the Homeopathic theory, and the rest. But when scientific methods, with careful observation, tabulation of results, and experimentation, secured a firm hold upon the leading minds in the profession, and especially among the teachers in medical schools, knowledge of disease became far greater and incomparably more precise and certain. It is high time that the same progress should take place in education. We ought to pass from the stage of theory, however plausible, to that of scientific knowledge.

No doubt scientific methods are more difficult to apply in education than in medicine. The effective use of experiment, such as is done with animals in cases of disease, is largely barred out in education, because we can try experiments in teaching children or young people only so far as we believe they are a benefit, or at least harmless, to the individuals themselves. We have no right to give anyone an intentionally bad education for the sake of observing the result; and experimentation so limited is robbed of a large part of its value. Nor can we make a pure culture of a mental process in a test tube, ascertain its nature by staining it, isolating and studying it under a microscope.

Moreover, differently as individual bodies may react to the same chemical substance or germ introduced therein, the results are relatively uniform compared with the processes in the human brain. We do not know what is already in the mind, what other agencies may be at work there, what may flow in by channels outside of the class room. That intellectual sponge absorbs all kinds of things and combines or transforms them into different shapes. The stream of thought is fed by many rills which we can neither stop nor analyze. In early childhood, in the first period of schooling, the problem is more simple and the results of teaching can be, and have been, measured with accuracy. But with advancing years the conditions become more complex, especially when we are seeking to discover, not the effect of a particular method of instruction on a knowledge of that subject, but the effect of different subjects on the development of the student's natural capacity. This depends upon so many factors, and so much upon the person himself, that little can be learned from a study, however thorough, of individual cases. A capable, vigorous man with a very bad education will in the race of life pass a dull, feeble one with a very good education. We must therefore deal not with single individuals, but with averages, and one of the few accurate ways to study averages is by statistics, large enough in number to overcome the effect of exceptions, and compiled so as to eliminate systematic errors. This is a highly laborious business, but it can be done, and must be done if we are to make any notable progress in the knowledge of college education. Each college could contribute its share to the result, and one of the great endowments for education could undertake a comprehensive study of the results in all the colleges. A prime difficulty is to find any true measure of the subsequent effect of a college course, since much depends in after life upon matters foreign to a man's own qualities, — upon getting a fortunate start, upon the influence of father or friends, upon wealth or poverty, marriage, health, and a host of other things. It would require an enormous mass of cases, and very careful, perhaps impossible, analysis to determine with perfect accuracy success in after life. The records of college graduates in professional schools have been used, and are trustworthy so far as they go. Doubtless other tests could be found that would yield at least approximate results.

It is probable, nay certain, that the qualities needed for training the intellectual faculties can be obtained from different subjects; just as in nutrition, protein, starch, and fat can be derived from a diet of beef, bread, and butter, or from beans, potatoes, and pork. The same effect will not be produced by a combination of any three of these six articles of food at random; and the same thing may well be true of subjects in education. No doubt the results attained by the study of any subject must always depend to a very large extent upon the object with which it is taught or studied. Latin in the high school may be taught, as it once was in many places, mainly as an exercise of memory in learning by heart rules and long lists of exceptions to them. It may be taught for the sake of grammatical construction, or chiefly for the literary value of the authors read.

William James early in life gave a college course on comparative anatomy and physiology. He told me that he could pick out the men who intended to enter the medical school because their attention was directed mainly to the small amount of human anatomy that figured in the course, to the neglect of the broader scientific relations which interested the other students. These two groups of men drew very different results from their studies. The elements that a man draws from any subject may also depend upon his type of mind and his previous studies. Many years ago two graduates of the Harvard law school were comparing what they had acquired from their studies there. They agreed that they had learned little substantive law which they had applied directly in practice. One of them, who had devoted himself in college mainly to history, thought that the chief benefit he had obtained from the law school was a greater ability to reason correctly; while the other, whose principal college work had been in mathematics, felt that his chief benefit had been in learning the importance of primary, as distinguished from derived, sources of authority.

The fact that men may obtain, or think they obtain, quite different benefits from a study of the same subject is not inconsistent with real differences in the ordinary effects upon the mind of the various subjects as they are usually taught in college. The two lawyers, it may be observed, thought, and no doubt rightly, that their minds had not been trained alike by history and mathematics. But of the intellectual effects of different subjects, and still more, of combinations of subjects, we know little or nothing. Surely we ought to investigate them, not by framing theories based on *a priori* reasoning, or on a few examples that happen to have fallen under our observation, but by the best scientific methods we can devise.

On one side we find teachers who believe that from our practical experience we know now all that we need to frame an adequate plan of education in all its stages; if, indeed, they do not think that our present practice is already just what it should be. On the other side we hear prophets who would construct a completely new scheme on the basis of a theory which they hold to be convincing if not self-evident. Neither of these would seem to point out the true path of future progress. Neither contentment nor dissatisfaction with existing conditions furnishes by itself a safe guide. The results achieved by long practical experience are worth much, but to adhere to them without improvement means stagnation and decay. They are incomplete, defective, and above all ill-adapted to a rapidly changing world. On the other hand, a new conception based mainly upon a protest against existing defects, although containing much which is useful and ought to be considered, does not point the way to the constructive work needed for the creation of an enduring fabric.

It is inconceivable that the vast expansion of human knowledge should not permanently change our education, as the fuller acquaintance with Greek literature changed education at the Renaissance; and it is not less inconceivable that we should remain in a state of educational chaos for lack of positive knowledge obtained by the methods of modern science.

We have met at a college of the Middle West justly held in high esteem; a part of the country inhabited by fearless men to whom people throughout the length and breadth of our land have a right to look for advance in education; — a country less bound by tradition than the older states, free to retain what is good in the past, but to leaven it with whatever is better that the future may have in store; a region that will possess the diversity of industries essential to a ripe civilization, but likely hereafter to be more homogeneous in population than the Atlantic seaboard. The destiny of this great central valley of the continent, and with it of our whole nation, will depend in large part upon its institutions of higher learning, — the colleges and universities founded in the early days of hard struggle in the wilderness, nurtured by the devotion of two generations of teachers, standing now in their mature strength, proud of what they have done and what they are, but looking forward confidently into the distant years to come. It is in this spirit that we are assembled in thankfulness and trustfulness to bring our greetings to Carleton College on her birthday.

THE ART OF EXAMINATION

ADDRESS AT THE INAUGURATION OF PRESIDENT BURTON OF THE
UNIVERSITY OF MICHIGAN, OCTOBER 15, 1920

WE HAVE met here not only to participate in the inauguration of Mr Burton as the new President of the University of
Michigan, and to express our hope and confidence in the
future of that great institution, but also to take an account
of stock in the educational progress of the nation. Everyone
will admit that the present condition of education in this
country has its merits and its defects. The product of our
schools and colleges shows a remarkable degree of resourcefulness and adaptability. This may not be wholly due to our
educational system, but in part to the environment, which
tends to develop these qualities in our people; for they are
shown also by men whose systematic education has been exceedingly limited. Nevertheless, it is easy to underrate the
effects of schooling. Men often attribute far too little to their
instruction, and too much to their own inherent qualities. It
is not only certain that our education has not tended to diminish natural resourcefulness and adaptability, but these
very traits have been shown most markedly among college-
bred men, as was seen in the late war. The two qualities of
resourcefulness and adaptability have been, indeed, those
that we have most needed in the past. They have been
absolutely essential for the great American achievement,
unparalleled in so short a period, of bringing under cultivation a vast wilderness, of developing the mines and other
natural resources of a continent, and of developing varied
industries for a hundred millions of people. But all this has
now been in large part done; the cream has been skimmed;
and the great need of the hour is a better conservation, a more
complete and scientific use, of our resources. In short, the

time for superficial treatment on a vast scale has largely passed, and the time has come for the greater thoroughness of an older civilization.

Wisdom consists, not in glorying in one's merits, but in curing one's defects; and the great defect in American education has been the lack of thoroughness. The European professional man is apt to have a wider knowledge and a broader foundation than the American. Professor Maurice Caullery, in his recent book on the universities and scientific life in the United States, in speaking of engineering education says, "The conditions of the training of the American engineer and his French colleague are very different. The latter has certainly a very marked superiority in theoretical scientific instruction. I am told, indeed, that since the war has brought into the American industries a rather large number of our engineers, this fact is well recognized. There is in the United States nothing to compare with the preparation for our competitive examinations for the Ecole Polytechnique and the Ecole Centrale. The first-year students — the Freshmen — in the engineering schools are very feebly equipped." On the other hand, he says, "It is not less true that the American engineer gives abundant proof of the combination of qualities which he needs." He then goes on to give an example from Mann's Bulletin on Engineering Education to show that of the Freshmen in 22 engineering schools only one-third could solve a simple algebraic equation. We are told also that the English physiologists have a great advantage over ours in a more comprehensive knowledge of physics and chemistry; and probably anyone familiar with learned professions in the two countries could give other examples.

As usual, a number of causes no doubt contribute to the lack of thoroughness in American education. One obviously is the briefness of time spent in study from birth through graduation from college. This is especially true in the younger years. Our children begin late and go slowly, apparently on the theory that the less conscious effort a boy puts into the process of education the more rapidly will he proceed. Another cause is the constant insertion of new subjects which are either not of a very severe nature or ought to be extracurricular activities, subjects which are inserted to the displacement of more serious ones. If someone suggests that rural walks and the observation of nature are good, the school, instead of providing them outside of school hours, inserts them in the school time in the place of language, history, or mathematics.

A third cause is the lack of rigorous standards which a few years ago pervaded most college work even more than it does today, and which I fear is still too prevalent in the schools. Last year a boy from a good high school not far from the central part of the country offered himself for the College Entrance Board examinations. He was the valedictorian of his class, and yet in five subjects — in all of which he had obtained a double A at school — his marks were as follows: English Literature 50; Latin 41; American History 37; Ancient History 30; Plane Geometry 33. In Physics, in which he had a B at school — which is, I suppose, an honor mark — his mark was only 28. The papers of the College Entrance Examination Board are not made out, nor are the books marked, by any one college, but by a body representing the colleges and schools. A difference in preparation might very well affect to some extent an examination in Literature and History, possibly even in Latin; but surely a boy who obtains an unusually high mark at school in Plane Geometry ought not to fail any entrance examination with so low a grade as 33 per cent.

The failure to maintain rigorous standards may well be connected with the American system of measurement by credits instead of by attainment. Courses, whether in school, in college, or in any kind of education, instead of being treated as an end, should be regarded as a means; and a test in them should be, not a final award, but a mere measure of progress.

At present the credit for a course is treated like a deposit in a savings bank, without a suspicion that the deposit is not of gold that can be drawn upon at its face value, but of a perishable article. To change the metaphor, we treat it like wheat poured into a grain elevator, whereas it is often more like the fruit in a cold storage plant without the means of refrigeration. Indeed, it is sometimes more like the contents of an incinerator.

There is an old saying in England that an educated man should have forgotten Greek. If the adage is true, it is not because the man had forgotten Greek, but because he retained something worth while from having learned it. Even if the material put into the mind be not perishable, we ought to distinguish between education and information. Let me quote again Professor Caullery. He says, "One must not confound education and information. There is in the American system, from the intellectual point of view, too much of the second and too little of the first." Storing of the mind is not enough; we must also train the student to use the store; and accumulating credits for things done is not the way to attain the result. When a man's life ends, we ask what he has done; but a diploma from a school or a degree from a college or university is not an obituary, and when a student's formal education ends we should ask, not what he has done, but what he is or has become.

Can we measure what the boy or man is or has become; can we measure him as he stands? It does not seem impossible. Yet most of our examinations are adapted to ascertain little except knowledge, and tend to promote mere cramming; whereas the tests in the great school of active life depend rather upon the ability to use information. Surely examinations can be framed to measure not only knowledge but the ability to comprehend and correlate what is known; in short, to test the grasp of a subject as a whole. Such a grasp requires a more rigorous training in fundamentals than we are in the habit of exacting. An examination of this kind

would be not only a measure of that which we desire to
ascertain, but it would tend also to direct attention to a field
of thought instead of to small isolated fragments of it. In
short, it must not be forgotten that examinations essentially
control the content of education. If examinations demand a
thorough knowledge of fundamental principles, the teachers
will provide it and the students will attempt to acquire it. If
they require merely a certain amount of miscellaneous knowledge, that will be the aim of instruction; and if, as in many
schools, there is no examination at all, there is naturally less
inducement to attain a very high standard of any kind.

The mechanical practice of credit for courses is, I believe,
the gravest defect in the American educational system, and
we ought to strive for some method of general examinations
testing the real grasp of a subject as a whole. But if such examinations are possible, it is nevertheless certain that they
demand a skill which can be acquired only by practice. The
art of examination is a difficult one, and in America it is still
in its infancy, particularly in the matter of measuring the
ability to use one's knowledge. The new psychological tests
are interesting as an attempt to do this, to measure the capacity of the boy or man as he stands. They are crude, and
for our purpose they suffer under the defect of assuming only
the most elementary information. We need tests that will
measure ability to use scholarly and specific knowledge. Anyone who attempts to introduce examinations of this kind will
be disappointed at first, because the art has not yet been sufficiently developed. To use them effectively, we need to learn
that the conduct of examinations is as important and worthy
a part of the educational process as giving lectures, and quite
as stimulating to the teacher. Ascertaining what the pupil
knows, measuring his progress and deficiencies, is, indeed, a
part of teaching, and quite as essential a portion of it as the
imparting of information. The true teacher should be constantly both developing the mind of his pupil, and ascertaining how rapidly and beneficially the process is going on. One

of the defects of much of our teaching — and especially of the lecture system — is that this second part of the function of education is to a great degree lost from sight. An improvement in our examination system which will measure the grasp of a whole subject is, I believe, the most serious advance that can be made in American education today.

STIMULATION OF THE ABLEST STUDENTS

ADDRESS AT THE ANNUAL MEETING OF THE PRINCETON CHAPTER OF THE
PHI BETA KAPPA SOCIETY, MARCH 17, 1921

THE Phi Beta Kappa has come recently into real distinction.
It has been criticized as being undemocratic. That is a mark
of progress. James Fitzjames Stephen years ago wrote a book
in which he attempted to show that liberty and equality are
not only things that do not necessarily go together, but that
as a matter of fact they are contradictory; that liberty produces inequality, propagating itself in geometrical ratio. He
said further that his observation led him to believe that democracy in the long run prefers equality to liberty, and would
take pains to suppress liberty when it interfered with equality. I have never heard, or read, a precise definition of democracy; but it is used to cover a multitude of sins. I expect
soon to hear that no cows ought to give more milk than other
cows because it is undemocratic. Why not? If the principle
of equality is the most important thing, why not? Why is it
not undemocratic for one man to own a cow that gives more
milk than another man's cow? Why should we not pass a law
that no cow shall be milked beyond a certain point; or that
all cows giving more milk than the average shall be slaugh-
tered so as not to improve the breed? You will answer me
very simply, "Because it is for the good of the community to
have cows give as much milk as possible."

But how about men? Is it or is it not desirable that men in
the community should yield as much intellectual output as
possible? If it is, how is it undemocratic in men any more
than in cows? Do not let us be deceived. Let us remember
that after all the greatest asset of a community is not its
mines, or its soil, but its men; and that it is for the interest of
the whole community that every man should be developed to
the utmost point to which he can be developed. If it is true

that it is for the interest of the community that cows should be so developed, it is far more for the interest of the community that men should be so developed.

Yet the principle that all men should be given an equal chance is often interpreted to mean that the bright boy ought not to go ahead of the dull boy; that the dull boy should get everything the bright boy gets — which means that the opportunities of the bright boy should be cut down to the level of the other. Is that so or is it not? Are we not right in saying this, that it is the right of every boy — and it is likewise to the interest of the community — that he shall have an opportunity to develop his talents to the utmost point of which they are capable; and that it is quite as important — nay, more important — that the unusual person shall develop his talents to the utmost than that the ordinary ones shall do it? If that is so, then it becomes the duty of everyone to cultivate his talents to the utmost point to which they can be developed; and this duty begins when he is born and does not end until his brain fossilizes. It is, above all, incumbent in the years he spends in college; because, let me tell you, gentlemen, you will never again in life have the same opportunity to expand your faculties in all directions that you have during your college years. You will have a time when you will develop yourself in the lines of your profession, but for the all-round development of your brain you will never have such another chance as you do in college.

Most men are born mediocre, because that is the definition of mediocrity. It is defined as that which most men are; but some men, though born with superior talents, achieve mediocrity, and some have mediocrity thrust upon them.

Why is it that some men achieve mediocrity and some have mediocrity thrust upon them? It is one of the results, I think, of a present tendency of popular prejudice. All through the community there is a certain lack of appreciation of superiority, a certain jealousy of it, a certain dislike of it. In our schools brighter boys, as a rule, do not get an opportunity to advance as fast as they are able — that is faster than the others. This college and the one to which I belong have the same entrance requirements, and there is constant complaint that we keep the standard too high, that we are not willing to admit everyone who has a certificate of graduation from a high school. It is the same old argument that the superior boy should not have superior opportunities, but should be kept down to the same level as others.

On the other hand, much fault lies at the doors of our colleges, for it is there that men achieve mediocrity, that they have mediocrity thrust upon them, and that for two reasons. In the first place, we do not stimulate the students to the extent that we should. Our whole educational system is saturated with the Herbartian idea; the view that no child ought to be made to work hard, that no education is good unless it is pleasant. Gentlemen, that is a very serious error. Make education as pleasant as you can, but, after all, no education is good for much that is acquired without effort; and, what is more, all real education is self education. Teachers aid, but they cannot impose it. To go through college without getting some education is not so easy as it used to be; but a man can still get through with very little, and it is almost impossible to prevent it. All real education is self education, and comes in proportion to the effort that is put into it.

I am afraid also that we do not stimulate as much as we ought the initiative of the student himself. What is most interesting to the student in the process of his education? Is it the course which is made simple and easy? Oh, no! The thing that is interesting is the thing on which he labors; the solution of difficult problems. To the man of virile mind the strongest pleasure comes from the vigorous exercise of his own talents. The thing that young men care for, and that is worth while afterwards, is the expenditure of effort in the exercise of their own faculties. Do men training for a boat race stop as soon as the exertion is fatiguing? Let us remember that the exercise of the brain is much like that of the body. It must be carried to a point that is uncomfortable or the power will never be fully developed.

There is another thing wherein we fail. We neglect to point out to the world about us the value of the man who does his college work well. We talk slightingly of the high scholar in this country in a way that is done in no other. Statistics prove that we are wrong. You can find published the proportion of Phi Beta Kappa men to others in "Who's Who." You will find it a very much larger percentage. You can take the proportion of men who have ranked high. You will find them larger again. At one time I compiled some figures on this subject which interested me. I took all the men who had graduated from Harvard College and later went into our Law School and Medical School. I took the Law School for twenty years, and the Medical School for sixteen years; and it was very striking how the men who had received a *summa cum laude* in college got a larger proportion of honors in those two professional schools than anybody else; the *magna cum laude* men came next; then those with a *cum laude*, and last came the men who had graduated from college with no distinction at all.

Wishing to carry the investigation farther, I took later the men from Yale who had come to the Harvard Law School. I should be glad to do the same thing for Princeton if I could get the figures. Dean Jones sent me the honors won by all the men who had come from Yale to the Harvard Law School for ten years. They have thirteen grades of honors at Yale, beginning with the philosophical orations. I took the actual marks of these men in the Law School, and averaging them for the men who had received each grade of honors at Yale, I found that the order of the groups was exactly that of the honors at Yale. The only difference was that the men who had graduated from college without distinction slightly passed those who had received honors of the lowest grade.

Now, that means something; especially in view of the well-nigh universal conviction that high rank in the Law School foreshadows much. In England men are recruited for the higher civil services by competitive examinations of the character of Oxford and Cambridge examinations for honors. In France, to enter the *Ecole Centrale* — one of the great engineering schools — there is a competitive examination over the whole country, and only a very small percentage of the men get in. In all other lands, in short, scholastic success is deemed an excellent test of a man's power. But with us many people prefer a man who has achieved a place on the football team. Statistics show that athletes in later life do on the average less well than the scholars. Why should they? Do we spend our time in later life in tackling men physically or mentally? The man with the brain trained so that he can really work with it is the man who will succeed. It is partly the fault of our college authorities that we do not put enough emphasis upon the man who has done well the things for which colleges exist. There is a great deal of talk in the community about the man with red blood, which means, being interpreted, blood that has never gone through the brain.

We are a young country. We have recently come out of the frontier state of civilization. We have not yet learned the value, the method, the use, and, above all, the measurement of education; and we have lost something during the period of expansion. Ask men who are now old what was thought of scholars in college seventy or eighty years ago when they were young, and you will find that in those days high scholars were esteemed more than they are today. If we do not succeed in building up a greater respect for the high scholar in our colleges, the colleges themselves will not achieve the respect of the community to which they aspire.

You remember what Daniel said about it, "They that be wise, shall shine as the brightness of the firmament; and they that turn many to righteousness, as the stars for ever and ever." The great minds of the world are the scholars, and the trained minds among our youth will be the stars of the future. All stars, remember, are not visible. We shall probably pass away and leave no trace. Our scholarship may not be great enough, or our originality striking enough, to be remembered in future generations; but there are hosts of stars in the universe unseen by men. I have been told that the stars which are not visible to the naked eye give in the aggregate more light than those which we can see, and I am inclined to think that the scholars whose names are not remembered have done in the aggregate more for civilization than the few whose names through their lustre pass down into history. We who aspire to be scholars, we men of the Phi Beta Kappa, whether our names are remembered or not, will forever be casting some light upon the civilization of the future, and that is what makes the institution to which we belong an inspiration.

ADDRESS AT THE UNIVERSITY
OF VIRGINIA

DELIVERED AT THE CELEBRATION OF THE HUNDREDTH ANNIVERSARY,
JUNE 1, 1921

IT IS a privilege to speak for the endowed universities of this country at the celebration of the hundredth anniversary of the University of Virginia, founded by the philosopher-statesman and architect as well. Here he lived during the struggle for independence, whereof he wrote the charter; and here he returned after his labors for the new-born nation, in France, as Secretary of State, and as President. In his later years of well-earned repose he lit here a beacon to diffuse the light of learning he held needful for the people he had served so long.

The examples of such farsighted men as he have been followed, until today a host of lights are shining over our whole country from shore to shore. The oceans that guard our land are the only things upon the planet that man does not, and cannot, change. Ulysses sailing forth from the pillars of Hercules, Columbus discovering a new world, and the Northmen on their voyage to Greenland, saw the Atlantic precisely as we see it today. The ocean is a symbol of eternity, eternally in movement and eternally at rest. In this it typifies the human spirit, unchangeable yet ever changing; and the universities, which embody that spirit in its most refined and keenest form, should ever be centres both of continual movement and of rest.

Bound together in a common cause, quickened by a common aim, faithful to a noble trust, our universities and colleges are constantly calling with their bells throughout this broad land — calling to one another to serve the needs of the present time, and to prepare the way for generations yet to come.

Your bells have called, and we, representatives of the great brotherhood of scholars, have come to pay our tribute of respect to this university, venerable in years, but ever young — more vigorous and more youthful as the years roll on. We come to tell you of our faith that, large as have been her services in the century that is past, the University of Virginia, in the century that lies before us, will be greater in works, in influence, and in renown.

ADDRESS AT YALE UNIVERSITY

DELIVERED AT THE INAUGURATION OF PRESIDENT ANGELL, JUNE 22, 1921

DAUGHTER of Learning and Mother of Men, Yale for two hundred and twenty years enlarged the circle of her influence, until it extended from the Atlantic to the Pacific, and across the Pacific to the heart of China. Her sisters have gathered here for the inauguration of her President; but first we want to speak of the great scholar who, to our regret, has laid the office down. Brilliant in thought, quick of wit, genial by nature, he has endeared himself to the men in other institutions, and we are proud to tell him of our affection and respect. We welcome his successor who, with unfaltering hand, takes the blue pennant, for a new advance in the unending course of progress.

In the courtyard of the Sorbonne are shown in the pavement the lines of the building of Richelieu; and, on a still smaller scale, those of medieval halls. The University of Paris has lived more than seven hundred years. It has survived the shocks that overthrew royal and imperial thrones, and stands erect through every storm.

Where Oxford lifts to heaven her diadem of towers there is a lane called "Dead Man's Walk" where men were shot for taking part against King Charles the First. Yet Oxford passed safely through those dangerous times, and the Wars of the Roses earlier still. She has survived all the dynastic strifes of English history, to come forth stronger than ever since the crown came under popular control. At Cambridge they point out in the Great Court of Trinity the small building by the gate where Newton, Macaulay, and Thackeray had their rooms — an inspiration to the youth of later days.

Universities have outlived every form of government, every change of tradition, of law, and of scientific thought, because they minister to one of man's undying needs. Of his creations none has more endured through the devouring march of time; and those who administer them, or teach therein, are but living links in an ever lengthening chain that stretches forward measureless to the unknown. They work not for themselves alone. Theirs, like the Vestal Virgins, to keep alive the sacred fire lit long ago, to furnish it to all who seek it, and add fresh fuel to the ever brightening flame.

It is in this spirit that, on behalf of the sister institutions here assembled, I congratulate you, sir, on the opportunities that lie before you, and this great University upon the fitting choice that has been made.

ADDRESS AT CORNELL UNIVERSITY

DELIVERED AT THE INAUGURATION OF PRESIDENT FARRAND,
OCTOBER 20, 1921

To THESE festivities I am charged to bring the greetings of
the older Eastern universities. But the message that I bear
to this great seat of learning, of congratulation for the work
that it has done, of confidence in that which it will do, is
shared by every college and every scholar in the land. No
different greeting can be brought where all must think alike.

Ponce de Leon searched our country for the Fountain of
Perpetual Youth. He sought in vain, not because the place
was wrong, but because he sought it out of time. He thought
that such a fountain should be nature's work, whereas it can
be made by man alone. The legend of the Greeks tells us that
where the winged Pegasus had struck his foot a spring gushed
out. No Pegasus makes springs for us; and yet, wherever
here — whether in the great city, in the smaller town, or on
the country-side — learning has set her foot, there has welled
up a fountain of perpetual youth. Go down to the river and
see. Go up to the playground and see. Look where the public
can not see; but where the real work is done, — by the student
alone with his books. Not that we who drink of that fountain
shall not grow old. We would not have it so. But there is an
ever rushing, ever growing, stream of youth that in these halls
comes upward to the light. It never ceases. Always bright
with youthful hopes, it flows to gladden and enrich our commonwealth.

Into that stream — the promise of the land — we pour
that which we have to give of knowledge and of wisdom,
drawn from the long heritage of thought and from discoveries of the present day. The various institutions have different
things to give; but each gives what it can, thankful that

others give what it has not; for all the colors of the spectrum must be blended to make the pure white light.

He whose light is partial sees partially. He whose light is dim sees faintly. Anyone has light enough to be visionary, but only he that clearly sees can see a vision. It is for all the watch-towers of learning so to throw their rays upon the path of life that our people may have clear white light to guide them on their way.

ADDRESS AT AMHERST COLLEGE

DELIVERED AT THE INAUGURATION OF PRESIDENT PEASE,
NOVEMBER 4, 1927

WHEN we meet on an occasion like this to install a colleague in an office of great opportunities and responsibility, our thoughts turn upon the work in which he is engaged.

To many, I hope to most, of us the proper function of the college appears not as vocational, not to train in the practical art of a profession or career, but to cultivate and liberate the forces of the mind that they may be employed with a broader outlook and larger power in anything a man may later undertake. Knowledge is, of course in part the aim of a college education; but only in part. The main object is to achieve intellectual freedom; not merely by escaping from the fetters of prejudice, ancient or modern, traditional or of recent invention, not merely by learning to look boldly at facts and ideas, but still more by becoming free to think.

The human mind was not at the outset free, moving at ease in a blaze of light. It began by groping its way in a dark cavern, until venturous spirits chiseled in the rock fissures that let rays of light fall upon some of nature's secrets. Still mankind gropes its way drilling for more light. But for the individual today constraint upon thought comes less from outside than from within himself, from his own apathy, indolence, and lack of practise.

Like everything solid, freedom of the mind has three dimensions. Its length is measured by alertness, an active interest in all that comes within its ken. This is an essential of all self-education. Its breadth is the range of its vision, and this should include some familiarity with the methods of different types of thinkers, — the literary and artistic, the scientific, the philosophic or abstract, and the students of human relationships. Its depth depends upon the mastery of some subject that is hard.

The forces of the mind are freed by use, and cannot be liberated otherwise. Nor can a fruitful use come from a mere intellectual manual of arms, or mental evolutions in the classroom. A man may be a walking dictionary or encyclopaedia without attaining freedom for his thought. To repeat a formula is not to grasp its significance. To be clever in discussion is not to be profound. To have a lively fancy is not to have genuine imagination. We may call it freedom; we may call it imagination; for these are two ways of looking at one thing, if by imagination we mean a real perception of the unseen. In any case, the use that gives the power must be personal, voluntary, and in time must be spontaneous.

Less in importance are a man's opinions when he graduates than the process by which he reaches them. If he has accepted them on the authority of his instructors, or by attraction or repulsion of an intellectual or social cult, he is not free from exterior constraint. If he has acquired them on his own account, but by crude reasoning, superficial study, or partial observation, he is not free from internal limitations. He has not experienced the search for truth that makes men free. Truth is a crystal with many facets, of which we see at best a few; but no man's mind has escaped bondage who does not see a real facet of the real crystal, and appreciate that there are different aspects that other men as truly see.

To liberate the intellectual forces, to teach the perilous art of thought, has been the mission of the New England college and of the colleges to which it has given birth throughout the land. To this heritage we welcome President Pease, so well equipped to maintain and improve the trust committed to his charge.

GENERAL EXAMINATIONS AND TUTORS IN HARVARD COLLEGE [1]

HISTORY OF THE SYSTEM

THE use of examinations as a measure of attainment never ceased at Harvard, and in fact, with the more rigorous training introduced by President Eliot into the Schools of Law and Medicine, the practice became general throughout the University. But with the growth of the elective system it came to have a special function. In the College that system began by permitting the substitution of an elective for some required course; at first in the senior year, then in the junior. The process was gradually carried farther and farther, — in each case substituting any elective for a course previously required, — until it reached the point that nothing was required except a course in English composition and one or two in modern languages if those subjects had not been included in the examinations for admission. Since the choice of electives was otherwise wholly free, it came about that the qualification for a degree was English A and any sixteen other courses, completion of each being proved by one or more examinations on what had been taught in the course. The examination paper had, therefore, to be prepared by the instructor who gave the course, for he alone knew the ground he had covered; and thus the degree was obtained by an accumulation of credits in independent courses. A similar process went on in the examinations for admission. At first these were rigidly fixed and were all taken at one time; then

---

[1] The following, which was published in 1927 to give information about the latest changes at Harvard, was written with the help of others; and, notably, much of the information was furnished by Professors Harold H. Burbank, Chairman of the Tutors, and Henry A. Yeomans, Chairman of the Board of Examiners, in the Department of History, Government, and Economics.

options were allowed, and finally the candidate was permitted to offer as few at a time as he pleased; so that admission, like graduation, was attained by a sum of credits which might be earned disconnectedly and at intervals.

The first departure from this system was made in pursuance of the report of a committee appointed in 1908 to "consider how tests for rank in college may be made a more generally recognized measure of intellectual power." On June 1, 1909, it recommended that rules for the choice of electives should be prepared, "based upon the principle that a student must take courses enough in some one field to lead to a degree with distinction, and must distribute the rest of his courses so as to leave none of the chief branches of learning wholly untouched." The report was adopted by the Faculty, and a standing Committee on the Choice of Electives worked out in detail a plan, which was enacted by the Faculty in December of that year. This change, like the provision for majors in other colleges, secured to the student something approaching a systematic knowledge of some subject, and laid the foundation for further progress.

A more direct breach in the practice of measuring by credits in courses was taken in the spring of 1910. All students who did not pass examinations for admission in both French and German had been required to elect, among their sixteen courses, one in the language that they had not so passed, or in each language if they had passed neither at entrance. Yet when they came to courses in which the use of French books, for example, was needed, a large part of the class proved unable to read them. The requirement in modern languages was therefore changed from that of taking a course to that of being able to read ordinary prose, to be proved by a special examination in so doing. This was a distinct step in substituting a direct test of capacity for a credit in the process of instruction.

Another advance in the same general direction was made in January, 1911, when an alternative method of admission

was adopted, still commonly known here as the "new plan."
The motive was a desire to open a door from schools in other
parts of the country that do not arrange their studies as a
preparation for college entrance examinations; but the result
was a new principle of measuring fitness for college work.
Instead of examining on all the subjects in the four years of
secondary school work, and doing it piecemeal, the fact that
an appropriate curriculum had been pursued was accepted
on the statement of the head-master, and the examination
was confined to four typical subjects, which must be passed
well, and at the same time. The object was to determine, not
what a youth had done at sundry times in the past, but what
kind of capacity he had obtained and what he had become as
the result of his schooling. It was an attempt to get an impression of the individual as he stands, rather than of the instruction he has been through.

In explaining the principle of concentration in his annual
report for 1908–09, the President remarked: "It may be
hoped that, under the new rules for the choice of electives,
some form of general examination at the end of the college
life on the principal field of study will be more commonly required." This hope was fulfilled first, not in the College, but
in the Medical School. Education for medicine is peculiarly
difficult because it requires the study of many subjects whose
interrelation, and whose connection with practice, is far from
self-evident. Hitherto, as was usual in all American education at that time, the degree had been conferred upon the
completion of a fixed number of courses, but complaint was
made that the system was inelastic, and lacking in stimulation. It was said that the student might graduate without
retaining sufficient knowledge of the subjects he had studied,
without coordinating them, and, indeed, without sufficient
inducement to do so. In the spring of 1910 a committee was
therefore appointed which examined the system prevailing in
American medical schools of granting the degree upon an
accumulation of credits in courses, and the European system

of two general examinations, the earlier upon the general scientific or laboratory subjects and the final one upon the clinical branches. The committee recommended the adoption of the latter system, and after its provisional approval by the Faculty of Medicine in March of the following year, another committee, mainly of different members, worked out a plan which was adopted by that Faculty in October, 1911.

At first it did not work well, for it was treated too much as a short review of the courses, and produced the meagre results of an examination of that kind. Moreover, the European plan of two distinct examinations, first upon laboratory and later upon clinical subjects, proved to be defective, because one of the main objects of such an examination should be to induce a correlation in the student's mind between these two parts of his professional knowledge, that is, between the basic sciences and the art that depends upon them. Not until after the war was the true significance of the principle appreciated. It was then seen that if the examination was to be general the questions must be general also, demanding an application of some portion of the laboratory sciences to the facts of disease. Of late years this has been done by a single general examination, partly written and partly oral, that closes the four years of study in the School; and it has become a real standard of achievement, fixing the attention of the students on the true aim of their work, and affecting to no small extent the teaching of the courses throughout. Curiously enough, while both the new plan of admission to college and the system of a general examination and tutors for undergraduates have been very widely adopted by colleges with problems akin to ours, the final examination in medicine, although for years highly successful, has not yet been followed by any other medical school.

Shortly after its adoption in the Medical School the idea of a general examination invaded departments at Cambridge. In the academic year 1911–12 it was adopted in the Divinity School for the degrees of Bachelor and Master of Theology;

and in this case it seems to have worked well from the start. Meanwhile the division of history, government, and economics had been considering the matter, and after a year of careful study formulated a plan which was sanctioned by the Faculty of Arts and Sciences in the winter of 1912–13. The examination was to be conducted by the division and in fact by a committee of three of its members appointed by the President, who were to be relieved of one half of their work of instruction. It was to consist of both written and oral tests, was to be required of all college students concentrating in that division, in addition to their courses, and was to go into effect with the class entering the following autumn. Authority was also given to supplement by tutorial assistance the instruction given in the courses. Thus the complete system of a general examination and tutors was set up for all undergraduates in one division, and the one which at the time had the largest number of concentrators.

The plan was put into effect without serious obstacles. The number of students concentrating in these subjects did, indeed, diminish, the weaker or more timid seeking departments where no such examination barred the way; but that was no harm, and proved to be in large part a temporary effect. The preparing of examination questions, which had been supposed very difficult, was exceedingly well done by an able committee. Yet the plan was not at once wholly successful. Tutorial work was new, and men equipped for it were not to be found. They had to learn the art by their own experience, and by what they derived from an exchange of tutors for a year with Oxford and Cambridge. In fact, after a few years of trial the plan seemed in danger of breaking down. The benefits were not at once evident; some men formerly in favor of it became skeptical, while opponents were confirmed in their opinions. Until we entered the World War the only other field of concentration which had adopted a general examination of all students for graduation was that of history and literature, although something of the kind had long been in common use in the case of candidates for distinction or honors.

The crisis came at the close of the war, when the changes made for military purposes in all instruction had left matters in a somewhat fluid state. A committee of the Faculty was appointed to consider what, if any, extension of the principle could profitably be made in other fields. There was a feeling that such a system ought not to be maintained in one class of subjects alone; that it should either be abolished or extended. After a study of the question in its various phases the committee reported, and in April, 1919, the Faculty voted that general examinations should "be established for all students concentrating in Divisions or under Committees which signify their willingness to try such examinations," and that they "be employed for the members of the present Freshman class." Thereupon all the divisions under the Faculty, except those dealing with mathematics and the natural sciences, decided to make the experiment. Some of them did so reluctantly, with misgiving, and under a condition that they should not be obliged to employ tutors. The plan of allowing each department or division to decide upon its own policy in so highly novel a matter was certainly wise, for it stimulated experimentation and made for permanent conviction. The system as a whole could be trusted to demonstrate its own merit, and did so. The divisions that set up a general examination without tutors found their students complaining that they were required to do a difficult thing without guidance, and the proportion of men who graduated with distinction was markedly lower than in the departments which had both general examination and tutors. By the academic year 1924–25, therefore, the students in all the divisions with a general examination had the benefit of tutoring.

Since that time the progress of the system has been gradual but continuous. Two years ago the department of mathematics decided to adopt it, and a year later biology and biological chemistry followed its example; leaving chemistry and physics as the only departments with a large number of concentrators that still retain the older methods, and their position is peculiar because so much work is done in laboratories. The only change in the system has come from a demand by the students themselves. We have not desired to abandon teaching or examination in courses, by copying the practice at Oxford and Cambridge of leaving instruction wholly to the tutor, save for such attendance at series of lectures as he may direct. That seems ill-adapted to our habits, and involves a loss of the valuable elements in course instruction. Nor on the part of the undergraduates has there been complaint of the burden of preparing for the general, or as they call them "divisional," examinations in addition to the work in courses, except in the case of candidates for distinction. These men are required to prepare theses that take much time, and for them a lightening of the course work has been asked. The Faculty, therefore, decided to permit, for such of these candidates as are recommended by the department and the Dean, a reduction of two courses in all, one of which may be in the junior, or both in the senior, year. The privilege has been granted sparingly, solely for the purpose of freeing time to be used for personal study and writing under the guidance of the tutor.

OPERATION OF THE SYSTEM

The General Examination

Not many years ago examinations were anathema over a large part of the country. Some teachers felt that they knew the progress of their pupils, and did not see the need of subjecting them to tests. An examination was often regarded as a reflection upon the pupil, and, if set by a stranger, upon the teacher also. It implied a doubt whether the instruction had given all that it purported to impart; it suggested a suspicion that taking a course diligently did not mean learning the subject taught. For pupils whose work had not been satisfactory it might serve as a discipline, but for the good scholars it was almost an indignity. It was like indicting an honorable man, and making him prove his innocence. Moreover, it distracted the attention of both teacher and pupil from the real object of education, turning it to preparation for an artificial performance, making the teacher a crammer and the pupil a learner of tricks. This conception of examinations has not been disproved, but it is being outgrown. Numerous conditions that might fill a treatise have brought a demand for the measurement of young people, for their classification in groups according to their natural capacity, their attainments, and their prospects. These have given rise to various kinds of tests, until educational thought and experiment have become deeply concerned with the subject of examinations. We hear much of intelligence tests based upon native ability, of aptitude tests, and of the new kind of examinations, where a large number of questions are given, to be marked rapidly Yes or No. These last, it is claimed, are more searching, more accurate, and more comparable than the older form of curricular questions in common use. Whether they will prove to be better or not for their purpose will be watched with interest, for it is highly important. But the excellence of any examination depends upon the degree in which it fulfills the object for which it is designed; and the intent of a general examination upon the main subject of a student's work in college is to ascertain not so much the amount of his knowledge as the use he can make of it; to measure his grasp, his power of thought, the extent to which his studies have moulded the fabric of his mind; in short, how far he has in that field become an educated man.

The aim of the system adopted here being the mastery of some subject as a whole, to be acquired so far as possible by the student's own work, a general final examination is needed to measure his attainment and still more to set a standard for achievement. This is the essential element, the foundation of the entire system on which all the rest is based; but in fact its importance is sometimes overlooked, because the tutoring, the frequent contacts with the students which it involves, and the personal influence of the tutors themselves, attract more attention. Yet it is the examination that marks out the goal for both tutors and students. Without it the system, except for a few undergraduates of exceptional scholarly tastes, would be like a football game without goal posts, or would degenerate into little more than tutoring in courses and lose its real significance. A general examination that was easy or superficial would hamper the tutors in doing their best work; one that was eccentric or unfair would discourage both them and their pupils; one that required only a memory of facts would make it hard for both to devote energy to the deeper relations of the subjects studied. The nature of the examination, therefore, determines the character and effectiveness of the whole system, and it is both the essential and the most difficult part thereof. The object is to enable the candidates to display their command of the subject and cause them to expose their ignorance, and this in the case of those who have much, or only a moderate amount, of either. To prepare such an examination is an exceedingly difficult task, requiring much time and labor; wherefore it is important that in the departments with a large number of students the examiners should be relieved from a part of their other work, and in the division that has had the longest experience with the system here, a single examiner in each of the three subjects comprised is excused from one half of his teaching.

Both written and oral examinations are used by almost all the examining committees, each being at liberty to apply them in accord with its own experience of their value. In fact the practice has varied, but the present tendency is to limit the oral to candidates for distinction and to students who on the written papers do not clearly earn a degree, it being thought a waste of time to give an oral examination in cases where it will have no effect upon the result. The number of written papers and the length of the oral vary. The division with the longest experience has three written examinations of three hours each, and others which have less are likely to find that an increase of their papers will improve the value of their tests. In the subjects taken by the largest number of students, history, government, and economics, ancient and modern languages, and history and literature, there are papers on both general and special fields. In history, government, or economics, for example, every candidate for a degree must take an examination of a general character in the two subjects in which his principal work does not lie, a second examination covering in more detail the one in which it does lie, and a third, more searching, on his special field therein. In the literary subjects every man, before trying the paper on his own field, must take an examination on the Bible and Shakespeare, and another on two modern authors if his field is classics, or on two ancient ones if his field is modern literature; the moderns being allowed to read the classic authors in translations, the classical students having the same privilege for some modern books in the less familiar languages. Candidates for distinction are usually required also to write theses, on which much labor is often expended. These are, in fact, most important in determining the grade of honors awarded. They may reach a high grade of excellence, and although far less elaborate than theses for the doctorate of philosophy, they are sometimes quite equal in quality.

The committee that prepares the examination must consider many things. It must maintain satisfactory relations with the instructors in courses and with the tutors. While, on the one hand, it must use its own judgment on the ground to be covered and the nature of the questions to be asked, it cannot, on the other hand, disregard entirely the content of the courses. They are part of the instruction offered by the Faculty and should be regarded as within the field included by the examination. This is true also of the work of the tutors, in the sense that they must be aware of the scope of the examination and the kind of question that will be set. The committee, therefore, cannot properly widen the field without warning to them. Students have a right to rely on them for advice about their reading and it would be demoralizing to conduct examinations so that tutors cannot give it. Yet the committee is naturally and properly testing the work, not only of the students, but also of the instructors, and especially of the tutors. For these last it must set a standard and by them it is likely to be thought a little severe. The scope of course instruction is in fact enlarged by the tutors, and the examiners require a more symmetrical and well-rounded preparation than course instruction alone would give. Moreover, it may be noted that the material with which to prepare for the examination must be accessible to the students. It must be in books. Undergraduates cannot be expected to make their preparation a matter of research.

The foregoing comes from the experience of the division that has longest used the general examination; as does also the following discussion how far the questions should measure a knowledge of facts and how far call for analytical or judicial capacity. To prepare a long list of things every student should know makes the tutor a coach; and while an occasional informational question may be necessary to expose the loafers, the main part of the test should involve the exercise of judgment. Facts should be required, but not facts for their own sake. The object should be to measure grasp, the power to deal with facts; and a question demanding a real grasp of a subject cannot be answered without an adequate knowledge of the facts with which it deals. The best opportunity to show judgment in dealing with a large subject seems to be given by a question that demands an essay, and one such essay at least should be required. But to find suitable topics for essays is among the hardest tasks of the examiner. If the question is too narrow, it does not give a chance to enough men; if too broad, there is encouragement to thin generalizations. The wise course seems to be to give fairly wide options among fairly specific subjects. Yet carelessness in the use of options may unwittingly affect the entire character of a paper by enabling a man to pass on a very narrow accomplishment. To arouse the student, a question that sharply challenges accepted opinion is sometimes useful. In this way the call for comment upon a quotation often serves. The danger here is irrelevance in the reply. Plenty of time must be given and responsiveness insisted upon.

There is a perennial question whether separate papers should be set for distinction and pass men. The strong argument against separate papers is that they mean separate preparations, and this means inability to encourage the able man who makes up his mind to try for distinction late in his college course. A better solution would seem to be an added paper for distinction candidates, or, better still, added questions on the regular papers. Groups of questions are frequently set from which distinction candidates must, and others may, make a choice.

These remarks, mainly drawn from a report by examiners in history, government, and economics, may be regarded as fairly typical of the difficulties in setting a fair and searching examination, and the methods adopted for meeting them. A few sample questions in history and English, in the form of quotations requiring something in the nature of essays, will illustrate what is done. They are taken from the papers of June, 1926.

Mediaeval History

6. "In the period which followed the Germanic conquests, by far the most decisive influence was the alliance of the papacy with the Franks; it was, indeed, one of the most eventful coalitions ever entered into in history." Explain.

History of the Renaissance

5. "For a variety of reasons the sixteenth century was monarchical in mind as the twentieth century is democratic."

Modern France

10. "Napoleon's work was to fuse the old France with the new." Explain.

American History

1. "The central problem of the American Revolution was the true constitution of the Empire."

English Literature

"Show by an analysis of the content, style, and diction of three of the following passages, in what ways they are characteristic of (*a*) their authors, (*b*) the times in which they were written."
Then follow passages of about 25 lines from Swift, Wordsworth, Ascham, and H. G. Wells.

The general examination increases not only the work required of the student, but also the danger of his losing his degree, and this is no imaginary peril. The records of the last two years show that in 1924–25 there were 577 candidates for graduation in all the departments having such an examination, and that 518 passed it, while 59, or 10.2 per cent, failed. In 1925–26 out of 549 candidates 508 passed, and 41, or 7.5 per cent, failed; the smaller proportion of failures being largely due to the adoption of tutors by the departments of modern languages. Of those who fail a number try again in a later year and many of them succeed in passing. Of the men failing at first about one half pass a subsequent examination.

THE TUTORS

Lacking guidance on his way, the undergraduate would be at a loss to supply the gaps between his courses, to connect them, to fill in the background and survey the whole subject. For that purpose the tutors are provided. As soon as the student, at the end of his freshman year, has selected his subject of concentration he is assigned to a tutor in that field who becomes thenceforth his adviser in all his studies. Looked at from the standpoint of academic organization, the function of the tutor is to help the student to cope with the general examination; not by coaching or cramming, — for an examination that could be passed by such means would have quite failed in its object, — but by making him competent to pass it. Looked at from its effect upon the pupil, the purpose of the tutor is to lead him to educate himself by a thorough study of his chosen subject; and, if the system works as it should, these two points of view are in fact two aspects of the same design from different sides, two ways of stating the same thing. There is always the danger that the tutor may degenerate into a coach, carrying his pupil instead of guiding him, saving him effort instead of stimulating him to effort; and that danger must always be watched, but so far it has not shown itself here.

In describing the work of the tutor it must be borne in mind that the office means a function, not an academic grade. In most of the departments it has been necessary at the outset to assign tutorial duties to young men. Whatever their capacity, old dogs are usually disinclined to learn new tricks. But as the young tutors have grown older, they have been promoted at the same rate as those who have been teaching in courses, until the tutors hold positions all the way from that of assistant or instructor to that of full professor; and such is the declared policy of the University. Some of the older professors have, indeed, preferred to use part of their time as tutors; and this is done by the whole department of mathematics. Tutoring is one form of teaching, not less difficult or honorable than conducting a course. In fact, a large part of the tutors do both; a rough survey of the departments indicates that at least one half of the tutors are also giving courses, and the proportion is tending to increase. In one of the subjects of concentration the head tutor thinks it desirable that every tutor should do so, not only for the stimulus to himself from teaching a course, but also because he believes that a man cannot know thoroughly the different mentalities of over fifteen pupils at the same time, and therefore should not have charge of more. At present the number of pupils to a tutor who devotes his whole time to this work runs from about twenty-five to forty-five, the general opinion being that the smaller of these numbers is not far from right.

The length and frequency of conferences with the tutor vary in the different departments. Sometimes they last only half or three quarters of an hour, but more commonly an hour is assigned for the purpose. In a few subjects the conferences for the Sophomores come less often than once in two weeks, but that is only in the smaller departments; the usual practice is once a week or fortnight for the Sophomores and once a week for the Juniors and Seniors. But there is much diversity, and, in fact, the meetings with the tutors are more frequent than any rules prescribe, especially in the case of candidates for distinction who are writing theses and are constantly seeking advice at odd times. Normally the students meet their tutors singly, but in some cases it has been found advantageous for them to meet in pairs or in groups of three to five. The departments are experimenting, and the individual tutors are allowed no small latitude, for much depends upon the personal quality of the students to be tutored.

The conferences with the tutor are by no means for the purpose of giving information; they are not in the nature of private lectures. Their object is to help the student to work out for himself the subjects that he is studying, and experience shows that the less the tutor talks, the better. He rather helps the pupil to work out his own difficulties. In short, the process is Socratic, not didactic. Moreover, it has as little to do as possible with the ground covered in the courses the student has taken. Sometimes, where the student has failed to grasp the subject of a course, it may be necessary to explain it to him; but in the main the courses are used, if at all, as bases for departure in other directions, or as fixed points to be connected in the field to be covered. In this the tutors seem to be almost universally agreed. The attempt to enlarge, complete, and, from various points of view, illuminate the field involves, of course, much reading quite outside the courses; and it has been found that one of the effective methods is to require the student to write a report upon the book or subject on which he has been at work, and discuss it with the tutor. These reports have been found very valuable, and their use has been increasing. Not only have they proved a valuable means of helping the student to a command of his subject, but one of the examiners reports that they have distinctly improved the quality of English composition as seen in the general examination.

The relation of the tutor to his pupil is peculiar, differing from any other in the College. It is that of a teacher, but not a teacher who sets examinations or gives marks. Nor is he supported by college discipline. Failure to attend the conferences he assigns is not reported to the Dean's office; and although the tutor has a right to prevent a pupil who has been grossly neglecting his work from trying the general examination, it has never been exercised. Failure to attend conferences was formerly not uncommon; but it has steadily diminished, partly, no doubt, because in preparing for the general examination the need of the tutor has come to be felt, and partly, it may be assumed, from the cordial relation that has grown up between tutor and pupil. The former is there to help the student as his guide and friend, and he is generally so regarded. His object is to develop the willing pupil, and provoke the listless to an interest in his subject. All this he could not do unless he were himself personally interested in his pupils. Naturally that is most obvious in the case of candidates for distinction, and the eagerness of the tutors that these men should succeed, and win as high a grade of honors as possible, is the more valuable because that spirit is caught by the pupils.

The system is tending to produce a broader type of tutor. Since he has to cover more ground with his students than the man who gives courses on his own chosen parts of a subject, he must keep up with a wider field, a fact that has manifest advantages. But after all, the system is still new, for we do not, and cannot wisely, copy the models of Oxford and Cambridge, but must seek to adapt to our conditions such methods as will make with our own a consistent whole. Every tutor is therefore very free to work in the way he finds most profitable for each student under his charge. Yet to compare experiences, to talk over their common problems, and to improve their methods, it is the custom of the tutors in the various divisions or departments to meet at luncheon every week or two for consultation. This is welding their work into an organic system.

EFFECTS OF THE SYSTEM

Before trying to judge the effect of the tutors and the general examination it is well to have clearly in mind the objects they are designed to attain. These are: to devote more attention to the undergraduate as an individual; to treat him as a whole being; to make him more largely educate himself; and to provoke in him an interest in so doing. The first of these hardly needs explanation. The former conception, drawn from Germany, that the function of a university is to provide wide opportunities for education, of which the student may or may not take advantage as he pleases, is passing into the background in America. Everywhere more attention is being given to the individual student, and that the tutor is a highly effective means to this end is self-evident.

The meaning of treating the student as a whole is not so clear. Owing to the process by which the elective system grew up, gradually substituting more and more electives for required courses, the course became the unit in education and a fixed number of credits in courses became the qualification for graduation. This was true whether the election was unlimited or restricted by certain rules of choice; and it was true both of colleges and of lower schools, so that in some form counting by credits became well-nigh universal in American education. It is a bad plan, because it measures by the process that has been gone through instead of by the result. It is bad also in making the course the unit in education when, in fact, there can be only one real unit — that is, the student himself. The course is merely a means to an end — the education of the student; and he is the end. The object of his education is himself, and that not as a conglomeration of intellectual fragments, but as a whole. The important thing is what he has become. Such a purpose would be most fully achieved if someone were omniscient enough to have the oversight of an undergraduate in all his studies; but this is impossible; and certainly, to have a tutor in a large field in which his principal work is done is far nearer to treating the intellectual life of the student as a whole than any system of courses can be; and, in fact, it does have that effect.

The third object mentioned — that of making the student more largely educate himself — is a highly important one. All true education above rudimentary, mechanical training is in the main self-education with assistance, under guidance and stimulation. The tutor can help, but he cannot supply the place of effort on the part of the student. Massage does not take the place of exercise in developing strength — a truth that applies not only to the learning of a definite subject, but still more to preparation for the battle of life. So far has this been forgotten that to the public, and probably to most members of the teaching profession, the words "education" and "instruction" are synonymous; whereas in fact instruction is a means, and only one means, to education. For that reason there has been a tendency to teach too much and study too little. What we need is to provoke personal thought as compared with receptivity, and this is exactly the function of the tutor. It is his business, not to supply the student with information, but to tell him where he can find it; not to present to him ideas, but to make him work them out himself by reading and discussion — in short, to help the student to educate himself from books and other material within his reach. The chairman of the board of tutors in one of the largest departments reports that in his opinion "the great gain due to the introduction of the general examinations and the tutorial system is twofold: first, the student has been taught to view a field of knowledge as a whole, not as a series of more or less unrelated parts; second, the student has learned through his intimate discussions with his tutor to probe more deeply and independently into his chosen field of knowledge, the result being that he is better able to do work by himself."

The fourth object is to provoke in the student a desire to educate himself, and this must be done by arousing his interest in some subject. It often happens that one loses sight of the end by fixing attention on the means. So strongly have American educators felt that a student cannot do good work in a subject in which he is not interested that they have been too much inclined to inquire in what he is interested, rather than to interest him in what he had better study. The fact is that most boys and young men have no very strong intellectual interests, and to ask them to select what they would like to study means in many cases a selection of that which they can study with the least effort. In short, the result of a selection according to natural interests has been in large part a reduction of effort and of the educational value that comes therefrom. To some extent effort will come from an existing interest, but to a much larger extent interest comes from voluntary effort. The normal youth who can be induced to throw his powers vigorously into any intellectual study will find it interesting. That is the function of the tutor. His business is to stimulate effort by interesting, and interest by effort. Partly for this reason, we have applied the system not only to men who at the outset desire to be candi-

dates for honors, but to all students, believing that all of them
will obtain a benefit and that many of them, who have the
capacity, will achieve a much higher grade of work than they
would otherwise do. This may be shown by a table of the
increase of candidates for degrees with distinction.

PERCENTAGE OF CANDIDATES FOR DISTINCTION IN SPECIAL FIELDS
JUNE, 1923–26

Year	Seniors and OCC [1]	All Classes
1923	21.7	23.2
1924	28.0	31.8
1925	30.5	41.0
1926	39.5	47.0

[1] OCC means out of course candidates — that is, students who do not take their degree with
their class, but are preparing to do so later.

Of course all these men did not win distinction, and the
fact that certain privileges relating to absence from classes
are accorded to those inscribed as candidates therefor has
helped to swell the list. Perhaps a better indication of the
effect of the new system may be found in the percentage of
men who have actually attained distinction at graduation.

Year	Degrees Awarded Omitting War Degrees	Degrees with Distinction		Degrees with Distinction in Subjects with General Examination	
		Number	Percentage	Number	Percentage
1922	547	114	20.8	82	15.0
1923	581	139	23.9	111	18.9
1924	584	171	29.3	120	20.5
1925	637	177	27.9	136	21.4
1926	648	184	28.4	143	22.1

It seems to be the general opinion of the chairmen of the
boards of tutors that a very large part, at least, of the increase has been due to the personal influence of the tutors,
the chairman of the board in one of the largest departments
remarking: "I view the entire increase in the candidacy for
distinction as attributable to the new methods of instruction. . . . I think it safe to say that 85 or 90 per cent of the
men capable of attaining distinction are now candidates for
distinction. Certainly not more than fifteen, and probably

not more than ten per cent of the non-distinction candidates for degrees have the ability to do much more than they are now doing." There is no doubt that the students work harder than they did. They have a more definite aim in their work; and it may be remarked also that something of the competitive spirit in their studies has been restored; for they regard the divisional examinations, as they call them, as a better test of ability and true scholarship than the examinations in the separate courses, where 'they feel that high marks can be more easily obtained by mere diligence and memory.

COST OF THE SYSTEM

The salaries of the tutors amount in the aggregate to a very large sum. In accordance with our practice of charging to a separate tutorial budget in many of the larger departments the salaries of the tutors, with the proportion of the salaries of men giving part time to that form of teaching, it is possible to make an approximate estimate of the cost. For the current year this comes to $173,114. That is certainly a large figure, and if the system had been adopted all at one time it would have been impossible to meet the expense without additional endowment; but in fact it was adopted gradually in one department after another, and therefore it has brought no sudden great increase of expense. Moreover, since — as already stated — the tutors in each department were at first young men, they have begun with comparatively small salaries, which have increased as they have grown older, and will not reach the normal cost for some time to come.

But the salaries of the tutors are by no means the only element in the problem. The question is not simply what they cost, but the expense of this system as compared with that which it replaced. Such a calculation, however, cannot be properly made in dollars, because all salaries have risen, or, to put it otherwise, the value of money has fallen so much that a comparison of the sums expended is meaningless. A far more accurate comparison is that of the number of students to a member of the instructing staff. This has the double advantage of eliminating the rate of salaries and also of eliminating the question of age, for about the year 1900 there was a large increase in the appointments of young men, and this happened again with the introduction of the tutorial system. In each case the salaries were at first small, but were certain to increase without an increase of numbers in the instructing staff. Taking, therefore, the number of students to an instructor at periods equidistant, we find for the years 1890–91, 1908–09, and 1926–27 that the numbers of students and of instructing staff, including tutors, were as follows:

FACULTY OF ARTS AND SCIENCES

| | INSTRUCTING STAFF | | | STUDENTS | | |
	In the Faculty	Not in the Faculty	Total	Harvard College and Specials	Graduate School	Total
1890–91	67	19	86	1339	110	1449
1908–09	135	53	188	2238	387	2625
1926–27	206	156	362	3329	864	4193

It may be observed that the number of students to an instructor was, in 1890–91, 16.85; in 1908–09, 14; and in 1926–27, 11.6. If the points representing these figures are plotted, it will be found that they fall almost exactly on a straight line. In other words, the rate of increase in the instructing staff to the number of students has been almost continuous, and unaffected by the appointment of tutors. What has in fact happened is that in the earlier half of this time the aim was to increase the number of courses as largely as the revenues would permit. The ambition of the University and of all its departments was to give as wide an opportunity of instruction, to cover as many fields, as possible; and an increase in the revenue was used to appoint additional instructors and give additional courses. During the later half this idea has changed. It has been felt that it is impossible to cover by courses every part of every branch of knowledge, and that there is no object in so doing. It has been thought that in the main the courses of instruction were sufficient, and the additional revenue from the income of gifts has been used to pay for tutors instead of for additional courses. Looked at from this point of view, it may be said that the tutorial system has cost the University no more than a continuance of the previous policy would have done.

On the other hand, the change of policy has brought a new problem. The students having increased more rapidly than the courses, the number of men in each course has, on the average, become larger; and this in turn has increased the labor of the instructor. Moreover, with the improvement in the education of the students, with their stronger interest in educating themselves and hence their greater proficiency in their subjects, the quality of the courses has become higher, and the demand on the instructor more strenuous. To this must be added the burden from the large growth in the number of graduate students. Meanwhile the tutors also have found that the call upon their time has been distinctly greater than the number of hours they were supposed to devote to conferences. In particular, the candidates for distinction, who are writing theses, drop in upon them at all sorts of odd times, and break into the continuity of their own work. Now, in order to get the best men as lecturers and tutors, we must see that they are not at a disadvantage as compared with those in other places. They should have fully as great an opportunity to keep up with their subject and to make and publish their own contributions to knowledge. During the current year this subject has engaged the attention of the Faculty, and, considered from the point of view both of the instructing staff and of the students, a plan has been devised for two periods in which, save for the elementary courses, there shall be neither lecturing nor tutoring, but reading by students on their own account. The first of the periods comes between the Christmas vacation and the mid-year examinations, the second from the seventh or eighth of May to the final examinations. During the latter period, indeed, both the general examinations and the examination of candidates for the doctorate of philosophy will take place, and the tutors' conferences with the Seniors, but not with other pupils, will continue. The object of these reading periods is two-fold: first, to relieve the work of the instructing staff, which is now believed to be more strenuous than in most colleges, by reducing the teaching period to about its length in a European university; and second, to make the student appreciate more thoroughly the fact that his improvement must come through self-education. For the Seniors there will be no difficulty in this regard. The candidates for distinction will be busy with their theses; the others sobered by the terrors of the divisional examinations. On the other hand, the Sophomores and Juniors are to have reading carefully laid out for them by consultation between the tutors and the instructors whose courses the men are taking; and the mid-year examinations will measure how far the reading has been conscientiously done. No doubt at first some Sophomores will not appreciate the importance and gravity of the task, will think they can do their reading in a few days at the end, will fall into mishaps, go on probation or have their probation closed; but that is the inevitable accompaniment of any improvement in education. It may be added that the Freshmen, who have no tutors, are not affected, the courses open to them being treated as elementary.

This is certainly a great innovation, but here we are accustomed to innovations. Among the most precious of our traditions is that of perpetual change. Change means experiment, and experiment means doing things which one does not at first know exactly how to do aright. This plan, which has now received the approval of the Governing Boards, is another long step in the direction in which the College has for a score of years progressed.

SELF–EDUCATION IN COLLEGE

REPRINTED FROM THE FORUM, APRIL, 1928

IN EDUCATION, as in everything else, a principle or hypothesis has its limitations, and is true only within the bounds of its appropriate application. Even within the region where it has validity its reaches a point at which it overlaps another principle not less true in its own domain. In this debatable area controversies take place, because there each principle is partially true, and the question arises which principle can be most properly applied, or how far a compromise between them is better than a logical deduction from either alone. The partisans of each, approaching from a situation in which their own theory is, or appears to them to be, absolute, are unaware that they have wandered over the frontier to a place where this is no longer true, and regard as a trespasser an opponent who preaches strange doctrines that seem to them to have no business there.

Now almost the whole field of education is a debatable land. Many principles are partly true; none absolutely so to the exclusion of all others. Hence the multitude of controversies, and the general superiority of the intelligent and experienced teacher over one who is guided wholly by a single theory. He who acts on the principle of discipline as the essential matter may do well in early stages, but falls into bad results later; while the teacher who believes that his pupils should think out all things for themselves does them little good before they have material enough to think upon. Children asked to reason for themselves about the agencies of commerce or the constitution of society usually do not reason at all, but accept passively the views of the teacher. They suppose, not always rightly, that he knows the facts, and from the facts as he presents them the conclusion follows almost inevitably.

From these remarks a belief on the part of the writer may be inferred that the divergent principles in education are not without value, and that their relative importance varies in its successive stages. In urging, therefore, the significance of self-education it must be assumed that there is no intent to exclude other factors, but merely to place emphasis on a matter that does not seem to have received all the attention it deserves. In America, indeed, from the grammar grades to the graduate school, too much reliance has long been placed on instruction as compared with personal effort in study apart from the teacher. Like other principles this one has an application in varying degrees throughout the educational process that ends only with life.

Self-education means two things — connected but not identical — first a desire on the part of the pupil to learn, and second a self-directed attention, a personal endeavor to inquire.

The first of these applies at all stages. Even in the rudiments of the three R's every teacher knows the difference in progress between the willing child who wants to master these arts, and the reluctant one who must be driven. The multiplication table must be learned by heart, and the earlier the better. It is less education than a tool of the trade; yet willingness to learn it helps the teacher greatly, and the effect of this attitude of mind is certainly not less as one rises into stages where thought counts more and mechanical mental action less. This aspect of self-education is obvious and need not detain us. The other concerns us here far more.

The second meaning of self-education — that of self-directed attention, a voluntary use of the mind for a conscious purpose — increases in importance with the maturity of the student. In discussing educational questions one is constantly tempted to use similes; they are so facile and so misleading. They have a proper use as illustrations to convey an idea; but they are not demonstrations to prove a principle, and the parallel is not close enough to sustain deductions. Therefore one must not try to reason from them. Merely for the sake of illustrating a meaning, the reader may permit a comparison of didactic instruction to being carried in a perambulator or an automobile, and self-education to exercise. By the former more ground is covered in less time, but the muscles are not thereby strengthened or skill in using them acquired. To pass from a simile to a general biological law, it is well known that an organ of the body performing its natural function develops, and one that remains idle tends to atrophy. The organ must not be overstrained, or it may suffer injury; but to attain its maximum efficiency it must be exerted to its fullest normal extent; and that is true of the mind as well as of the muscles, the heart, or the lungs.

If the acquisition of knowledge were the sole aim of education the quickest way to reach the result would be presenting it to a willingly receptive mind in a form easily remembered. That is the way the rules of Latin grammar were formerly taught, and setting them to rhyme helped the memory. That was also the basis of the old method of teaching law and medicine by didactic lectures, carefully prepared and read to the class. They might have been printed in book form, given to the students and by them learned almost verbatim. But if the object of education is rather an ability to deal with knowledge, then the student must learn to do it by practice on his own part. Education has, in fact, many objects. One of them is a mechanical training — as in the use of figures — which must give speed and accuracy, and applies to all direct use of the formulas that enter to some extent into most occupations. Another is to acquire what has been called codified knowledge, that is facts and ideas generally recognized as true and valuable. A third, with which we are concerned here as one of the chief objects of education, is to give the power to deal with facts, conditions, and ideas new to the person who confronts them. He must consider them in the light of a principle studied in other connections. He must apply to a new situation the principle he has learned, or more frequently some modification thereof because the facts do not accord with its rigorous application. We are often told that we ought to equip our young men in college for the problems of the day, and that is well, but not all; for by the time they have reached a position where their opinions count weightily the problems will have changed. We must equip them to deal wisely and profoundly with questions that have not yet arisen and of whose nature we may have no conception. Such a capacity is called resourcefulness, and it is one of the greatest benefits to be obtained by a college education.

To acquire the quality of resourcefulness the mind must not be passive but active. It must have the habit of initiative, which does not come from the mere reception of information systematically prepared by the instructor. Professor William B. Munro has told of an experience he had when a young instructor at a small college. Thinking it would be well for his men to read some of the great books on his subject he assigned reading to be done by the class. Consternation followed among the students, for such a demand had never been made before; and one of them said to him "Frankly, Mr Munro, we do not think you are treating us fairly. As we understand it, you are paid by the College to read these books and tell us what is in them; and now you make us read them ourselves." This is excellent as a statement of education by the method of the perambulator, without effort on the part of the student; but such a mechanical process is ill suited to the development of the brain. Professor Munro's class had misconceived the function of lectures, which should be in the main a stimulus to thought by a portrayal of a system of relations, a picture of a group of things, or an analysis of a subject, rather than a means of imparting bare facts. These in the case of mature students had better be obtained by reading. Lectures have great value, but only to a limited extent does it lie in stating facts. Much no doubt can be done by conducting the mind of the pupil through a difficult train of thought, but this has no-where near so durable an effect as his going, where possible, through the process for himself, and then having a discussion with the teacher, and best of all with fellow students also. One should seek to prevent a mere following of the guide. In the early days of our tutoring system we obtained the services of two Oxford tutors, and their pupils observed a difference be-tween their methods and ours at that time, in that when the pupil found himself confused or in error our tutors explained the matter, whereas the Oxford men sat still and made him work out his difficulty for himself.

Moreover, the moral effect of personal effort is important. To few men does mere receptivity give a vigorous impulse. For most students the motive power for mental action is not strong unless it comes from within. We hear a great deal about the need of stimulating teachers, but an exhilaration that does not cause a desire to go farther by personal effort, although by no means without marked value, has only a limited influence. It is said of a professor that after an even-ing with undergraduates the books he had been using were taken out of the library to a notably larger extent during the succeeding week. That means far more than being interested at the moment. It means inoculation with a curiosity to read more, which may come from the teacher, and is his most valuable qualification, but grows by what it feeds upon. It enlarges by use and is sustained by a sense of searching and solving until it becomes a desire, sometimes a passion, for discovery. This is one of the main objects of the case system, and the laboratory method, of teaching; much slower, both of them, as means of learning facts than the didactic lecture or the text book, but far more enlivening to the student, who becomes thereby an active agent in his own development, capable of carrying it on until he becomes an educated man. He is not, indeed, truly educated until he has acquired the power of self-direction, of seeking knowledge, and discerning its import.

No subject is really mastered until the student has made it his own; until, instead of repeating what he has been told, he has worked it over in his own mind so much that it does not seem to him a thing he has been taught, but a thing he has learned and can use as his own possession. All higher education in its best form is, indeed, self-education under guidance.

The necessity for personal effort and initiative is clearly understood and applied today in all the best law schools, in the preparation for a doctorate of philosophy, and is slowly gaining recognition in medical schools; but it has not been generally appreciated in college. Excellent examples there have been of professors who have long demanded from their students personal work of high grade, and some institutions have made it a requirement for graduation with honors. Only of late years, however, has the principle gained a foothold that self-education should be to some extent an essential element among undergraduates.

At the present day the college presents the most difficult problem in American education. This is true because the acceptance of authority and discipline which is a force in elementary, and to a less extent in secondary, schools is largely outgrown in college; while the purpose of preparing for one's career in life that gives an earnest tone to the professional schools is little felt as a motive. College is too often regarded as an interlude between school days and the serious work of life. Parents not infrequently take this view. They do not understand the value of the education to be obtained; they do not see what it leads to, measuring it too much by its practical application, and perceiving more clearly the social and physical benefits of the many so-called outside activities. Woodrow Wilson, when President of Princeton, remarked that the side-shows had overshadowed the main tent; whereas an alumnus is said to have complained that the President had turned that dear old college into a damned educational institution. The outside activities are a highly important part of student life, yet they are not the primary object for which colleges are maintained, nor if they were so treated would such institutions long survive. In fact a disproportionate view of the various aspects of college life is on the whole less common among the undergraduates than with the alumni and the public at large.

The main object of a college education is to lay a broad foundation for thought in the whole of the student's later life; and although his studies may have a more or less vocational trend, yet, save for those who intend to teach the subjects they are learning, the connection between the basic matters taught and their use in practice is by no means so clear as in a professional school, where the atmosphere is, or ought to be, thoroughly professional. The connection is, in fact, remote and the true aim is not to make the undergraduate perceive a direct relation to practical affairs which may not exist, but to stimulate a zeal for achievement that will confer greater intellectual and moral power.

In college the obstinate pupils who at school positively resist instruction have disappeared, for they rarely get so far in their education; but the indifferent who incline to use their brains no more than is necessary to get through are common. Among these are many men of natural ability, who, though capable of intellectual tastes and achievement when aroused to exertion, are listless at set tasks. The most obvious form of exertion is the reading of serious books, but here there arises a difficulty from the fact that freshmen, as a rule, cannot read such books. While they can, of course, read words and passages, even a few pages pointed out to them, they have not the power of sustained attention to follow the thread of thought through its convolutions in a book. This must be acquired by practice, that is by a process of self-education which requires personal effort, stimulated by interest and a determination to master the subject.

To create artificially a voluntary effort seems a contradiction in terms, and there has been a tendency in American education to avoid the paradox by making the effort as effortless as possible; that is by making the work easy, or at least pleasant, for the pupil. A variant of the same method is to assume that since the effort should be voluntary it must be exerted in some subject in which the student has a natural interest, with the result that he often proves to have a more natural interest in play, or in doing nothing, than in study. The fact is that in most people interest in serious things is not inborn. They do not do things because they are interested in them (although they think so) so much as they are interested in things because they do them. The thousands of people who spent hours in working over cross-word puzzles did not do so because they had a natural interest in making words out of odd combinations of letters, for if they had, this pastime would not have gone so largely out of fashion in a few months. On the contrary, the very effort to solve the puzzles created for a time an ardent interest in work that had no other attraction or value. Some people keenly enjoy mental exertion, to more it is a pleasure in moderation, but almost everyone desires to find the solution of a problem in which he is engaged if it does not require too hard labor or too much drudgery. In the case of the undergraduate, therefore, the aim should be to get him at work on a problem which he thinks will be interesting, and which will become so as he engages in trying to solve it.

A skillful tutor, whose field was history and literature, was fortunate in holding the belief that every student had a natural interest in something, although he might not be aware of it himself. He asked one of the young men assigned to him why he had selected that subject for his principal work in college. The student replied that he was not interested in any other. "Are you interested in this one?" "No." That seemed discouraging; but the tutor inquired what books he liked to read, and, Scott's novels and other fiction of the period being mentioned, he told the pupil that his interest lay in romantic literature, and that he would enjoy finding the connection between that literature and the French Revolution. In two weeks the pupil was reading earnestly. The tutor had won a victory, not so much by discovering, as by creating, an interest; and if the pupil had intellectual faculties his whole life was probably affected thereby.

To arouse a strong interest the problem or subject should not be made easy, but hard; for it is only by strenuous mental exertion that power is developed. Moreover, a series of short unrelated problems does not sustain the interest. For those who have no keen enjoyment in thinking for its own sake the appetite for such problems is likely to diminish. The subject on which the student is working had better be continuous, engaging his attention for as large a part of his college course, and aiming at a knowledge of as large a field, as possible. That is the meaning of requiring the student to elect a major subject, a provision to be found in the rules of almost all colleges at the present time.

No doubt, as an old sailor used to say, there are many ways of killing a cat beside choking it with butter; and that is true of education. One method of reaching the result, now spreading among the Eastern colleges, is that of stimulating an enduring interest by making the mastery of a subject a visible object. This is done by demanding for graduation the passing of a general examination thereon after two or more years devoted mainly to studying it. Such an examination is by no means a review of the courses of instruction, for it includes ground that they do not cover; and the preparation for it must be made by personal reading outside of course instruction. The examination is remote enough, comprehensive enough, and tangible enough to be a conscious object of endeavor. At the same time the papers, if properly prepared, are not such as can be passed by cramming. Hence, the goal is not the passing of the examination, but the mastery of a subject, the student knowing that this will enable him to pass and that nothing else will. The success of the method depends upon the skill of the examiners. The art of examination is a difficult one, little understood in America, and this general form is the most difficult of all. To make it effective tutors are no doubt important, if not essential, because a student can hardly be expected to find his own way through a field of knowledge without a guide; but the main thing is the general examination, rather than the tutor whose duty is not to teach but to help the student to learn. That the system has stimulated many undergraduates to a keen interest they would not otherwise have had has been proved by experience, and the future success of the plan will be watched by all men engaged in the problem of college education.

REMARKS AT THE INAUGURATION OF CLARENCE A. BARBOUR AS PRESIDENT OF BROWN UNIVERSITY

OCTOBER 18, 1929

SIR GALAHAD on one occasion missed finding the Holy Grail because he forgot to ask the meaning of what passed before his eyes. So it may be that we, in institutions of higher learning, may sometimes forget to ask why we are here, or what we are doing, and thus through absence of mind fail of our object, if we have one. This is particularly true of the undergraduate department, or college, because it is, by all odds, the most difficult and least successful part of our universities. The object of a professional school is obvious and concrete, whereas that of the college is indefinite and confused. Of course one can easily state its purpose in glowing terms which have little bearing on the actual direction to be followed; but that is like trying to lay one's course at sea by taking an observation of St. Elmo's fire at the masthead. In the college we are dealing with imponderables, so heavy that we lack weights with which they can be measured.

Now I hear someone, connected perhaps with the press, who is saying to himself that we all know perfectly well what our colleges are for. They are here to furnish spectacular games for the alumni and the public. The alumni give us panem and we provide them with circenses. We do it abundantly; but, alas! defectively. Great as is our duty in this matter to the public, it is even greater to our own alumni, and they are not satisfied merely with an exciting contest, even with one that is a good fight, for they crave victory. Therefore we must do everything we can to win. But unfortunately the other college has the same idea, which prevents on these occasions perfect content all round, both at the moment and for some time thereafter. So the unalloyed pleasure the circenses should give in return for solid panem is most regrettably impossible.

Moreover, to give the fullest opportunity for enjoyment we must build larger and larger amphitheatres — at least as large as that of a rival, who may thereupon build a larger one — a prospect that has no finite limits. In my home town we refused this year to increase the seating capacity of our stadium beyond the temporary seats already used, and we cherish the strange belief that the bulk of our alumni hold their entertainment secondary to the welfare of the student body; while the attitude of the undergraduates as a whole toward these things, their estimate of relative values, is highly rational. Recreation and competitive sports are excellent — nay indispensable — in the training of youth; but they may be overdone. Two great nations of antiquity, whose language, deeds, and thoughts our colleges have always taught, both had sports publicly attended and attracting wide interest; but conducted on different principles. No people have set more store by competitive athletic contests than the Greeks, none have valued success more highly, yet with them the object was, and always remained, the cultivation of physical excellence in young men. With the Romans the primary object was the entertainment of the spectators, while training of youth in health and strength was in these shows lost from sight almost altogether. Is not the Greek principle preferable to the Roman for our colleges? As an abstract proposition probably no one would deny this, but we do not conduct our athletic sports in the abstract. With our frequent intercollegiate games, attracting huge crowds at short intervals, and continuous publicity, are we not slipping into the Roman attitude of mind? The Greeks thought one great contest of a kind a year enough to sustain ardor in athletics; may it not be that a single intercollegiate meet in each sport would do the same?

Without contending against those who think otherwise, let us assume that the object of our colleges is the welfare of the students, that the aim should be the utmost development of which each is capable, and their fitness to play their parts in the vast drama of our nation. Our numerous Bills of Rights tell us that "All men are born free and equal, and have certain natural, essential, and unalienable rights; among which may be reckoned the right . . . of seeking and obtaining their safety and happiness." We are repeatedly told at the present day that our constitutions are out of date, and in this particular it is certainly true. Judging from the state of the public mind it is probable that the next revisions will assert the right of every man and woman to seek and obtain a college degree. But in order to bring to pass that amiable result we must adapt the standard to the end desired. We must set it within easy reach; for if all men have a right to obtain a degree, they are entitled to do so by a very moderate effort on their own part — the main object of a college education being social rather than intellectual. The popular demand is for professors who can stimulate interest and infuse a modicum of information without distasteful or degrading labor on the part of their hearers. Like all other modern operations this must be painless.

But here again, the colleges are not succeeding in doing what is expected of them, for the simple reason that it cannot be done. One might as well expect to train a crew by having them listen to the instruction of the coach and watch him row. Every capacity worth having can be developed only by personal effort, and brought to a high point only by carrying the effort far. To build on any other supposition is contrary to human nature and especially to the nature of youth. In the main young men do not take seriously what can be got without striving; nor do they desire to have the things they care about made easy. Students who take part in intercollegiate sports do not want the effort, the fatigue, the strain, or even the risk of injuries reduced. It was the administrators of the colleges, not the players, who insisted a score of years ago that the rules of football should be so changed as to lessen the danger of serious injuries and fatal accidents. Youth longs to exert all its powers to the utmost, if it can be brought to see that the exertion is worth while, and that the test applied measures the qualities that it admires.

There stands our problem and the road to its solution. In part it lies in eliminating those who are unable or unwilling to make the effort, and make it fruitfully. The attempt to include large numbers, by admitting too freely, spells reduction in standards to somewhere near the slowest members of the class; and, what is worse, a lowering of the aspirations of the whole body. Is this undemocratic? It is certainly at variance with conclusions often, but wrongly, drawn from the statement that all men are born free and equal. Equal in standing before the law they are intended to be, but they are very far from equal in capacity for intellect and energy — a fact that no political platitudes can reverse. It is not undemocratic in Pasteur's sense that democracy allows every man to put forth his utmost effort. Democracy, no less than every other polity, needs for the public welfare the full use of its best minds.

In part the solution lies in making intellectual excellence appear worth while by demanding and honoring qualities that strong young men admire, rather than those which mediocrity can attain by mere plodding. The tortoise that beat the hare has never excited youthful enthusiasm, and never will. Nor for that matter has the hare either, and there was something wrong in the conditions that suffered him to go to sleep. Conducted as they are, our colleges have far too many sleepy hares, in an active, if not feverish, age. If we can wake them up by putting before them something that whets their hunger and ambition, the tortoise will not win, nor will the fear of his doing so detract from the interest of the race.

Now, President Barbour, let me welcome and commiserate you. One of my predecessors, the Rev. James Walker, remarked some years after he had left the office, and not long before he advised President Eliot to accept it, that it was a respectable way of earning one's living, but it was detestable. The position has changed in some respects since those days, but it is still a place of struggles, of trials, of perplexities, of disappointments. Yet, like the young athletes, we would not remove the effort, the fatigue, and the strain; for work that is all pleasant, simple, and facile leads to little that is much worth doing. We, who are engaged in education, may be pardoned in believing that the future of our country depends in large measure upon the character, the aspirations, and the ripened wisdom of the young men to issue from our institutions of higher learning; and if so yours will be a place of vast opportunities for good, not to them alone, but also to the nation they must help to ennoble. Such an opportunity is as great as any man may crave; and therefore, President Barbour, from the bottom of my heart I congratulate you.

EXPANSION OF KNOWLEDGE AND EDUCATION

PART OF AN ADDRESS AT THE UNIVERSITY OF PENNSYLVANIA, JUNE 2, 1933

FOR the last two centuries the advance in knowledge has been more rapid than ever before, and it has been proceeding with greater and greater acceleration, until the accumulation has become so large that men are perplexed in dealing with it. In education they are as much puzzled to know what to leave out as what to include. From time to time profound basic principles have, no doubt, been discovered which have simplified knowledge and made possible an arrangement or crystallization of known facts in a more systematic form. Such were the Conservation of Matter in the eighteenth century, and in the nineteenth the Conservation of Energy and the Theory of Evolution. But while these made it easier for men to cope with the growing mass of facts they have not been enough to counteract difficulties flowing from the enormous growth of knowledge. Principles of this kind which render disparate facts more manageable by making the distinct items parts of a more inclusive whole, may be expected hereafter, but they are hardly likely within any near future to reduce the burden of learning, retaining, and using the vast, and ever increasing, store.

The accumulation of knowledge has, indeed, gone far beyond the capacity of any single mind. A Casaubon, supposed to know all that could be known, became long ago impossible. Natural Philosophy, once regarded as a single subject in which a man might acquire proficiency enough to teach a college class, would provoke a smile today. Owing to the growth of scientific knowledge its fields became sharply sundered into Physics, Chemistry, Botany, Zoology, and others; and these again into subdivisions so small as to give rise to the jest that men of science were learning more and more about less and less. The greater the magnifying power of a given lens the less the space included in its scope. The principal fields were so distinct that if a man cultivating one of them looked over the wall into the next he was liable to be considered inquisitive, and, if he wrote about it, almost as an intruder.

In recent times another factor has come into play, counteracting the segregation of the sciences, although arising from the same extension of knowledge. So many sappers have been digging under the walls that separate the fields, and coming up on the other side, that the walls themselves have become much dilapidated, no longer a protection against interlopers. In places the very boundaries of the fields are not clearly marked, and what was in fact no-man's land is now explored by every man who can stake out a rational claim. No one can say whether the electron and its derivatives should be more at home in a chemical or physical laboratory; whether the organic cell develops more happily under a botanical or zoological microscope; whether physiological chemistry is more properly studied as a branch of chemistry, physiology, or medicine. Obviously, the true answer is by all three in close cooperation. All the sciences are reaching out into new lands to cultivate, often alongside of their neighbors, overlapping and intersecting each other as they go.

Moreover, each science is in constant need of the others in tilling its own field. An institution for any one of them alone deprived of ready means of access to the rest would find itself crippled, or confined to the collection of specimens. The tendency of science has been from classification to structure, from structure to function; and function involves change, chemical, physical, physiological, and ultimately adaptation, both material and psychological. To understand any of these processes one must know much beyond the limits of any one traditional branch of science, and the more he knows the more fully he will be equipped.

Clearly this means that anyone who aspires to contribute to scientific knowledge, or to teach it on a high plane, must have some familiarity with other basic sciences, not necessarily in great detail, but enough to be able to obtain and comprehend the collateral information that he requires. Does it mean also that he needs nothing else? Every aspect of thought has its limitations, that of science as well as others; and on the whole the broader the approach the better.

.   .   .   .

Didactic instruction in everything is not indispensable. In later life every man with social instincts and an inquiring mind learns a vast deal from conversation. Let us imagine a group of eminent scholars in diverse fields, who for reasons of health and otherwise had established themselves with libraries and laboratories in some remote spot, and had drawn about them many young men, not directly preparing themselves for a specific career, but eager to learn, to think, and to understand. Suppose that these young men should be, not of course exclusively, but constantly, conversing about their own and one another's subjects, often too with the eminent scholars who teach them, what an education would they obtain! Would they not leave, not only with a mastery of their own field, but a broad culture of a very valuable kind and much understanding of things in which they had received no didactic instruction? They need not be bookworms. They might be in physical strength and skill equal to the best in the land, for the number of hours spent in study ought not to be excessive. The question is rather the use of leisure, and mental attrition in social intercourse, keeping the mind at all times keen and full of interest.

Suppose that were the picture of a real college, would you send your son to it? Suppose that were a fair description of all American colleges, what would it mean for the future of our country? Would it not leaven the whole lump and bring our people to a higher plane? But many people will think

such a supposition absurd, because in view of the natural indolence of youth, and indifference to higher things, the condition is impossible. Granted that to attain the picture fully
is a fantastic dream, it is not beyond conjecture that it might
be approached. Youth when aroused is neither indolent nor
indifferent, as the late war showed. Youth longs to spend
itself for something it believes worth while; and it is highly
susceptible to the opinions of others on what is worth while.
My own experience is that the students, as a rule, have a
better appreciation of the relative value of scholarship and
athletic victories than the public at large, in spite of the influence of the press in magnifying the latter as the only thing
worth consideration. In fact the greatest benefits of college
life are not spectacular or adapted for current publications.

Approach to the dream requires faith; faith on the part of
the instructing staff that it is possible; faith on the part of
parents, alumni, and the public that it is desirable; and mark
you, if even an approach is made no man can predict how far
it may be carried.

EXAMINATION IN THE EDUCATIONAL PROCESS

THE MASSACHUSETTS INSTITUTE OF TECHNOLOGY, COMMENCEMENT, 1933
REPRINTED FROM THE HARVARD TEACHERS RECORD

I

FROM teachers to committees of the United States Senate, inquisitors are apt to be unpopular with their victims. A generation ago an examination was often looked upon in the schools as unnecessary and objectionable. The teacher asserted that he knew how his pupils were doing, and regarded it as much like an indictment — a thing not to be used against good citizens — and as implying at least a suspicion of misconduct. As recently as 1926 Professor Grover T. Somers made some investigations on the attitude towards examinations of students and teachers in schools and colleges, and discovered that both bodies disliked them and thought them of little value. This is not unnatural; for examinations are as a rule given mainly for purposes of discipline — that is, to see whether the pupil has really done his work, the exact rating of individuals being of less importance. Now discipline and all its methods are obviously unpopular both with those who employ and those subjected to them. Moreover, the value of examinations conducted as discipline depends on the difficulty of evasion; and the offense of trying by various illicit means to circumvent or impose upon the examiner is not always regarded by youth as partaking of mortal sin. To pass the examination without possessing the knowledge it is intended to require is sometimes regarded as more clever than wrong.

Another object in examination — that of measurement rather than discipline — has lately become prominent. The increasing number of applicants for higher education, the conviction that too many college students benefit little from instruction, a desire for a better criterion of what we are trying to do and how well we are doing it, have caused a greatly increased interest in tests of ability, of attainment, and of promising qualities. Of course every examination partakes somewhat of the nature of discipline and somewhat of that of measurement; but the primary object and the emphasis may be very different, and the large amount of recent study and experiment in examinations would never have been made with a mere view of discipline. It has arisen from a feeling of the practical need for accurate measurement of the quality and prospects of young students. Its value depends on its accuracy, and although no examination can be perfectly fair, the object is to make it as objective and unbiased as possible.

Now one of the chief causes of uncertain results in examinations comes from the personal judgment of the examiner. To eliminate this, resort has been had to questions susceptible of answers absolutely right or wrong, which can be marked and graded by anyone who has the key. That such tests are highly valuable there can be no doubt; but what they actually measure, and how accurate they are, remains to be proved. In their nature they give little scope for fine discrimination, or the display of careful reasoning on the part of the person examined. They are based largely on speed and give little time for thought.

Now there is a third function of examinations, where the main object is neither discipline nor measurement, but education; and that aspect of the matter has not hitherto been much discussed. I hope I may be pardoned if I draw illustrations from things under my own observation, where I can speak with personal knowledge. In the middle of the first year of the Harvard Law School there are examinations offered to those who choose to take them. Their object is clearly not at all discipline, for they are voluntary; and they are not used for measurement on behalf of the School, for the results do not count toward marks in the courses, and except in the matter of student aid no effect is given to them. They are offered that the student himself may know how he is doing, and improve his own work thereby. Hence their object is almost wholly educational. Let me give another example, that of the discussion of cases in that School, according to the method of Langdell. These are not formal examinations, and yet they partake of their character. When I was in the Law School, out of a class of about forty men, some eight or ten took part in the discussions every day. They tried to expound the problems presented by the cases, and did so in a highly competitive spirit. They were, in effect, being examined, or examining themselves and one another, before the class. Now the object of this was certainly not discipline, nor, except in the sense of rivalry, was it measurement, for of course no record of it was ever kept; and so far as it may be called examination, its effect was purely educational. The same thing is true, to a lesser degree, of all themes, reports, and problems to be written or done, where no doubt discipline and measurement enter, but the primary intent is education — that is, training in the acquisition and use of knowledge.

Such cases, if not all of them examinations in the ordinary academic form, are in substance a species thereof, and they are certainly a part of the educational process. Now, someone will say, that may be true of such things when intermediate, taking place during a period of study; but how can a final examination that occurs at the end of the period be a part of the process? In three notable ways: by setting a standard; by requiring the expression of thought; and by promoting the association of ideas. These things interlace, of course, and yet they may be discussed separately.

II

Every examination at the close of a period of instruction tends to direct attention to the matters on which it lays stress. If it demands bare facts, dates, and formulae, these will be uppermost in the mind of the teacher and prevalent in the thought of the students. If the information required is such as can be rapidly crammed, many of the class will be tempted to put off work until near the end. But if the questions require a real comprehension of the subjects dealt with and their significance, the nature of the examination will color the character of the instruction given and received. I am assuming that where the examination is written, the questions are printed and published, and that where experimental or practical, the scope is made known. If so, these things will be considered by the students as the goal they are expected to attain; and for that reason it is an advantage to have a distant one. If the nature of the examination is not generally known, it loses much of its value as part of the process of education.

May I be pardoned again if I use an illustration within my own observation? The principle of a general examination was introduced into the Harvard Medical School in 1910. It went through different forms, and several years passed before a series of experiments showed how it had best be used. In its definitive shape it is truly general — that is, it is obligatory for all students at the end of the four years' course and covers all the subjects studied both in the laboratory and the clinics. It is, of course, a measurement, but that is not its chief aim; and, in fact, the proportion of failures is very small. For a time its nature was not understood, and some of the faculty seemed to consider its purpose a review for the assigning of marks; but its real object is quite different, that of requiring a correlation between the various subjects included in the whole four years' course. In medicine this is peculiarly difficult because, studied separately, the relations between these subjects are not easily grasped. The connection beween anatomy, chemistry, the diagnosis and treatment of disease, and the curative processes of surgery are not at the outset obvious to the student, or always so taught as to make them so. The art of medicine deals with man as a complete, self-consistent organism, and the art of the general examination is to cause the student to regard it as such. For this purpose the questions are not special but comprehensive, each calling for the bearing of different subjects on one another. Let me repeat, the essential thing about this examination is not the measurement in itself, but the attitude it engenders; and although nothing accomplishes its ends perfectly,' it has had a notable effect in causing the students to reflect upon medicine as a whole, as well as an influence on the teaching of diverse subjects.

Every examination whose nature is known, set at the close of a period of study upon the subjects studied, will affect the attitude of the students towards those subjects for good or evil, becoming to that extent an integral part of the process of education; and the more it is considered by the examiners from this point of view the better its effect is likely to be.

III

The second way in which an examination may be a valuable part of the process of education is by requiring a systematic expression of thought. Some wise man has remarked that no one knows a subject in an intellectual way unless he can talk or write about it; that is, can express his ideas upon it; for to express oneself involves arranging one's thoughts in order, formulating and thus clarifying them — a very different thing from answering Yes or No to a series of questions formulated by the examiner. The great art in life lies less in solving problems than in discovering the problems to be solved, and to that an examination may, in part at least, direct attention. By so doing it can reduce the comparative weight of mere memorizing and cause the student to make the subject his own, leading him to work it over in his mind until he can express it, not in the terms of a book or a statement by a professor, but as it comes to stand in the fabric of his own thought. If he knows that at the close of his studies he will be called upon to do this, he will be inclined to prepare himself for an orderly statement of what he has learned.

Now to be fair such an examination should comprise options, for one man will have thought more on one point and his neighbor more on another. Moreover, the answers cannot be marked by mere clerical labor because every student's formulation and expression of his ideas is, and should be, somewhat different from that of every other, and can be valued only by a person thoroughly conversant with the subject. Of course this entails the uncertainty that lies in any personal judgment, but it is a case where the precise mark is of less consequence than the effect on the educational process.

IV

The same is true of the third potential influence of examinations — that of promoting the association of ideas. For students it is very easy to think of their work as amassing facts and formulae, and this is strengthened by examinations framed for the sole purpose of measurement, for they tend naturally to require such things. But the true object of education is only in part the acquisition of bare knowledge. Much of that will vanish away. More important is the art of dealing with facts — of correlating, comparing, and combining them. Not least is the sense of proportion that comes from looking at things from more than one point of view; and this the type of examination may encourage or depress. If I may turn once more to the experience of the Medical School: at first the European plan of one general examination at the end of the laboratory subjects and another at the close of the clinical years was tried, but it was found that the real object was to correlate these two kinds of knowledge, and a single examination was substituted where each question involved the use of both.

The end sought by education is enlarging and refining the mind of the student, inducing keen perception, correct reasoning, and above all an appetite for knowledge and thought for their own sake which will not vanish, but once acquired is well-nigh insatiate, unquenchable and capable of being turned in many directions. Examinations consciously treated as a part of the educational process are more likely to promote that purpose.

Education is a vast and complex thing of which we have learned something by experience, by theory not very much; and verily the art of examination is difficult, for it aims at several distinct objects at once. These things are not to be solved by a formula, nor are any formulae either exact or essential, for there may be many roads to the same end. But one matter that has not yet received the attention it deserves is that of examinations as a vital factor in the educational process.

UNIVERSITIES, GRADUATE SCHOOLS AND COLLEGES

THE ATLANTIC MONTHLY, AUGUST, 1933

I

DANIEL COIT GILMAN did a great work, making in the highest ranges of education the largest single advance in the annals of our country. Yet he made one mistake; but, before discussing this, one must first know his purpose, for an error is a failure to adapt the means to the end sought.

From Gilman's inaugural address in 1876 as the first President of Johns Hopkins University it is difficult to discover a definite plan of operation. Perhaps it was not so clear in his own mind at that time as it became later; but the object was perfectly distinct, for it was the largest possible freedom in advanced teaching and study, in an atmosphere of liberal culture, and under the guidance of the greatest scholars, eminent or of high promise, that could be secured. How the result was to be attained he does not state. He was thinking of an aim rather than a formula. While speaking of the essential difference between colleges and universities, and rejecting for Johns Hopkins the traditional four-year college course, he says nothing that shows a clear intention to restrict admission to those who had already obtained the bachelor's degree. He notes that Harvard "has essentially given up its collegiate restrictions and introduced the benefits of university freedom"; that Michigan and Cornell "quite early adopted the discipline of universities"; and that "the University of Virginia from its foundation has upheld the university in distinction from the college idea."

In none of these cases was he referring to a graduate school. In fact, he does not use for his own project the terms "graduate school" or "instruction for graduates." His idea seems to have been a high method of education, not a series of degrees. "The exact standard," he says, "is not yet fixed. It must depend on the colleges and schools around us; there must be no gap in the system, and we must keep ahead, but the discussions now in progress, respecting the City College, Agricultural College, and St. John's College, must delay our announcements. Our standards will doubtless be as high as the community requires." Later he remarks that many students will come to them excellent in some branches of a liberal education and deficient in others. "I would give to such candidates, on examination, credit for their attainments, and assign them in each study to the place for which they are fitted. A proficient in Plato may be a tyro in Euclid. Moreover, I would make attainments rather than time the condition of promotion." Apparently he meant the test for admission to be qualification for the instruction offered, not the possession of a college degree; and this accords with his conception of freedom in a university.

Johns Hopkins, under his lead, started like Pallas from the head of Zeus. The selection of the first faculty, and of the younger men who joined it, was extremely skillful; and in a few years the University was a Mecca for many of the most promising college graduates in the country, attracted by the spirit of freedom and investigation and the absence of emphasis on numbers. What its destiny might have been but for the misfortunes of the Baltimore and Ohio Railroad, in which most of its funds were invested, no one can say. Its medical school prospered, but its graduate teaching was crippled at the very time it met the competition of richer institutions, for graduate schools were soon established in most of the large American universities. These were by no means wholly a copying of Gilman's idea, since doctorates of philosophy and science had been regularly conferred at Harvard for three years before his inaugural address — one of them on a subsequent professor at his university — and the masters of arts for advanced studies already exceeded a score. No doubt the same had been done elsewhere; but the example at Baltimore greatly stimulated the movement, and its fame set a fashion. Whatever he originally intended, his plan led to the graduate school as we see it today.

II

Now for President Gilman's one mistake, if it was a mistake; and if so it was certainly not his alone. It was that of conferring degrees. If — for we are dealing with conjectural matters — if his main object was to develop original thinkers, men expected to contribute deeply to knowledge, who cannot be very numerous in any generation, he would have done better to confer on them no degrees and let their productions speak for themselves. Granting degrees had an unforeseen but inevitable result.[1]

However it may be in continental Europe where competition is extreme, and there are often examinations conducted by the state, in America the higher degrees are sure to be used as qualifications for teaching, and there is a strong temptation to reduce standards to meet the demand. Instead of the most advanced work being limited to future productive scholars, the doctorate has become the passport to the faculties of universities and the better colleges, while a master's degree is commonly required for teaching in the high schools of large cities. "Raising the standard" this is called by the appointing authorities, and to some extent it is, but not so much as they suppose, because to require a result above what can be produced lowers either the amount of the production or the test actually applied. Attempts to fix the price of bread have often been tried, and within narrow

[1] "Fifty years ago a fair proportion of the students in the University came without any idea of obtaining a degree; and Mr. Gilman was continually expressing the hope that the proportion would be larger. . . . To-day it is safe to say, I believe, that practically every student in the University is working purposely for a degree." (President Ames of Johns Hopkins: *Annual Report*, November, 1931, p. 4.)

limits they may be successful,' but if the cost is too high for the price fixed either the bakers are driven out of business or the amount of wheat in the loaf falls off.

Take the case of the master's degree. Not all teachers in high schools are capable of really advanced work. Many of them can be excellent teachers, sufficiently competent in the knowledge of their subjects, but without originality or high scholarship. A man unfamiliar with the intricacies of potential functions, non-Euclidean geometry, or the higher differential equations may teach algebra, geometry, and trigonometry in a secondary school well, and sometimes better than an eminent mathematician. What is taught in any college of high grade will serve his needs, if he has been proficient at it, and the same is true of other subjects. The demand that he, or she, must have done really advanced work becomes largely illusory. Often it may consist of scoring a number of credits, one at a time after school hours or in the summer. As evidence of a desire to improve one's self, and as a means of doing so, this is excellent; but it is not really advanced study in the sense of university work for scholars of distinction. This the secondary teacher does not need and does not get. The demand for such instruction as he does need is large, and the graduate schools have set themselves to supply it, with the result of bringing into their student body a large mass of earnest, industrious young people who can never rise above moderate intellectual attainments. That this work should be done is clear, but whether it should be combined with the attempt to develop great scholars is a very different question.

To a less extent the same is true of the doctorate of philosophy, since it has come to be regarded as the essential requisite for teaching in a good college. The qualification for doing so has become the measure of the degree, and in the best universities it is a high one; but it is not quite the same as an atmosphere of enthusiasm for original thinkers. Every preparation for a degree involves, especially if the numbers are large, a certain amount of routine, of fixed rules which impair the complete freedom that should be enjoyed at some stage in a true scholar's career. At what age that point is reached is not easily determined, but, for a man with the qualities for contributing greatly to the world's thought, it should probably be placed earlier than is commonly assumed in America. Newton had the essential elements of the calculus in his mind while still an undergraduate at Cambridge. Evariste Galois left the theory of determinants in a letter to a friend written the night before he was killed in a duel at twenty; and many such examples might be cited. We are turning out every year in this country a multitude of doctors of philosophy, and yet there is often complaint of difficulty in finding men of the quality needed for positions in our universities. The fact is that graduate schools do not attract men of aggressive ability as much as they should. To attribute this to the small remuneration of professors is beside the mark, because men with scholarly tastes and comfortable fortunes, to whom this is not an important consideration, go in much larger numbers into other occupations, like law or business, that are certainly not less exacting.

Economists have long been familiar with Gresham's Law, to the effect that money coined from a cheaper metal will drive that of more intrinsic value out of circulation; and the principle has a wider application. Other things being equal, a professional school will attract in the main men of the general quality of its members. Graduate schools are now mainly seminaries for teachers of high and not so high, grade, predominantly the latter, and they draw chiefly men of that type. Many people have thought that more ambitious and talented youths would come if they were offered large fellowships; but surely this is the wrong approach. It is making life easy during the period of preparation, and was tried in the divinity schools a hundred years ago, with the result of helping to lessen rather than increase the proportion of forcible men in the ministry. In fact the pecuniary advantages

hitherto offered in graduate schools in the form of scholarships, and often of lower tuition fees than in other parts of the
university, have not had an altogether good effect on their
students. They are less provident, marrying before acquiring
a settled means of support much more frequently than the
students in schools of law or medicine.

The graduate schools are doing an excellent and much
needed‹ work; but they are not what we have supposed
President Gilman had in mind. They produce some extraordinary scholars, but they are not on the whole well adapted
to attract, and stimulate to the utmost, young men of that
kind. For this purpose a new — I will not say organization,
for the word implies the very rigidity we would avoid —
rather, a new method is needed which will provide a more
stimulating atmosphere, broader contacts with eminent men
outside the special field, and a more definite independent
opportunity and productive purpose.

III

Graduate schools have had one effect that has not been
sufficiently noticed. They have tended to block the advance
of the college. This appears clearly when we trace the history
of the American college from its inception. It began as a
transplantation to the newly founded colony in Massachusetts Bay of the institution with the same name in Cambridge
and Oxford. These colleges were residential and teaching
bodies, without the power to confer degrees which belonged
to the university alone. From its foundation, however, Harvard assumed this power without authority, but by tacit
acquiescence of the colony, and thus acquired control of its
own affairs. In so doing it had usurped a royal prerogative,
yet its right was not contested in England, and Dunster, the
first president, obtained from the two great English universities recognition of its degrees as equivalent to their own,
a privilege that seems to have been dropped only when they

ceased to give the same treatment to foreign degrees. This modified type of the English college, with a power to grant degrees and therefore to determine its own standards, was universally followed until the Revolution, and became the traditional form of the American college.

For two hundred years there was little advance here, and in fact the eighteenth century was a time of somnolence in the universities of Europe also. They awoke to greater activity early in the nineteenth, and at the same time a literary revival came in this country, together with expansion of teaching by the creation of schools of law and medicine. But the stirring of the waters had no large effect on the colleges or the standards of their education until after the Civil War, and then the eyes of scholars were turned to Germany. Some of our best men had studied there, and, instead of trying to raise the college to a much higher level, they sought to do here for the graduates what had been done for them at Göttingen, Leipsic, or Berlin. So they superposed on the American college a graduate school modeled on the German university.

Now there was in Germany nothing beneath the university analogous to our colleges, and it was not clear how they would fit into their new environment, or what would be their educational position. If the graduate school was to be a place for independent study and research by a few selected men, their position would have resembled that of the prize fellows at Oxford and Cambridge, while the colleges would have been free to develop, and in the strongest institutions probably would have evolved, education of a high order. But if the graduate school was to be, like a German university, the sole place for advanced study, the college had no adequate function in higher education. It must be confined to a lower grade of work, and in most places that has happened. Such is, indeed, the view often held by American professors. They are constantly giving as a reason for preferring one offer to another that they will be expected to teach only graduate students. The expression "the university, that is the graduate school" has become common, and with such an attitude on the part of many, perhaps most, of the members of university faculties, the lack, still frequent, of serious effort to raise the standard of undergraduate education to a much higher level is not surprising.

Everywhere in Europe the university follows directly on the secondary school, and so it should. A tendency is therefore observable in America to associate the college with secondary work. In his article in the April *Atlantic*, Mr. Abraham Flexner sets forth the conventional point of view when, referring to the colleges before the advent of graduate schools, he writes, "Such scholars and scientists as we then possessed led double lives — teaching boys at one time, pursuing their studies in their scant leisure. The graduate school at Baltimore shut out mere boys." Why mere boys? In the early nineties, when the graduate schools had begun to grow large, the age of entering Harvard was on the average nineteen years and four months, about the same as that for the English and German universities. No doubt the training in the secondary schools was inferior to that in Europe, largely because primary teaching here begins late and proceeds slowly. But the secondary schools have improved, must improve, and it is noteworthy that the average age of entrance at Harvard has in the last four decades declined just one year, although the requirements for admission have not been lowered.

To treat young men from eighteen to twenty-two and more as boys is not only an unpardonable waste of time and money, but also demoralizing to them. No excuse will justify continuing their secondary instruction to that age, or indeed any education not of university grade, by which term I mean such as is fit for maturing youth well grounded in the discipline of school. If by that time they are not capable of this, they have reached the limit of profitable advance, and should not remain to slow down the progress of the other students. We are thus brought to the alternative of raising the college to a higher level, encroaching thereby on the sphere of the graduate schools, or abolishing it in its present form by reducing its period to that required for completing secondary education — a year for the product of the best schools, two years for that of those less good.

Of course the college might be abolished altogether, and the secondary teaching relegated wholly to subordinate institutions such as the junior colleges common in the West, and especially in California. This has been proposed, but never carried out completely, for the universities which admit graduates of the junior colleges generally treat the work done there as a substitute for the first two years of their own undergraduate course. If the system were adopted fully, the university might become, like the German, a congeries of professional schools, but without the traditional background of culture that envelops the whole. Moreover, at present at least, the junior college cannot provide the highly trained teachers of the German *Gymnasium*, or the selected body of students preparing under rigorous discipline for the university. Such a system thoroughly tried would be interesting, but the results might be problematical.

Abolishing the college in its present form has serious drawbacks. Not only in this country, but also in England and Germany, the two nations from which we have borrowed our ideas of higher education, it has been the habit during the formative period of early manhood to bring together in a community with an atmosphere of culture men who will later follow many careers — future lawyers, physicians, statesmen, public servants, teachers, and here, and to an increasing extent in England, young men who will engage in business. The contacts made, the mutual attrition, have been thought valuable, for it is not the direct education alone, but the common life also, that has been sought and has caused much of the affection and loyalty of alumni, who esteem it highly. In England and Germany this common life for young men has been supplied in varying forms by the universities, in America by the college. Not long ago a student from one of the state universities remarked to the writer that in his part of the country the undergraduates deemed the instruction less important than learning to deal with men. Without exaggerating the value of close contacts between young men of very different destinies, we may observe that if the colleges were abolished nothing for the purpose would take their place, for the students in our professional schools cannot, and had better not, be merged into a single community. Certainly the graduate schools, composed as they are almost exclusively of prospective teachers, cannot take the place. Therefore these schools are not, and cannot be made, social counterparts of their German prototypes. In short, the attempt to superpose a German university upon an Oxford or Cambridge college has resulted in most cases in producing neither. Each has tended to denature the other. Speaking of American universities in general, the college and the graduate school have been doing in succession separately some things that had better be done at the same time together.

IV

The graduate school, being practically confined to the education of teachers and of technical experts, cannot by itself be a university, nor can a law school, medical school, or any other that prepares for a particular profession; but the college, if raised to a level high enough, can. To many people this may seem chimerical, yet in some of the most progressive universities it has been largely done. Their honor graduates are in many subjects fairly equal to those of Oxford and Cambridge, and certainly can be made fully equal if there is a determined effort to do so. No doubt it will be said that we have undergraduates who take no real interest in learning and neglect their work. Such men are found everywhere. In England they take the degree with a pass, formerly a very low measure of scholarship; but happily both the standard for the pass and the proportion of men who try for honors have been greatly raised. In Germany under the Empire, when we were extolling her system, a large fraction of the students never attempted to get a degree or study seriously, but after a few years' residence went home to manage their estates. Men of this kind are the vexation and despair of all higher education, not strictly professional; but in good colleges here many of them are dropped out early, and others are provoked to a respect and desire for scholarly attainment. Moreover, to win any degree in these colleges requires more work than to obtain the pass in England, and it is needless to make a comparison with the German student who seeks no degree.

When we speak of raising our best colleges to a level commensurate with that of European universities we are, of course, using a vague and grandiose term. We do not mean that they will cover the same ground as any one of those institutions, and, indeed, in no two countries are these in all respects alike. Our colleges, however developed, will not give the professional training of the German university, which is in marked contrast with the less vocational tone of Oxford and Cambridge. We are referring, not to technical details, but to the general range and quality of the education. Our institutions of higher and of professional learning should not attempt to copy those elsewhere, and must be adapted to our own conditions, but they need not be inferior, or distorted by an effort at imitation.

Raising undergraduate instruction to a higher level by no means implies discarding the graduate school, although part of its work will naturally pass to the college, as it has already done where graduate courses are open to upperclassmen. The graduate school has essential functions with which we cannot dispense: first, in supplementing the education given in colleges less well equipped; second, in preparing men to be teachers in institutions above the secondary grade — not by imparting a technique of instruction, which in higher education is of slight importance compared with learning and personality, but by giving the specific knowledge required in the subject to be taught.

To raise the level of the college does mean readjustment of the graduate schools to different conditions, for as the quality of undergraduate education rises it overlaps work formerly done later, a fact of which the graduate schools must take more account than they do now. They must be more elastic, pay more regard to individual attainment, relax their routine, and leave the progress of the proficient student more in his own hands. They must not think of themselves as essentially the university, and hence treat everyone entering as if he had received only secondary education. They must not follow for mature students methods of measuring advance by scoring credits in courses, inappropriate in a real university, and wholly out of place for graduates of high-grade colleges. The fact is that the practice of graduate schools is no longer adapted to the improvement made by the best colleges, and should be revised in accordance therewith.

V

This takes us back to the point of beginning — President Gilman's ambition to foster prospective great scholars. I do not say to train them, because that connotes a formal process; or to educate or instruct, for these in common usage mean imparting information, not in this case the chief object sought. The aim is to incite to ardent exploration, not in a line pointed out by a superior, but in an untrodden path perceived by the imagination of the explorer. One may ask if young men have such visions. The genius does, and must seek his road in his own way. Of course he must be equipped for his travels, and all the resources of the university must be open to him, all its vast storehouse of knowledge and experience; but he must not be trammeled by conventional rules and processes, good for the ordinary man but not for him. Nor, if he is, as a friend expressed it, cutting a fresh diagonal through human knowledge, can he always know at the outset all the equipment he will need.

Devotees of the existing system will maintain that there are now such opportunities in the graduate schools, that they now produce some men of mark, and that the number of these is at best small. That is true, but the conditions might be better than is possible in the present composition of such schools. The crowd of less capable and less ambitious students, with the routine inseparable from mass production, has not the attraction or driving force of a small selected group of men of rare abilities. These should not be candidates for a degree, because their attention should be directed, not to courses and examinations, but solely to progress toward their own objectives. They should live in contact with one another and with older men, both in their own subjects and in others.

Let us suppose such a group chosen in early manhood from the whole country, each member having some important project of his own that he hopes to work out. Let us suppose he is appointed for a definite term, renewable if his progress toward his goal is promising; that he is comfortably lodged, and supplied with all the opportunities for counsel, research, and experiment the university provides. Imagine these young men around a dinner table once a week with some of the greatest productive scholars it contains, to talk not about their own work so much as the currents of thought in the ocean of knowledge, the less charted the better; for the object is not to acquire codified knowledge, but to rouse the imagination by the intellectual ferment that conversation with such men instills. What an atmosphere that would be!

The Foundation Thiers in Paris is based on such a plan, save that the social life of the members is only among themselves, without the presence of older scholars. More complete is the resemblance to the prize fellowships in Trinity

College, Cambridge, which have produced an extraordinary number of distinguished men. Such a group can be most effective only in a university whose object is not merely to preserve and impart knowledge, but also to reveal fresh sources and produce the men capable of finding them. To do so it should attract the most creative minds and place them in a tingling atmosphere of eager thought, not with large mixed masses but in selected groups, with the give-and-take of ideas and aspirations and the stimulus of ripe scholars. A plan of this kind is well worth a trial. It has been called here a Society of Fellows.

UNIVERSITIES AND COLLEGES

THE YALE REVIEW, WINTER, 1934

THAT our institutions of higher learning have not been, and in spite of many improvements still are not, in a wholly satisfactory condition will be generally admitted. In fact, what should be done about them has been actively discussed for many years; but until their organization is more nearly perfect, suggestions of any reasonable kind should be welcome.

Apart from professional schools preparing for the ministry, the bar, medicine, and engineering, the American college was sixty or seventy years ago the only body that carried education beyond the high school or academy. Its curriculum was in general rigid, its minimum standard by no means high, but it gave a certain amount of culture, and there was respect for those who attained high rank. In the older colleges — and no doubt the same was true of others — the first scholar and his close rivals were held in esteem. Their names were known both to their contemporary students and to their teachers, who expected something from them in after life. Partly from the evolution of the elective system which destroyed the significance of a first scholar, that esteem diminished later — for, as President Hadley observed, we have forgotten that a curriculum meant a competitive race, and competition can be effective only when the endeavors are commensurate as they cannot be when men are pursuing wholly diverse subjects under different instructors. Other causes, too complex to be considered here, helped to reduce the respect for high rank, and the athlete or social favorite became the prominent figure, the respect for scholarship fading into the background. A college graduate of the early eighties remarked that his mother was pleased at his being at the top of his class, but that no one else took notice of it; whereas, a few years later, when he made a first at Oxford, he received a score of congratulatory letters, and while travelling afterwards on the Continent people spoke to him about it. Since that time even mothers seem to have lost delight at the rank of their sons.

At about the same period as the elective system the graduate schools arose, at first for a few men whose aim was to contribute notably to knowledge; and later for all who intended to make teaching their profession — the master's degree being gradually required for positions in the great urban high schools, and the doctorate for the universities and colleges. The result has been a large mass of intelligent, industrious, and docile students, with a smaller number of men of marked talent. Yet the professors, as a rule, have deemed teaching them more honorable than teaching undergraduates; and the expression has come into vogue that the graduate school is essentially the university. Such an attitude, combined with the indifference of the undergraduates, has hampered the raising of the college to a higher scholastic level, and at the same time reduced the graduate school from the place for exceptional scholars designed by President Gilman at Johns Hopkins.

In discussing reforms it is well to have a clear idea of the object sought before considering the means of attaining it. The statement that the primary purpose of a university is scholarship will probably be accepted by everyone, if it includes imparting as well as extending knowledge; for if the term refers to the latter alone, a university should include only creative scholars and a few men, let us say two or three score, with a high promise of becoming their successors. This would certainly rule out nine-tenths of both graduate and undergraduate students. Such an institution may be invaluable in special lines, but by itself it cannot fulfil the functions of a university, which we will assume is for all who desire, and are competent to attain, scholarship.

A plan commonly proposed by those who regard only the graduate school as the real university is that the first two

years of the college should be treated as a continuation of
secondary education, to be relegated to junior colleges, that
is, continuation high schools, or retained as a subordinate,
preparatory, department for work of true university level in
the graduate school.

In this connection, it is urged that the preliminary work
should be concerned with general education, which should
be finished before true scholarship begins. Perhaps, like so
many discussions, the question turns merely on the meaning
of words; but if I grasp their idea aright, I take issue with its
advocates at this point. As I understand it, general education, or cultivation of the mind, is a continuing process that
should end only with life; and one measure of it is the ability
to get pleasure and profit from wide reading and from conversation with men interested in a large variety of subjects.
A mind so cultured is ever expanding, its ideas are constantly
enlarged, and its imagination stimulated by fresh contacts
with the written or spoken thoughts of others.

That secondary schooling alone can produce men and
women with a high grade of cultivation few people would be
willing to assert. Nor are the graduate schools as now organized well adapted for imparting it. Their instruction and
their atmosphere are too highly technical, too much directed
to a specific end. That end is the preparation of teachers,
and, to a less extent, of young people who aspire to make
substantial contributions to knowledge. For the graduate
schools are in fact as distinctly professional as those of law
and medicine which train for a distinct career. Almost all
their students are looking forward to positions in schools,
colleges, or universities; very few to entering later the bar,
medicine, the church, or business, or to study with no more
definite objective than cultivating the mind and increasing
its power. In its report the Committee on College and University Teaching, of the Association of University Professors,
observed, "It is from the college, during their undergraduate
careers, that young men and women must get an inspiration

to breadth of intellectual interest. If they do not get it there, the graduate schools can hardly make good the deficiency."

Since the graduate schools are essentially professional schools for students preparing for academic pursuits, we may ask whether it would be wise to confine higher education to this class, whether the welfare of the community is not promoted by having in all the professions, in occupations of all kinds, many men with more than secondary schooling. This I think no one will deny. But if so, the university, that is, in the language of our friends, the graduate school—and probably on reflection they would add the other professional schools — must be greatly changed. For if these schools are in fact to attract all young people with a serious desire to be scholarly, without intending to make scholarship their means of livelihood, they must be very different from what they are today.

A transformation of this kind has not yet been proposed, or at least attempted. If it should be made with such an objective, our friends would be right in thinking that four years of undergraduate preparation would be needless and therefore, as now commonly conducted, harmful. But we may well ask whether even two years of secondary work in college would not in such a case be excessive. We begin primary education too late and for the more capable children follow it up too slowly. A friend of the writer said long ago that the trouble began in the nursery; and hence, as another friend remarked, men are now taught to make a forward pass at the age their grandfathers commanded ships around the world. Their more remote ancestors translated in college the Hebrew scriptures into Greek at a time of life that would now seem incredible. Young people, with the natural aptitudes, are quite capable of doing scholarly work, or indeed any work requiring responsibility, distinctly earlier than they do at present. The records of one large college show that the freshmen enter now almost exactly twelve months younger than they did forty years ago; yet the requirements for admission, and certainly the standard of work demanded thereafter, have not been lowered in that period. Investigation would probably reveal that this is by no means an isolated case, and that the age can be still more reduced.

A change in the nature and objectives of the graduate school, making it the true core of the university, is by no means impossible. It would become more like a European university, more like what the earliest of our colleges was intended to be, when President Dunster procured the recognition by Oxford and Cambridge of Harvard's degree as equivalent to their own and to those of Continental institutions. No doubt a primary object in the founding of Harvard was the training of ministers, who were the teachers of that day, but from the outset its students were by no means so confined, about one-half of them not being, in fact, destined for the church. No doubt the college in those days was primitive, but so, for the most part, were the European universities from which the present ones have grown. We think of those in modern Germany as highly specialized, and so they were so far as their seminars, their examinations, and formal requirements for a degree were concerned; but, in fact, they were much more than that. I refer, of course, to the period of their greatest reputation before the war, with which I am better acquainted than with later conditions. A large part of the students attended courses of lectures outside their own fields, and a not insignificant proportion did not attempt to take the specialized examinations for a degree. When Bismarck said that one-third of the students killed themselves by overwork, another third went to the devil, and the remaining third ruled Europe, he meant that those who did not become specialists got something that gave them capacity. His last third were a type of man that rarely attends our graduate schools today, but goes to college in large numbers, and is a strong element among the high scholars at Oxford or Cambridge. To make the graduate school attractive for such men at the close of their secondary education would probably be regarded by many professors therein as lowering its aims and standards; and, as already remarked, does not seem to be seriously contemplated.

There is another method of reaching the same result: that of raising the college, or undergraduate department, to a true university level. This is by no means impossible, and would probably have been done, if graduate work had, as originally conceived by President Gilman, been confined to a small number of highly talented students capable of making substantial contributions to knowledge. Raised to that point the college would become the core of the university, the graduate school receiving only the few who by their undergraduate theses had shown marked originality, and whose work in the school would be strictly limited to actual research and preparation therefor. We should, no doubt, be confronted by the present incubus of professional requirements of higher degrees for teaching positions, which render all reform difficult; but if education is to advance, the public must be taught that the important thing is personal attainment, not symbols too often delusive.

To bring the college to the point desired, admission must be restricted to young people who show aptitude for study of university grade, and the work required of them should be placed at that level as soon as possible, preferably now at the end of the freshman year; those who do not rise to the opportunity being remorselessly dropped out. Of course, the student body must be inspired with a different attitude towards scholarship from the one it has generally had in the past; and although that is the most serious obstacle to the project, it is by no means insuperable. Men who know undergraduates best are aware that most of them will do whatever is required when they are convinced it is worth the effort.

Such a change does not mean so much an alteration in any particular curriculum, or factor in student life, as a new atmosphere. The outcry against excessive prominence of athletic spectacles, for example, is not to be met by abolishing them, but by increasing the interest in things of more permanent value. Children are not made serious by forbidding play. They are merely made sulky; and youth is led to higher pursuits not by prohibiting sports, but by recognizing them as proper play, whose true value in the process of normal development is better understood than in the past. The essential point is the attitude of mind; the means are important only so far as they contribute to the result. So long as college is regarded by students, and their parents, as primarily a social institution, the present situation will endure; but by a sufficient effort on the part of university authorities it can be greatly, and indefinitely, improved. The method of doing so will vary with the conditions, for there is no universal recipe for scholarship. The highly cultured man knows a little of everything and something well; for without this last he is liable to be a mere smatterer who grasps no principle thoroughly. General culture may well involve, therefore, a considerable amount of special study in college. For practical purposes also it is generally, though not universally, easier to provoke serious interest in a subject that is carried far than in one of which only the elements are taught; and intense curiosity in anything scholarly lies at the base of all self-education.

Raising college education on these lines to a university plane has in fact been attempted in varying degrees of thoroughness. In all our better colleges the standards, and the desire for scholarly attainment, have risen of late years, and in some of them the improvement has been notable. In those that have gone farthest the attempt to attain a real command of a subject, such as would, for example, bring honors at Oxford or Cambridge, is far more widespread than formerly — at Harvard College last year 32.8 per cent of those who graduated did so with honors in special fields — and it is not very infrequent for some undergraduate thesis to be presented quite as good as those accepted for a doctorate of philosophy. In such colleges it may safely be asserted that a bachelor of arts *cum laude* in a special field signifies at least as high scholarly attainment as a master of arts conferred anywhere in this country.

The writer is by no means urging a plan for general adoption by American universities and colleges, for he believes that at the present time experiment, and therefore diversity, is much better than uniformity. His object is merely to point out that if American universities are to become what they might, and should, be they must contain a central structure designed for all young men really seeking scholarship, whether they are preparing for an academic career, or intend to practise some other profession, or to engage in business or public service. This might be accomplished by a radical transformation of the graduate school; but that is in itself highly improbable, and if universally carried out would involve the abandonment, or reduction to a secondary status, of the independent colleges, historically the backbone of American higher general education. The central structure may, on the other hand, be provided by raising the undergraduate department, and in its train the best independent colleges, to a true university level. This entails, of course, difficulties, requires firmness in resisting opposition, preconceived opinions, and social ambitions; but it can be done. In fact, it is now being tried not without a measure of success.

DEGREES, PRIZES, AND HONORS

THE HARVARD TEACHERS RECORD, JUNE, 1934

DEGREES now conferred by American universities resemble in their sequence the mediaeval usage more nearly than do those conferred in Europe. That seems strange, — what is the reason? It is not from a conservative clinging to past tradition, for most of these degrees are late arrivals here. Although first devised in the thirteenth century or thereabouts, we regard them as very modern advances, adopted by us from no antiquarian motive, but in the name of educational progress. Let us trace briefly the history of degrees, and then consider their significance and effect.

Universities are a heritage from the Middle Ages, when students attended them in greater numbers than at any later period until very recent times. In order to establish a curriculum of studies, and make sure that it should be duly followed, a certificate, or degree, at its completion was needed, and this was especially important in the case of men who proposed to teach; wherefore the degree of Licenciate — otherwise called that of Master — was the earliest conferred. But the practice soon evolved farther; and, with many variations of time and place, the typical custom became that of three degrees in ascending scale: Bachelor, Licenciate or Master, and Doctor; the first coming at the completion of the trivium and quadrivium, and the last given in each of the four faculties of Theology, Law, Medicine, and Philosophy or Arts. Such was the general scheme at the close of the Middle Ages; and it is interesting to observe what has become of these degrees in modern Europe, though for our purpose it is necessary only to glance at France, England, and Germany.

The University of Paris was the first to reach a full development, and in spite of its many vicissitudes has preserved the early forms with singular tenacity. There the *Baccalauréat* has been transferred to the Lycées, or public secondary schools, where the course of study corresponds in grade fairly well with that for which this degree originally stood. The university, on the other hand, has retained the two upper degrees: the *Licence*, continuing under its older name, being conferred after two or three years of study and the passing of examinations in all the principal faculties save that of medicine. The Doctorate follows later, usually after two years, generally involving the preparation of a thesis. Of course the details vary in the different schools, and there is a distinction between Doctorates that relate to public employment and those that do not; but for us the important point to observe is that —except in Medicine, where only the Doctorate is conferred — there are still two degrees, one superposed upon the other.

In England and Germany the change from the mediaeval plan has been greater. At Oxford and Cambridge the only modern degree regularly given in course was, until recently, that of Bachelor; and this was conferred in Arts, Science, Letters, Medicine, Law, Divinity, and some minor subjects. It signified the completion of the university course of study in the subject; and, save that the candidates for the degree of Bachelor of Letters or Science at Oxford and Bachelor of Law at Cambridge must already have had that of Arts, one such degree was rarely superposed upon another. The Master's degree in Arts, though given, had ceased to signify any farther academic advance; for it was automatically conferred on any Bachelor who kept his name on the books for a certain number of terms by the annual payment of a fee. The Doctorate was indeed given, but in Law, Medicine,[1] and sometimes other subjects it might be acquired by presenta-

---

[1] The barrister, physician, or surgeon must complete his training at the Inns of Court or in the London hospitals, which are not connected with the two universities.

tion of an approved printed book, — being, therefore, rather in the nature of a decoration than a degree; and in the Arts and Sciences no Doctor's degree was conferred after a course of study until a few years ago, when Doctorates of Philosophy and Science were offered to attract colonial and foreign students for advanced work. If these were to become practical requisites for appointments to positions in the colleges of the old universities, as is the case in America, they might have a serious effect on the significance of the "honour schools" at Oxford and the "triposes" at Cambridge; but so far they have been used almost wholly for export.

The German universities developed later than those in France and England, and on the whole have retained less of the mediaeval tradition. They were largely reorganized on new lines, and the success with which they promoted advanced study and research attracted from all over the world students who were convinced that their methods were far the best, and their degrees the only ones that stood for high scholarship. Dropping, as in France, the Bachelor's degree below the university level, and that of Master altogether, except in a few places where it is given with the Doctorate, they have in substance kept only the highest of the old trio. The degree of Doctor is conferred in each of the four faculties of Theology, Law, Medicine, and Philosophy; and as the last of these includes almost all subjects not essentially practical, the degree of Doctor of Philosophy is considered in many countries the expression for the most complete academic training, and therefore has been much copied.

In America the earlier colleges, inheriting English traditions, conferred only the Bachelor's degree, that of Master being later added after five years on the payment of a fee. There was, indeed, one exception to the rule; for when medical schools were opened the degree of Doctor was conferred upon their graduates, since that was the term in common use for practising physicians and surgeons. So matters remained until after the Civil War; but in the early seventies two changes began which virtually brought in two new degrees. One of them came by requiring a year's residence and examination for the degree of Master of Arts; while the other, that of Doctor of Philosophy, was imported about the same time from Germany. These two degrees have been adopted throughout the country, so that now American universities confer in the Arts course the three superposed degrees of Bachelor, Master, and Doctor, as their mediaeval prototypes did six hundred years ago. Sometimes there is a cumulative series of a similar kind in the professional schools; and it is certainly clear that in America the universities have more superposed degrees than in Europe, and that during the last seventy years the number has tended to increase.

Having looked at the facts we may turn to the purpose and significance of degrees. Their objects are three-fold. From the standpoint of the university itself some kind of formal certificate or diploma — called in this case a degree — is almost essential for securing a measurement of its own work and that of its students. Otherwise the institution would be like the caucus race in Alice in Wonderland where everyone ran as far and as fast as he pleased, — a most excellent plan in a body of earnest scholars, each working on his own account at the discovery of truth, but futile in a school where the aim is teaching. From the standpoint of the student the degree is an incentive to keep him up to his work, — a reward if well done, a censure and a disgrace if so poorly done that he loses his degree; for he does not, like the Hindoo, print on his visiting card "Failed Bachelor of Arts." Thirdly, for the public the diploma is a certificate of definite progress and accomplishment.

A degree signifies, or should signify, something definite. But mark! by its very nature that something must be a minimum requirement. That is not true in the case of the English Doctorates in Law and Medicine already mentioned, for they are in essence really decorations; but it is true of any degree conferred in course, especially when the number of candidates is considerable. It cannot be awarded arbitrarily, and anyone who qualifies is entitled to it. This does not mean that the minimum is low, but that there is a minimum, and on everyone who attains it, whatever it may be, the degree must be conferred. Such a plan is excellent for fairly large bodies of students, many of whom cannot be expected to rise much above the minimum; and some do not care for more than a margin of safety. It may be noted that in fixing the minimum the element of competition enters indirectly and only to a small extent.

Now some conscious effort on the part of those who give the marks is needed to maintain the minimum, especially when the degree has a vocational value, for kindliness leads the other way. Except in a mechanical kind of test the means of measuring is not exact, estimate enters in; and if the case is near the line there is a tendency to give the student the benefit of the doubt. One dislikes to cut off his future prospects where his work is so little below grade, and in fact may be regarded as quite equal to that of another candidate previously let through — a fatal way of lowering the minimum by placing it at the worst ever yet passed. Of course the scale does not usually go down, but that is because of a deliberate effort to keep it up by those who care more about the standard than the effect of failure on the individual near the line.

Mere mechanical devices for improving the standard are untrustworthy. Sometimes an attempt is made to do so by requiring for credit a higher mark, but this is in large part illusory, because to the students whom he deems worthy of passing the instructor will give the passing mark. If, for example, the marks range from A to E, the last being a failure, and a faculty should decide that in future C shall be the passing mark, the instructor will give to some students — not to all — that mark where previously he would have given a D. In fact, experience has shown that where in the same course a higher mark is required for graduate than for undergraduate credit the grading is not always quite so strict for the former.

We have seen that cumulative degrees in an ascending series on the same general subject are carried farther in America than in other countries; and where this is done there is a tendency to construct an educational pyramid of superposed blocks with a degree between each of them and the one above. Each fills its own allotted space to which it is confined by the plan of the structure. In other words each member of the edifice tends to have its appropriate place, and should not encroach on what is reserved for others; so that the system tends to rigidity, by deterring each division from expanding upward into the one over it, since to do so would throw the whole scheme into confusion. In many universities, indeed, the courses are sharply divided into those for the college and those for the graduate school; and in such a case the difficulty of raising college education to a higher level is obvious. If Oxford, when introducing the "honour schools" at the beginning of the last century, had conferred for them a Doctorate, while retaining for other students the Bachelor's degree, it is improbable that a large majority of the undergraduates would enroll themselves in these schools as they do today. By keeping them open to all ambitious candidates for the regular degree, Oxford and Cambridge have greatly raised their undergraduate level. In short, the effect of superposed degrees is likely to be crystallization *in situ*. When in an American university a general examination was proposed for graduation from the college, someone referred to it as a little Doctorate, which seemed to imply trespassing on a superior province. Of course that is not a condemnation, but it is an aspect of the matter to be pondered.

In contradistinction to degrees, which signify a minimum of accomplishment, there is another kind of academic recognition which we may call prizes. The name is not popular in this country, where it suggests a schoolboy coming up to receive a medal for good conduct; but it is used here in the larger sense of any academic award, whether money, honor, token, fellowship or other appointment, won by a competition which may take the form of examination, judgment of written work, or other method of selection, provided it is truly competitive. In Europe it is more used than it is here. Admission in France to the Ecole Normale, the Ecole Centrale, the Ecole des Beaux Arts, and others is strictly by competition, and often at the examination the candidates are many times the number of places to be filled. A competition of some kind is the very essence of a prize, which without it would have no meaning, and unlike the case of degrees, there is no temptation to lower the standard of prizes, because it is maintained by the competitors themselves. Being awarded only to the best in the contest a prize signifies a maximum, and differs thereby from a degree conferred upon everyone who attains a minimum. If, therefore, the object sought in an educational institution is to produce a considerable number of persons who attain a certain standard the appropriate symbol is a degree; but if, on the other hand, the aim is to stimulate and select excellence the proper instrument is a competition for what is herein generically called a prize.

Although degrees and prizes are very diverse in their nature and effects, they are not incompatible, and the benefits of both may be combined in the same system. This has been done very effectively by the "honour schools" of Oxford and the "triposes" of Cambridge, where every graduate receives the same degree, with the same legal rights and privileges, but is incited to strive for special distinctions, which are not only gratifying but of practical value in starting him on his career. These are not, indeed, wholly competitive in the sense that the number in each of the three or four grades is strictly limited, for the number varies from year to year, but the element of competition enters largely, and the examinations are so recognized by the candidates.

Now it is noteworthy that while honors of various kinds, and of generally competitive character, are commonly awarded in American colleges, yet in our graduate schools, where it is most important to attract and stimulate excellence, the element of competition is absent. They confer only degrees without distinction of quality. In Germany this is not so, for the Doctorate is given in four different grades, plain, *cum laude, magna*, and *summa*; and unless one obtains the highest of these he has very little chance of being appointed to a professorship in a German university. We may well ask why, when this degree was imported, the distinction in grades that counts for much there was not brought with it. Was it overlooked? Was it thought unimportant, or was it deemed inconsistent with our preconceptions? Few American professors know that there are such grades in the German degrees; still fewer are aware of the weight attached to them, or inquire how high a rating in Germany a Doctor of Philosophy obtained. Perhaps the lack of competition may in part explain why our graduate schools have become so different from what they were at the outset. Johns Hopkins was at first a resort for young scholars of the highest ambition, and drew a band of notable students; but that is certainly not true of the average membership of graduate schools now. Perhaps if they were not so large and recruited, or weeded out, by competition, or the élite were a group by themselves, or the degrees were awarded in grades, it would be better.

American students, who understand their own psychology much better than their teachers, use in athletics the factor of competition to the greatest possible extent. The lack of scholastic ambition and respect for scholarly attainment by the average American undergraduate has been due in part to the comparative absence of genuine and serious competition; in part to the fact that he has been inclined to believe that college grades as ordinarily given indicate diligence and docility rather than real superiority; while the faculties themselves have not been convinced, and certainly have not tried to convince the public, that academic distinction is a harbinger of later success. Statistics compiled by various men in different ways all agree that to a large extent, and with many exceptions, it certainly is so, but in this country it seems to go against the grain. The writer strove for years to have the honors won by students at Commencement noted, as in England, in the catalogue of alumni; but in vain, until official position became a lever to put it through.

In Europe high academic achievement is far more valued and receives wider recognition than it does in America. The winner of a First-Class in Classical "Greats" at Oxford, or a "Wrangler" in Mathematics at Cambridge, is expected if entering the Law to take a high position at the Bar, and to have opened a door that leads towards the Bench, in a way that has no parallel here. Glancing at the English and American Who's Who one may observe a difference in the autobiographies therein. The Englishman commonly includes a statement of the honors he received at graduation from his university, and of the most notable prizes he won there. The American lists his degrees but not the honors or prizes, and if he did so he would be thought — well, somewhat odd.

For reasons too complex to be discussed in a short article, higher education in this country tends to shun the use of prizes with the competition they involve, preferring a series of superposed degrees with the minimum standards of achievement they signify. This is not a deliberate policy; it is rather instinctive, assumed, absorbed, and all the more noteworthy on that account. It is a fact, and as such not without food for reflection.

FROM THE ANNUAL REPORT, 1908–1909

CHANGES IN THE ELECTIVE SYSTEM

IN THE affairs of the College the most significant movement during the year was that looking toward a modification of the elective system, and this resulted from an effort of much wider scope to improve the condition of scholarship among undergraduates.

It has been truly said that the opportunities for education in our universities are now enormous, and that the immediate problem before us is to bring the undergraduate to make the best use of them; for the benefit of a college education to a student consists, not in the abundance of opportunities he neglects, but in those of which he takes advantage. From colleges in different parts of the country have been heard general complaints that students not engaged in professional work have far too little desire for sound scholarship, and slender respect for those who work hard; while athletic triumphs are regarded as of vast importance. Now, it is a very significant fact that this condition is not due in the main to a sincere belief that prowess in sports is intrinsically of greater value than intellectual achievement. Almost every undergraduate would be proud to be told that he was destined in after life to write a remarkable history, or to make a notable scientific discovery, and would be shocked to hear that he was to be the best professional baseball player in the world; yet he often submits willingly to drudgery that would tend to prepare him for the latter, though recoiling from study that would fit him for intellectual work. This shows a disproportion between immediate ambition and relative permanent values, even as they stand in the mind of the undergraduate himself. Of course, the disproportion is due in large part to a contrast in the amount of applause won by the two forms of activity in college, for few men at any age are so self-contained as to be impervious to apparent estimates of success on the part of the general public. But there is another cause for the distortion of values. Undergraduates are prone to believe that athletic sports are a good measure of red blood, while high rank in studies indicates only industrious plodding. They often rate the two occupations much as savages do hunting and husbandry. That athletics develop essential moral qualities is undoubtedly true; but that is no sufficient reason why intellectual things should be undervalued; and it was the feeling that either our tests for rank were wrong, or that the students failed to recognize them at their true worth, that gave rise to the appointment of a special committee of the Faculty of Arts and Sciences in the spring of 1908.

.   .   .   .

The committee believed that the best policy for the normal undergraduate is to concentrate a considerable part of his work on one subject, and distribute the rest widely; and that if this were true every student might reasonably be required to show cause why his choice of electives should not be based upon that principle.

.   .   .   .

The object to be attained was two-fold: first, to require every student to make a choice of electives that will secure a systematic education, based on the principle of knowing a little of everything and something well. Such an education would ordinarily be measured by the courses taken in college, but instruction elsewhere or private study would also be taken into account, and latitude enough must be given to make the system elastic in exceptional cases. The second object in view was to make the student plan his college curriculum seriously, and plan it as a whole. This is presupposed by the theory of the elective system, but, in fact, it is by no means always done, as is shown by the very large number of changes of electives, and often radical changes, made in the first few weeks of every college year.

. . . .

Obviously the value of the new system, so far as the first of these objects is concerned, depends upon the mode of insuring a sufficient amount of concentration on the one hand, and a broad enough distribution of courses on the other. Concentration is attained by providing that every student shall take at least six of his courses in some one department, or in some field for a degree with distinction covering a group of related subjects taught in more than one department. Distribution is a less simple matter. It has been secured by classifying all the subjects taught in college among four general groups, and requiring every student to take something in each group. These groups are based not primarily upon the subject-matter of the course, but upon the method of treatment, because the object of a liberal education is not so much knowledge as an attitude of mind and a familiarity with processes of thought. The first of the four groups contains the arts of expression, — language, literature, fine arts, and music; the second, the natural or inductive sciences; the third, what might be called, for want of a better term, the inductive social sciences, such as history, politics, and economics; the fourth, the abstract or deductive studies, that is, mathematics and philosophy, including law and diverse kinds of social theories.

. . . .

Need of More Interest in Scholarship

A modification of the courses of study pursued in Harvard College was not the only problem before the committee. It was not, indeed, the principal object in view. To provide that no student shall graduate with a merely superficial education, or one that is too narrow in scope, is certainly an advance; but to stimulate a more general interest in scholarship is a far greater and far more difficult matter. It cannot be done merely by raising the standard for a degree, for that is merely raising the minimum. This has, no doubt, its value. It spurs on the laggard, but it neither stirs enthusiasm, nor provokes ambition. A minimum requirement can never be really high nor act as an incentive to exertion for men of superior capacity; and it is not impossible that by constantly harping upon the minimum we have actually lessened the desire for excellence.

We are tending in America to make a fetish of degrees. Our universities are beginning to require a bachelor's degree for entrance into the professional schools; and in many colleges a doctorate of philosophy is virtually a condition for an appointment to the faculty. So far as these things are designed to raise the standard by insisting upon a definite amount of preliminary education they are good, but the measure applied is not very accurate, and it is far from assuring a high level of attainment, for a degree can indicate at best only a good grade of mediocrity. Nothing that is given in course, and is not keenly competitive, can be reserved (that is awarded only) for superior excellence.

Moreover, in conferring the degree itself we are in danger of relying too much on mechanical rating. Where all students are pursuing the same curriculum, or where there is a conventional body of learning which they are required to possess, their proficiency can be ascertained with more or less precision by a general examination covering the whole ground, but with the increase in specialized courses and the progress of the elective system this has become an impossibility. We have therefore fallen into the habit of giving all degrees, except the doctorate of philosophy, on a certain number of courses passed with satisfactory marks. We have thus made the passing of courses the measure of education. No doubt examinations, framed apart from a specific course, to test a candidate's general knowledge of a subject, are defective and tend to hurried cramming as a preparation. But that should

not blind us to the shortcomings of our habit of counting by
courses, or lull us into indifference to its perils. The ordinary
student is too apt to treat courses as Cook's tourists do the
starred pictures in foreign galleries, as experiences to be
checked off and forgotten. To have taken a course is by no
means always equivalent to possessing any real command of
a subject. We require at Harvard that every undergraduate
shall either pass an entrance examination in French and German, or take a course in the language in college; and yet
when thereafter an instructor in another subject needs to
refer his pupils to a book of not more than ordinary difficulty
in a foreign tongue, he finds that scarcely one-half of them
can read French and very few of them German. A remedy
for this particular difficulty is now under consideration;
but it remains true that a course with a pass mark to one's
credit may mean fair work done with little of permanent
value to show for it. It may be hoped that, under the new
rules for the choice of electives, some form of general examination at the end of the college life on the principal field of
study will be more commonly required.

The chief evil of laying exclusive stress upon the degree,
and of counting by courses, is that it fixes attention upon the
pass mark. Too many of the more capable undergraduates
today are inclined to set their ambition on getting through
college in three years with a respectable record, and then
taking a master's degree, instead of spending four years on a
smaller number of courses and doing brilliant work, although
the latter is far the more valuable training. In short, they
prefer an additional degree, without mark of distinguished
excellence, to winning scholarly distinction in college. They
value quantity more than quality, and a similar tone is naturally prevalent among their less gifted or less ambitious classmates. In order to correct this impression, and create a
stronger desire for excellence, the institution of distinct honor
and pass degrees, akin to the practice of the English universities, has often been suggested. Whether it would be

wise to have different curricula for honors and for a pass, as in England, is by no means clear; and certainly there is no object in having distinct degrees. In fact, the degree conferred by Oxford and Cambridge is the same for both classes of candidates. The vital point is the importance which those universities have attached, and persuaded the public to attach, to the winning of honors. In their calendars, or catalogues, they print every year a list of the honor men from the time when these lists were established. They make much of high honors, which are, indeed, always remembered and constantly referred to throughout a man's life. It is that spirit which must be cultivated here if we would foster a desire for scholarship in college. So long as the distinctions achieved in college are not worthy of perpetuation, or are not deemed to be so by the university itself, it is idle to expect the students or the public to value them highly, or to hope that undergraduates will have any great ambition to excel in their college work. If we are to succeed in making scholarship in college an object of ambition, we must lay stress not exclusively upon the degree, but also upon the grade with which that degree is taken, and upon literary and other prizes that are won. In short, we must fix the attention of the student not upon minimum requirements, but upon the highest grade of excellence that lies within his power.

.   .   .   .

The Age of Entrance

The age at which boys enter college is a matter of serious consideration. The average has not, indeed, advanced of late years, but the increase of technical knowledge, and the consequent lengthening of professional training, is bringing to bear a constant pressure to reduce the length of the college term. For those who believe in the value of college education, who feel that there are great numbers of young men in all parts of the country to whom four years of college will be a lasting benefit, the question is not to be put aside. There are, of course, many youths who are properly anxious to begin their professional studies early, and in other colleges and universities with combined degrees there is abundant provision for them. But it is well that there should also be colleges for those who will profit by a longer period of liberal education. For them it is important to reach college younger than they do now. They are mainly the brighter boys, who can be prepared for entrance earlier than others, and who gain a great deal more from a fourth year in college than from another year at school. Some interesting statistics have been collected in regard to the age of candidates for admission to Harvard College, from which it appears that during the last five years the average of those who were admitted clear was eighteen years and four months, of those admitted with conditions eighteen years and eleven months, and of those rejected nineteen years and three months.[1] It is evident, therefore, that the brighter boys are prepared earliest, and it is these boys that Harvard College desires to recruit throughout the country. At present the age is artificially advanced by the fact that boys who are fully prepared are not infrequently kept out a year on the theory that they are too young for college. Sixty-six of those who passed the examination this year failed to come to college, and in reply to inquiries thirty-six of them gave their reasons. Of these four went to other colleges, while twenty-two postponed their coming for a year, and although most of them were from the eastern part of Massachusetts the rest were scattered over the country as far as Milwaukee. Some of these boys were not yet seventeen, but many more were between seventeen and eighteen years of age. No doubt others were held back in the same way of whom we have no information; and there are certainly many boys whose education at school is intentionally delayed in order that they may enter college

---

[1] These were the ages at the opening of the college year at the end of September.

later than they could easily be prepared. With the pressure of time for professional training, and the consequent temptation to cut down the length of the college course, it is a pity that the period of liberal study should be shortened by delay at school; more especially as holding a boy back in school, and above all holding him back after he is prepared for college, is a detriment both to his intellectual progress and to his moral energy.

There is thus good reason to suppose that boys could be prepared for college younger than they are, and that it would be an advantage for them to come younger. The chief difficulty is the reluctance of parents to allow their sons until decidedly mature to embark in the freedom of college life at Harvard. A greater degree of supervision and friendly advice is one of the advantages that will come with the institution of a Freshman dormitory. Rigid discipline will not be needed there if more careful oversight and closer intercourse between instructors and students are provided. A community life suited to boys who come from the stringent rules of school to the larger freedom of the university will not be difficult to establish, and will be readily accepted without the use of vexatious regulations. A boy's career in college is largely determined by the conditions of his Freshman year, and it ought to be possible to organize that year so as to improve the whole state of the college intellectually and socially. To build a series of dormitories with dining halls for this purpose will be expensive, and an effort is now being made to raise the money required.

.   .   .   .

Scholarships in the Graduate School

We hear a great deal at the present day about the necessity of attracting into the career of university teaching men of first-rate ability, and about the great difficulty in doing so.

We are commonly told that meagre salaries present the prime obstacle.

The main difficulty would seem to lie at the other end of the career, at its beginning rather than at its end. It would seem to be due in great part to the fact that our students while in college are not attracted enough by scholarship. To them it appears too much a mere matter of plodding or grinding. Then it may be doubted whether the graduate schools in American universities are conducted upon the wisest principles. They pride themselves upon the number of their students, and in order to attract them they compete with one another all over the country by offering many scholarships. It is universally believed that generous aid given too freely in the theological seminaries lessened the calibre of the ministry in the last century, and there is grave danger that a similar policy in our graduate schools may have the same disastrous effect upon college professors.

.   .   .   .

The ratio of the total amount of aid given to the whole number of students in the department is in the Graduate School four and a half times as large as in the College, about five and a half times as large as in the Medical School, seven times as large as in the School of Business Administration, and more than ten times as large as in the Law School. In fact, the school that most attracts ambitious and self-reliant young men is the one that offers them the least amount of aid.

A fellowship of considerable size granted to assist in research is a very different thing from a scholarship given to enable a man to study in the school. It should be awarded only to help on a definite piece of productive scholarship which is likely to be of material value to the world, and it should be extended only to exceptional men.

.   .   .   .

The danger of giving scholarships too freely is insidious. It is urged everywhere on the ground that it is necessary in order to attract to the university the best men, and it does attract men who are good scholars, but it attracts mainly the docile and studious youth who has not the vigor and aggressiveness to attack the world without aid and is prone to follow the path of least resistance. The presence of such students in large numbers tends to discourage others of a more vigorous type, for Gresham's law applies to men as well as to currency. If we want to recruit the most forcible of our youth for the future members of our faculties, we must not make the path too easy at the outset.

. . . .

Here, again, Harvard is by no means the worst offender, but it would be a service to sound learning if such scholarships were combined into a smaller number of better-paid fellowships which should be given only to men of proved productive capacity. The best men who stand in need of assistance would thus be led to compete more keenly for such appointments, and the successful candidates would be able to devote their whole time to the productive work which it should always be the highest aim of a graduate school to promote.

FROM THE ANNUAL REPORT, 1909–1910

READING OF MODERN LANGUAGES

PRACTICALLY, it has been found that an undergraduate is commonly unable to use with ease French or German books in his college work. Quite apart, moreover, from the benefit of knowing modern foreign languages, an oral examination in reading them has a meaning of no little importance. It involves the principle of examining a student upon his command of a subject, instead of upon the ground covered by a particular course. The principle, wisely applied, can be extended far with manifest advantage. It is a test of power, of the grasp of a subject, as compared with minute attention to particular tasks. It throws the responsibility for acquiring knowledge more consciously upon the student, who sees that a single course is not an end in itself but a means to an end. He learns that formal instruction is merely one means to an education; and thereby he may be led to appreicate the value of reading outside of his courses, a habit that many observers think has tended to decay under the influence of an educational bill of fare displaying all knowledge chopped into small morsels whereof any seventeen are enough for intellectual nutrition. Examinations upon a subject, conducted by persons other than the instructors, are commonly used in some form in connection with foreign universities, and while if carried too far they involve dangers, they also have advantages of which we might avail ourselves more fully in our colleges.

FROM THE ANNUAL REPORT, 1910–1911

THE MEDICAL SCHOOL

DURING the year the Faculty discussed a radical change in the process of examination leading to the degree of Doctor of Medicine. Hitherto the degree has been conferred upon the completion of a fixed number of courses, those in the first three years being required and those of the fourth year elective; and, since the intensive method is pursued, the student, in the earlier part of his course at least, devoted his whole energies for a certain length of time to a single subject, passed an examination upon it, and bade it farewell. Complaint was made that the system was inelastic, lacking in stimulation; and that the student might graduate without retaining sufficient knowledge, without coördinating it, and without inducement to review it. In the spring of 1910, a committee was appointed to consider means of lessening the rigidity of the medical curriculum. Members of the committee examined carefully the system prevailing in American medical schools of granting the degree upon an accumulation of credits in separate courses, required or elective, and the European system of holding general examinations, first upon the general scientific or laboratory subjects, and later upon the clinical branches. The committee was convinced that the latter plan afforded a better test of medical preparation, gave to the student more latitude in his work, and directed his attention more to acquiring a thorough command of medical science. It reported, therefore, in favor of two general examinations, partly practical, partly oral, and partly written, designed to measure the student's comprehension, judgment, and skill, rather than to test his detailed information; the first examination to cover the laboratory subjects taught in the first year and a half, the second to cover the clinical subjects studied later, the examination in special courses to be retained only for the purpose of certifying that the student has completed the courses required and can be allowed to present himself for the general examination.

.   .   .   .

General examinations of this character involve a marked departure from the prevalent American system of counting points and accumulating credits by examinations passed in separate courses. It will be observed that they are based upon the same principle as the new plan for entrance and the oral examinations in reading French and German already introduced in the College; and their possible application is by no means limited to the Medical School. Examinations are in all cases defective instruments. In a primitive golden age, if the college consisted of a log with the president on one end and the student on the other, examinations might perhaps be dispensed with altogether, but in an institution of any size they are a necessity, and where they exist their character and scope will inevitably determine in large measure the attitude of the student toward his studies. If he obtains his degree by passing examinations in separate courses, each course will be to a great extent an end in itself; whereas if he must look forward to a general examination in the future, the course becomes a means to an end, a part of a larger whole. The difference is even more marked where the courses are elective than where they are required, because in scoring points toward graduation the indolent student is tempted to select courses which require little work, and is attracted therefore to those which cover ground already in part traversed; whereas, if he is preparing for a general examination, he is drawn to choose those which will give him the knowledge he will require. The value of any general examination must depend upon the skill with which it is administered; and that skill can be attained thoroughly only by experience. The art of conducting examinations is not less difficult and worthy of cultivation than the art of passing them; and in the Medical School the organization of committees for the purpose seems to promise good results.

FROM THE ANNUAL REPORT, 1911–1912

GENERAL EXAMINATIONS

IN DESCRIBING the general examinations for the Medical School something was said of the principle on which they are based; but the subject merits fuller treatment, because it involves a more radical change in American educational practice than anything the University has done for many years. It means a change not so much in machinery as in object; not of methods alone, but of the point of view. So far as I am aware, general examinations of some kind exist in all European universities, except for a degree with a mere pass in Scotland and the provincial universities of England. They have been used in the past in American colleges. In a very crude form they were at one time prescribed for graduation from Harvard; and in some other colleges they lasted until after the middle of the last century. Since the curriculum of those colleges comprised many subjects, the examination, which covered them all, was open to the criticism now heard of the general examination for graduation from the German gymnasium. It was almost of necessity a review of unconnected studies; an effort of memory, preceded by a strenuous cram. But whether in such a test the disadvantages outweigh the benefits or not, it was quite inapplicable after the elective system had been adopted in a thorough-going form at Harvard, and more or less completely by other colleges. The student being allowed to select as he pleased among all the courses of instruction offered by the Faculty, a general examination would have covered a different ground for each student; would have been merely a repetition of the examinations in several courses which the student had already passed; and could not have required reading outside of the courses, or demanded a correlation of information obtained in courses in diverse fields. But now that every student is obliged to take six courses in some one field, the situation has changed, and the way is open for this valuable instrument of education in that field. To the courses distributed among other subjects it is still inapplicable; but in the field of the student's concentration his attention can be directed, as it should be, to the subject pursued, rather than to the particular courses taken, which then become not ends in themselves but only efficient means to an end. By examinations well devised for the purpose the student can be made to reflect upon the subject as a whole, correlating the several parts; and the interest of an intelligent man follows his efforts. Moreover, he can be induced to read books outside the strict limits of his courses in order to fill in the gaps; for the habit of independent reading has fallen sadly out of use among undergraduates at the present day.

A general examination has drawbacks as well as merits. If it tends to fix attention on a subject wider than any single course, it tends also to make the passing of that examination the goal, and to lessen interest in matters unlikely to appear there; and hence, unskilfully used, it may lead to the cramming of information by expert tutors without serious effort to master the subject. But if skilfully used, it may be made a powerful instrument for promoting coordination of knowledge, a broad comprehension of the subject, a grasp of underlying principles instead of memory of detached facts, and in some subjects may provide an incentive to intellectual effort such as no other type of examination can offer.

.   .   .   .

If the general examination stood alone, the optimism of many undergraduates would lead them to postpone preparation until the time drew near, and then it would be too late. This could be justified only on the assumption that the function of the College was limited to providing earnest men with opportunities for education, probably with the result, witnessed in the German universities, that a large part of the students would make no attempt to obtain or earn a degree. No one would advocate such a plan for undergraduates here. American colleges must strive to form character, to induce habits of diligence; and they must do so all the more because, unlike the German universities, they are not groups of professional schools with the stimulus of direct preparation for one's career in life. It is not proposed, therefore, to abandon examinations in the several courses except so far as they occur at the same time as the general examination. Moreover, if the student is expected to study a subject, to regard his courses as means rather than ends, to do some outside reading, he must have special guidance beyond that which is provided in the courses he takes. There must be tutors, not unlike those at the English universities, who confer with the students frequently, not about their work in courses alone, but also about their outside reading and preparation for the final test that lies before them. Tutors of this kind are an integral and necessary factor in the plan. . . . The great advantage for the average student of a general examination upon his principal field of study lies in forcing him to correlate what he has studied, to keep it in mind as a body of connected learning, to fill in gaps by reading, to appreciate that all true education must be in great part self-education, a personal effort to advance on the difficult path of knowledge, not a half-reluctant transportation through college in perambulators pushed by instructors.

No one in close touch with American education has failed to deplore the lack among the mass of undergraduates of keen interest in their studies, the small regard for scholarly attainment; and a general examination upon a field of concentration seems to offer the most promising means of improvement. It was the method adopted in England a hundred years ago. The class tests at Oxford based on general public examinations began in 1802, and five years later they were divided into the Honour Schools of *Literae Humaniores* and Mathematics and Physics.[1] The effect in stimulating interest in scholarship and respect for high rank was rapid, profound, and permanent. Success in the examinations has been universally accepted as a test of ability and a gateway to the careers entered by Oxford and Cambridge men. The failure of American undergraduates, and, following their lead, of the American public at large, to value excellence in college scholarship is due in part, as the students themselves declare, to the fact that rank in courses depends upon the varying standards maintained by different instructors. It is due also to a sincere doubt whether one who can accumulate the largest number of high marks in short stretches of work is really the ablest man. Much must be ascribed, moreover, to the absence of competition on a large scale. So long as college men are all treading separate paths, crossing at many points but never leading to a common goal, there can be little of that conviction of superior qualities which attaches to the man who succeeds in achieving what many others are striving for. A well-ordered general examination avoids all of these imperfections, for it provides a uniform standard, a competitive test, and a run long enough to call out the whole power of the man. The stimulus is not only good for those who hope to win high distinction, but will tend also to leaven the whole mass.

[1] The Mathematical Tripos at Cambridge began in 1747, the Civil Law Classes in 1815, the Classical Tripos in 1824. The other triposes at Cambridge and Honour Schools at Oxford were established at various dates after the middle of the nineteenth century.

FROM THE ANNUAL REPORT, 1913–1914

THE AGE OF ENTRANCE

THE report of the Chairman of the Committee on Admission contains much that is interesting, and among other things a statement of the average age of candidates. It appears that those who were admitted averaged about eighteen and a half years old, while the rejected were about nineteen. The difference ought not to surprise anyone familiar with the problems raised by the age of students. Carefully compiled statistics referred to in the report of last year show that the men entering college young are on the average better, both in their studies and their conduct. On the whole they are the more intelligent and industrious youths; and this appears in the examinations for entrance, as well as in college work. Yet even those who are admitted come late. This subject was discussed in the last annual report, but it will bear repetition. With the long period of special training now required in every profession, there is a universal cry that men are beginning their careers in life too old, and that the period of education is too long. Disease and death are not postponed because a man starts upon the practice of his profession a year or two later than is necessary. His period of active life, his achievements, and his usefulness are simply curtailed to that extent; and a part, at least, of the time wasted could be saved in the school days before coming to college. Boys of ordinary capacity could, by beginning young enough, be ready to enter college a year earlier than most of them do now, and they would be perfectly competent to pursue the courses even of the best colleges. The advantages, indeed, would seem to be almost wholly in favor of entering college young. Seventeen is a more appropriate age than eighteen to begin the life of college. The real pleasures are more fully and innocently enjoyed. Under a proper environment the moral dangers are in fact less. The means of education are quite within the reach of the youth who is well prepared for admission at that time; and, paradoxical as it may appear, he is in fact more likely to take advantage of them. He is at the period of life when his intellectual powers are growing rapidly, and when it is a natural process to develop those powers by exercising them without too much regard for the direct use to be made of the knowledge acquired. In short, there is a normal time for general education. A man who is too old, if a serious student, seeks to prepare directly for his career, to study his profession; or if not, is in danger of treating his studies lightly. Much has been said about maturity, but that is the result less of age than of environment and responsibility. Maturity may easily become over-ripe. Finally, the boy who enters college older begins life later; unless, indeed, he cuts down his time in college. If twenty-one is the best age to begin the study of a profession, — and the signs of the times seem to point to this, — then one must enter at seventeen or remain only three years. In the last analysis the practical problem of the community at the present day is narrowing itself down to shortening the college course or entering younger, to the question whether it is better to stay longer in school or have a fourth year in college. The question needs no answer for those who believe that the Senior year is the most profitable, not only because it is the last, but because it is the fourth.

FROM THE ANNUAL REPORT, 1914–1915

THE FRESHMAN HALLS

THE Freshman Halls are not an isolated project, an attempt to treat the newcomers by a method peculiar and distinct. They are a part of a general tendency to be seen in all American colleges, the object of which is to bring the strongest possible influences for good to bear upon the student, instead of merely offering opportunities to be seized or neglected as he may please. The unlimited elective system presented to the student the broadest and most diversified opportunities, placing upon him the responsibility of making a wise use of them. The attention of the college authorities was naturally directed to the list of courses given, in an effort to make the offering as rich, as varied, as comprehensive as possible; and the conscientious instructor strove to make his own course as valuable as he could. Save in the case of candidates for distinction in a special field, or men who proposed to carry their studies in one subject far, it was not the duty of an instructor to inquire what courses other than his own a student might be taking, or might thereafter elect. Nor was it the business of anyone but the student himself. The single course inevitably became the unit in college education, and the degree was conferred upon the accumulation of a fixed number of those units. They might be well or badly selected; they might form a consistent whole, or be disconnected fragments of knowledge, according to the earnestness and wisdom of the student. If he selected well, he obtained an excellent education, not because he had to his credit so many units, but because he had so chosen them that together they gave him the development he required.

THE TRUE UNIT IN EDUCATION

But in fact, the single course is not, and cannot be, the true unit in education. The real unit is the student. He is the only

thing in education that is an end in itself. To send him forth
as nearly a perfected product as possible is the aim of instruction, and anything else, the single course, the curriculum, the
discipline, the influences surrounding him, are merely means
to the end, which are to be judged by the way they contribute
and fit into the ultimate purpose. To treat the single course
as a self-sufficient unit, complete in itself, is to run a danger
of losing sight of the end in the means thereto.

. . . .

In the College the problem of making the student, instead
of the course, the unit in education is more difficult than in
the other parts of the University, because general education
is more intangible, more vague, less capable of precise analysis and definition, than training for a profession. Nevertheless, in the College, some significant steps have been taken
which tend in this direction. The first was the requirement
that every student must concentrate six of his seventeen
courses in some definite field, must distribute six more among
the other subjects of knowledge, and must do so after consulting an instructor appointed to advise him.

. . . .

The General Examination

The second step in treating the student, instead of the
course, as the unit in education was taken by the Division
of History, Government, and Economics, when, with the
approval of the Faculty, it set up the requirement of a general examination at graduation for students concentrating
in that division. . . . This is a marked departure from the
plan of earning a degree by scoring courses; and it will take
time to adjust men's conceptions of education to a basis new
to the American college, though familiar in every European
university. To assist the students in preparing themselves
for the general examination each of them at the beginning of
his Sophomore year is assigned to the charge of a tutor who

confers with him about his work and guides his reading outside of that required in the courses.

.   .   .   .

EVIL OF CREDITS IN COURSES

All these changes are in a direction away from the mechanical view of education which is the bane of the American system. We see that view displayed everywhere, prominently at the present day in efforts to raise the standard of premedical training. This is commonly expressed in terms of courses taken and credits obtained, not of knowledge acquired. If a young man has passed a course and learned little or nothing, or forgotten all he knew, he fulfils the requirement; but if he has mastered the subject in any other way, and can prove it by examination, it avails him nothing. Counting the credits scored in courses is, no doubt, the easiest way to apply a requirement, but it is not a sound system of education. What a man is, what knowledge he possesses, and what use he can make of it are the real measure of his education. All persons who desire to improve the American system from the common school upward ought to strive not to lose sight of the end in the means, not to let the machinery divert attention from the product.

.   .   .   .

THE WIDENER LIBRARY

The most notable change in the aspect of the University within the year has been wrought by the completion of the Harry Elkins Widener Memorial Library; but the contribution thereby made to its working power as a seat of learning has not been less significant. During the summer, with rare administrative skill, the books were transferred to the new building and rearranged upon the shelves, the catalogue improved, and the whole library put into working order. The far greater ease and comfort in using the collections was reflected at once, both by the larger number of books used in the Reading Room, and by the larger number taken from the building. And yet the principal advance made in the new university library has been due to the facilities for using the books in the stack itself by members of the instructing staff and advanced students. There are about sixty private rooms for the professors in immediate contact with the stacks; and the open stalls in the stacks, with windows and places for table and chair, number nearly three hundred. Such an ample provision for work among the books exists in no other library in the world; and the relief from the intolerable conditions in Gore Hall cannot be without effect on the productiveness of our scholars. In the old conditions scholarly work was done under grave difficulties; but the professors' rooms in the new building, so apportioned as to be as near as possible to the collections a man will chiefly use, furnish all that a scholar could desire. The instructing staff look forward to, and the friends of the University expect, an era of productiveness greater than was possible when our scholars were hampered by the *res angusta domi*.

Independent Research Fellowships for Young Men

It is not only among the instructing staff that we ought to foster productive scholarship. The habit of writing ought to begin young; younger than is usually the case in America. Contrary to the common impression, writing becomes more difficult the longer it is put off. As a man grows older he becomes more fastidious, more self-distrustful, less ready to grapple with a large theme, less ready to put pen to paper until he knows all about a subject, which no one can ever do. A certain crudity of youth is inseparable from early and great productiveness, and ought not to be too much repressed. It would seem that American graduate schools do sometimes, quite unintentionally, repress it too much, by prolonging the period of study too long. Real capacity for truly productive work is no doubt rare even among learned scholars, but where it exists it might perhaps be encouraged, and encouraged younger, than it is today. Perhaps fellowships, like those in the English universities, or like those in the *Fondation Thiers* in Paris, might be created with good results. The holders of such fellowships ought not to be members of any school, because the atmosphere of a school is essentially that of study, and the atmosphere of study is not the same as that of production. The fellows would, of course, be in close contact with the professors, and go to them for criticism and advice; but that is not the same thing as studying under them, or working up under their direction a thesis for a degree. It assumes that the period of study under tutelage has passed, and the period of independent work has begun; and this means a subtle but real change of attitude. It may be early to devise any plan of this kind, but it seems to be worth consideration.

FROM THE ANNUAL REPORT, 1915–1916

LECTURES AND BOOKS

LECTURES are an excellent, and in fact an indispensable, part of university work, but it is possible to have too many of them, to treat them as the one vital method of instruction. This has two dangers. It tends to put the student too much in a purely receptive attitude of absorbing information poured out upon him, instead of compelling him to extract it from books for himself; so that his education becomes a passive rather than an active process. Lectures should probably be in the main a means of stimulating thought, rather than of imparting facts, which can generally be impressed upon the mind more accurately and effectively by the printed page than by the spoken word.

Then again there is the danger that if lecture courses are regarded as the main object of the professor's chair, the universities, and the departments therein, will value themselves, and be valued, in proportion to the number of lecture courses that they offer. This matter will bear a moment's consideration, for it is connected with certain important general considerations of educational policy. To make the question clear, and point out its bearing upon our own problems, something may be said about the relations that exist between instruction in the College and in other departments of the University.

Many American universities have adopted a combined degree, whereby the earlier portion of the professional instruction in law, medicine, and other technical subjects is taken as a part of the college course; and at the same time they maintain separate faculties for the college, or undergraduate academic department, and for the graduate school of arts and sciences. At Harvard we have gone on the opposite principle in both cases. We have separated each of the professional schools almost wholly from the college, with a distinct faculty and a distinct student life of its own. We have done this on the ground that a strictly professional atmosphere is an advantage in the study of a profession, and we believe that the earnestness, the almost ferociously keen interest, of the student body in our Law School, for example, has been largely due to this fact. We believe that the best results in both general and professional education are attained by a sharp separation between the two. On the other hand, we have not established a distinct faculty for the Graduate School, but have the same faculty and to a great extent the same body of instruction for undergraduates and graduates, each man being expected to take such part of it as fits his own state of progress. We have done this because we have not regarded the Graduate School of Arts and Sciences as exclusively or distinctly a professional school for future teachers. If it were so, it would probably be necessary to give it more of a pedagogical character than it has today. Indeed there has appeared to be no serious disadvantage, such as exists in the case of a purely professional school, in our practice of not separating the graduate school wholly from the college. Although there is a single faculty the two bodies of students are quite distinct, and the graduates take no part in the athletics or social activities of the men in college. They are in no danger of any lack of industry, nor do they suffer from contact with the college students taking courses primarily for graduates. The best Seniors who have reached the point of electing advanced courses are by no means inferior in capacity, education, or earnestness to the average graduate. And, on the other hand, competent undergraduates benefit greatly by following instruction that would not otherwise be open to them.

NUMBER OF COURSES

Our system, by closing professional education to undergraduates, obliges them to devote their college course entirely to academic studies; and at the same time it opens all academic instruction to undergraduates and graduates alike. By so doing it treats the whole list of academic courses as one body of instruction whereof the quantity can be readily measured and the nature perceived. In this way our system brings into peculiar prominence a question that affects the whole university policy in this country. A university, as its name implies, is an institution where all branches of learning are studied, but this principle easily transforms itself into the doctrine that a university ought to offer systematic instruction in every part of every subject; and in fact almost all departments press for an increase of courses, hoping to maintain so far as possible a distinct course upon every subdivision of their fields. This is in large measure due to the fact that American graduate students, unlike German students, tend to select their university on account of the number and richness of the courses listed in the catalogue on their particular subjects, rather than by reason of the eminence of the professors who teach them. Some years ago it happened that a professor of rare distinction in his field, and an admirable teacher, who had a large number of graduate students in his seminar, accepted a chair in another university. His successors at his former post, however good, were by no means men with his reputation. Under these circumstances, one would have supposed that many of his pupils would have followed him, and that fresh students would have sought him in his new chair. But in fact the seminar at the place he had left was substantially undiminished, and he had a comparatively small body of graduate students in the university to which he migrated.

The real reason for increasing the list of courses, though it is often not consciously recognized, is quite as much a desire to attract students as a belief in the benefit conferred on them after they come. The result has been a great expansion within the last score of years in the number of courses offered by all the larger universities.

.   .   .   .

Nevertheless, it is a proper subject for consideration whether the policy of offering courses of instruction covering every part of every subject is wise. No European university attempts to do so. No single student can take them all in any large field, and his powers would be deadened by a surfeit of instruction if he did. For the undergraduates a comparatively small array of staple courses on the most important portions of the subject, with a limited number of others on more highly specialized aspects thereof, is sufficient. For the graduate students who remain only a year to take the degree of Master of Arts, and who are doing much the same work as the more advanced Seniors, the same list of courses would be enough; and for those graduates who intend to become professors in universities and productive scholars it would probably be better — beyond these typical specialized courses, which would suffice to show the method of approaching the subject — to give all the advanced instruction by means of seminars where the students work together on related, but not identical, paths, with the aid of mutual criticism and under the guidance of the professors. Fewer courses, more thoroughly given, which would free instructors for a larger amount of personal supervision of the students, would be better for the pupils, and would make it possible for the university to allow those members of the staff who are capable of original work of a high order more time for productive scholarship. Many a professor at the present day, under the pressure of preparing a new course, cannot find time to work up the discoveries he has made, or to publish a work throwing a new light on existing knowledge.

In making these suggestions there is no intention of urging

a reduction of our existing schedule. But it is time to discuss the assumption, now apparently prevalent in all American universities, that an indefinite increase in the number of courses provided is to be aimed at in higher education. The question is whether that policy is not defective in principle, and whether we are not following it to excess, thereby sacrificing to it other objects equally, if not more, important.

FROM THE ANNUAL REPORT, 1916–1917

ACADEMIC FREEDOM

THE war has brought to the front in academic life many questions which are new, or present themselves to many people in a new light. One of these is liberty of speech on the part of the professor; and it seems a not unfitting time to analyze the principles involved, and seek to discover their limitations. In so doing I shall deal only with higher education, that is with universities and colleges.

Experience has proved, and probably no one would now deny, that knowledge can advance, or at least can advance most rapidly, only by means of an unfettered search for truth on the part of those who devote their lives to seeking it in their respective fields, and by complete freedom in imparting to their pupils the truth that they have found. This has become an axiom in higher education, in spite of the fact that a searcher may discover error instead of truth, and be misled, and mislead others, thereby. We believe that if light enough is let in, the real relations of things will soon be seen, and that they can be seen in no other way. Such a principle, however, does not solve the actual problems, because the difficulty lies in the application; and for that purpose one must consider the question in various aspects. One must distinguish between the matters that fall within and those that lie outside of the professor's field of study; then there is a difference in the professor's position in his class-room and beyond it. These two cross divisions raise four distinct problems that may profitably be discussed in succession.

The teaching by the professor in his class-room on the subjects within the scope of his chair ought to be absolutely free. He must teach the truth as he has found it and sees it. This is the primary condition of academic freedom, and any violation of it endangers intellectual progress. In order to make it secure it is essential that the teaching in the class-room should be confidential. This does not mean that it is secret, but that what is said there should not be published. If the remarks of the instructor were repeated by the pupils in the public press, he would be subjected to constant criticism by people, not familiar with the subject, who misunderstood his teaching; and, what is more important, he would certainly be misquoted, because his remarks would be reported by the student without their context or the qualifications that give them their accuracy. Moreover, if the rule that remarks in the class-room shall not be reported for publication elsewhere is to be maintained, the professor himself must not report them. Lectures open to the public stand on a different footing; but lectures in a private class-room must not be given by the instructor to the newspapers. That principle is, I believe, observed in all reputable institutions.

This brings us to the next subdivision of the inquiry, the freedom of the professor within his field of study, but outside of his class-room. It has been pointed out that he ought not to publish his class-room lectures as such in the daily press. That does not mean a denial of the right to publish them in a book, or their substance in a learned periodical. On the contrary, the object of institutions of learning is not only the acquisition but also the diffusion of knowledge. Every professor must, therefore, be wholly unrestrained in publishing the results of his study in the field of his professorship. It is needless to add that for the dignity of his profession, for the maintenance of its privileges, as well as for his own reputation among his fellows, whatever he writes or says on his own subject should be uttered as a scholar, in a scholarly tone and form. This is a matter of decorum, not of discipline; to be remedied by a suggestion, not by a penalty.

In troublous times much more serious difficulty, and much more confusion of thought, arise from the other half of our subject, the right of a professor to express his views without restraint on matters lying outside the sphere of his professorship. This is not a question of academic freedom in its true sense, but of the personal liberty of the citizen. It has nothing to do with liberty of research and instruction in the subject for which the professor occupies the chair that makes him a member of the university. The fact that a man fills a chair of astronomy, for example, confers on him no special knowledge of, and no peculiar right to speak upon, the protective tariff. His right to speak about a subject on which he is not an authority is simply the right of any other man, and the question is simply whether the university or college by employing him as a professor acquires a right to restrict his freedom as a citizen. It seems to me that this question can be answered only by again considering his position in his classroom and outside of it.

The university or college is under certain obligations to its students. It compels them to attend courses of instruction, and on their side they have a right not to be compelled to listen to remarks offensive or injurious to them on subjects of which the instructor is not a master, — a right which the teacher is bound to respect. A professor of Greek, for example, is not at liberty to harangue his pupils on the futility and harmfulness of vaccination; a professor of economics, on Bacon's authorship of Shakespeare; or a professor of bacteriology, on the tenets of the Catholic Church. Everyone will admit this when stated in such extreme forms; and the reason is that the professor speaks to his class as a professor, not as a citizen. He speaks from his chair and must speak from that alone. The difficulty lies in drawing the line between that which does and does not fall properly within the professor's subject; and where the line ought to be drawn the professor can hardly claim an arbitrary power to judge, since the question affects the rights both of himself and his students. But serious friction rarely arises, I believe, from this cause, and a word of caution would ordinarily be enough.

The gravest questions, and the strongest feelings, arise from action by a professor beyond his chosen field and outside of his class-room. Here he speaks only as a citizen. By appointment to a professorship he acquires no rights that he did not possess before; but there is a real difference of opinion today on the question whether he loses any rights that he would otherwise enjoy. The argument in favor of a restraining power on the part of the governing boards of universities and colleges is based upon the fact that by extreme, or injudicious, remarks that shock public sentiment a professor can do great harm to the institution with which he is connected. That is true, and sometimes a professor thoughtlessly does an injury that is without justification. If he publishes an article on the futility and harmfulness of vaccination, and signs it as a professor in a certain university, he leads the public to believe that his views are those of an authority on the subject, approved by the institution and taught to its students. If he is really a professor of Greek, he is misleading the public and misrepresenting his university, which he would not do if he gave his title in full.

In spite, however, of the risk of injury to the institution, the objections to restraint upon what professors may say as citizens seem to me far greater than the harm done by leaving them free. In the first place, to impose upon the teacher in a university restrictions to which the members of other professions, lawyers, physicians, engineers, and so forth are not subjected would produce a sense of irritation and humiliation. In accepting a chair under such conditions a man would surrender a part of his liberty; what he might say would be submitted to the censorship of a board of trustees, and he would cease to be a free citizen. The lawyer, physician, or engineer may express his views as he likes on the subject of the protective tariff; shall the professor of astronomy not be free to do the same? Such a policy would tend seriously to discourage some of the best men from taking up the scholar's life. It is not a question of academic freedom, but of personal liberty from constraint, yet it touches the dignity of the academic career.

That is an objection to restraint on freedom of speech from the standpoint of the teacher. There is another, not less weighty, from that of the institution itself. If a university or college censors what its professors may say, if it restrains them from uttering something that it does not approve, it thereby assumes responsibility for that which it permits them to say. This is logical and inevitable, but it is a responsibility which an institution of learning would be very unwise in assuming. It is sometimes suggested that the principles are different in time of war; that the governing boards are then justified in restraining unpatriotic expressions injurious to the country. But the same problem is presented in war time as in time of peace. If the university is right in restraining its professors, it has a duty to do so, and it is responsible for whatever it permits. There is no middle ground. Either the university assumes full responsibility for permitting its professors to express certain opinions in public, or it assumes no responsibility whatever, and leaves them to be dealt with like other citizens by the public authorities according to the laws of the land.

All this refers, of course, to opinions on public matters sincerely uttered. If a professor speaks in a way that reveals moral obliquity, he may be treated as he would on any other evidence of moral defect; for character in the teacher is essential to the welfare of the students.

Every human attempt to attain a good object involves some compromise, some sacrifice of lesser ends for the larger ones. Hence every profession has its own code of ethics designed to promote its major objects, and entailing restrictions whose importance is often not clear to outsiders. But for the teachers in American universities and colleges the code of professional ethics does not appear to have been thoroughly developed or to be fully understood either by teachers or trustees. That result requires time, and for this reason few difficulties arise in institutions that have had a long and gradual growth.

Surely abuse of speech, abuse of authority and arbitrary restraint and friction would be reduced if men kept in mind the distinction between the privilege of academic freedom and the common right of personal liberty as a citizen, between what may properly be said in the class-room and what in public. But it must not be forgotten that all liberty and every privilege imply responsibilities. Professors should speak in public soberly and seriously, not for notoriety or self advertisement, under a deep sense of responsibility for the good name of the institution and the dignity of their profession. They should take care that they are understood to speak personally, not officially. When they so speak, and governing boards respect their freedom to express their sincere opinions as other citizens may do, there will be little danger that liberty of speech will be either misused or curtailed.

FROM THE ANNUAL REPORT, 1917–1918

The Student as a Whole

THE disturbance of the ordinary college routine caused by the war has furnished an occasion for reviewing our methods of education and considering whether we ought not to proceed farther in the direction we have pursued for some years — that of paying more attention to the student as the man to be educated, or provoked to education, and less exclusive heed to the single course of instruction as the means of educating him. We need among the students, and even among the instructors, a better sense of proportion, a clearer conception of the aim of the college and of what means are best fitted for attaining it. Too few of the students have a definite idea of their object in coming to College, even after completing half of their work for a degree. Too many have a disproportionate idea of the value of intellectual as compared with athletic strength, rating exceptional physical achievement too highly, exceptional intellectual power too low, and thinking far too little about the importance to the ordinary man of cultivating both his mind and his body. The conscientious instructor, on the other hand — and instructors who are not conscientious are rare — is too much inclined to deal with his own subject as a final aim in itself, a thing apart from every other side of education, instead of one element among others in the training of an immature mind. This is true not only of the subject, but of the fraction of the subject that falls within the limits of a single course. A professor of history in a great foreign university remarked some years ago that there were some advantages in an institution smaller than his own, because in his university no one taught history as a whole, but each occupant of a chair only a small part of it. The tendency to cut the knowledge of a subject into fragments separately taught in distinct courses, with nothing to weld them into a whole in the mind of the student, is artificial and harmful. An exaggerated importance seems to be attached by teachers in our universities and colleges to the dignity of giving courses as compared with other methods of instruction or of directing study, or with exerting a control over the whole system of education by conducting examinations of the kind used in foreign universities. This is partly because the value of a department is too often measured by the number of courses offered, rather than by the proficiency of its students, or the quality of its productive scholarship.

The college years are not the time to form highly trained specialists; that comes later; and although an undergraduate must specialize to a considerable extent in order to grasp any subject thoroughly, his main object should be to acquire habits of intellectual application, of clear and accurate thought, and of lucid expression. He should cultivate the power to understand the intricate relations of things, and above all that subtle quality of substantial imagination and resourcefulness which comes from constant and profound thought on difficult problems. Both the older advocates of the doctrine of formal discipline with its division of the mind into distinct faculties, and those modern protagonists of pedagogy who assert that any particular study gives only a capacity to deal with the subject matter that it covers, appear to overlook the effect which one mental process has upon another. Anyone who has mastered the calculus, for example, tends thereafter to regard all things from the standpoint of ratios rather than quantities, of movement rather than position, of tendencies rather than present conditions. Anyone who has learned to seek for truth in original sources, or by primary proof, tends in any serious matter to be dissatisfied with secondary sources or evidence. The human mind would seem to be, not a collection of thought-tight compartments separated from one another, but an exceedingly complex whole wherein every method of reasoning, every intellectual conception, and every body of knowledge has an influence upon all the habits of thought. If so, education should be directed to improving the mind as a whole; and the different subjects of study, still more the several courses of instruction within any one subject, should be considered in their relation to that whole, — not for the sake of bringing the various minds into conformity with any one type, but that each whole mind may be as good of its kind as it can be made.

The subject has been discussed more than once in these reports, in seeking to maintain the principle that the single course of instruction is not, and cannot be, the unit in education, that the only true unit is the student himself; and the principle cannot be too often repeated or too earnestly urged. The steps that have already been taken to give it effect have also been described. In the attitude of the student toward his work, in the regard paid to his development as a man, there has been a marked improvement of late years; but much remains to be done. The new psychological tests, much in vogue during the war, are based upon the idea of seeking to measure the capacity a person possesses, instead of the process he has been through to acquire it; and imperfect though as yet they may be for the purpose, the idea is sound. One of the most serious evils of American education in school and college is counting by courses — the habit of regarding the school or college as an educational savings bank where credits are deposited to make up the balance required for graduation, or for admission to more advanced study; whereas the only place where education can be stored to be drawn upon when needed is the student's own brain. To some extent the constant checking off of work done throughout the curriculum is necessary, both to avoid a mere cramming for a final examination and because the art of comprehensive examination, to measure the actual attainments and abilities of candidates, is still imperfectly developed here. But such checking off should be only a record of progress, not the final test of attainment.

A Prophecy of Materialism

The rapidity with which our whole community has turned from the excitement of the war to the conditions of peace has already been noted, and it may well provoke serious reflection. During the war many people felt that the heroic temper, the spirit of self-sacrifice for an ideal, the exaltation of sentiment called forth, were certain to raise our civilization permanently to a higher level, and to produce a lasting effect on the national character. But that has not been the experience with great wars hitherto. The wars of Napoleon were followed by an era of material progress, where interest was centered in the accumulation of wealth. Our own Civil War was followed by the lowest state of political morals that we have ever known, reaching its climax in the Tweed Ring in New York. The war of 1870 was followed in Germany by the growth of materialism that culminated in the present attempt to exploit mankind by force. Nor are these unnatural results. On the material side, war destroys vast quantities of property which have to be replaced, rolls up debts that have to be paid, and it is natural that after a war people should seek to repair the damage it has caused. On the spiritual side, also, any great moral effort is liable to be followed by a period of moral relaxation. After a great war, therefore, and not least, perhaps, after a war that has awakened so great an enthusiasm and devotion, it is wise to beware of a materialistic reaction. Among the strongest agencies to prevent such a relapse ought to be our colleges and universities, which should feel more than ever their duty to keep before the minds of young men the eternal values and the spiritual truths that endure when material things pass away.

FROM THE ANNUAL REPORT, 1918–1919

TRAINING FOR THE UNKNOWN

THE war has shown the necessity of expert knowledge and therefore of specialized training when a people is called upon to put forth its utmost effort; but it has shown also the value of general education. The excellence of college-bred men as material for military officers, their adaptability and resourcefulness, has been widely recognized in the army. The same qualities are not less important in peace than in war. One of the principal functions of our colleges is to give a broad preparation for citizenship. The expert with a high degree of special training is a necessity in every modern country, and perhaps he was sufficient for a state autocratically ruled; but under a free government the large-minded citizen also is essential. For this purpose education in the immediate problems of the day, political, civic, social, and aesthetic, is often urged; but it is not enough, because the problems that in later life will confront the youth of today will not be altogether those of the present hour. He must be prepared to solve the problems of the future, and these are as little known and foreseen by us as the questions now pressing were by our fathers, or theirs by an earlier generation. With that object before us we must lay a foundation large and solid. We must train our students to think clearly; to see facts as they are; to be broad and tolerant from the study of past experience, profound from communion with the thoughts of great men, and thereby to distinguish the superficial or ephemeral from the fundamental and enduring. This is the true meaning of the humanities, — the study of what man has thought and done, not excluding what he is thinking and doing at the present time.

THE NEED OF DORMITORIES

The annual report of two years ago contained a paragraph upon the moral influence that can be brought to bear on undergraduates, and the means of exerting it. The subject is surely important enough to merit further consideration with a view of suggesting one line of practical approach. College students can be made to feel the necessity of precision and industry by a high standard of attendance and achievement, or they can be allowed to contract habits of carelessness and slothfulness by laxity of requirement; but their characters cannot be formed by disciplinary regulations, because the object sought is not instinctive obedience to rules, but self-discipline, self-control, and self-direction. They can, however, be profoundly influenced in these matters, either directly by personal contact, or indirectly by the creation of good traditions. Direct personal contact of an intimate character is not possible with a large number of students enjoying the freedom of college life. A few can thus be reached, but unless they affect the rest the influence cannot extend very far and seriously permeate the whole body. To influence a large number of men they must form a community, with common sentiments, aspirations, and interests. In short, they must have a strong consciousness of being bound together by common ties. They must have *esprit de corps*. The fact that this exists to no small degree among college men was observed by officers of the Reserve Officers' Training Corps, who remarked that one of the first efforts in forming any military unit was to create in it such a spirit, but that in the college they found it already developed. Intercollegiate sports have had a considerable effect in producing it; but the community spirit they have fostered has been little used as a means of influencing the student body in other ways; nor is it sufficiently continuous or pervasive to be a basis for affecting the personal characters and standards of the great mass of undergraduates. In order to weld the students into a closely bound community, with traditions strong enough for permanent moral effect, it is highly important that they should be housed in college halls, with an opportunity, at least, to take their meals together. Under such conditions a strong influence can be brought to bear upon the natural leaders, and through them upon the whole body. If wisely and sympathetically used it can do much good; and that without in any degree making the students all alike or reducing their individuality. Both the Athenians and the Florentines had a remarkably strong community feeling, but they certainly did not suffer from uniformity. At Harvard we believe that compulsion should be as small as possible, and there is no suggestion of extending it in the matter of residence beyond the Freshman year; but it would be a great benefit to have sufficient college dormitories so ordered as to attract the rest of the undergraduates. Private dormitories, maintained for profit, do not accomplish the result, for they inevitably seek to gather those men who can pay a fair rent, and hence tend to segregate the students on the basis of wealth. In the professional schools university dormitories are not so essential, because the students are more mature, their characters and standards nearly formed; yet even in this case provisions for housing them have great advantages.

.   .   .   .

Stimulating Creative Work

Stimulating creative scholarship is a matter to which we ought to pay more attention, and we may well try to devise effective means of doing it, for many a professor abundantly capable of contributing to the world's stock of knowledge is so hampered by the burden, or rather distraction, of teaching and administrative work that he postpones writing to the time that never comes. In the humanistic subjects, at least, the difficulty arises not so much in what is commonly called research, for the professor of literature, history, politics, economics, or philosophy must be constantly reading and investigating if he would keep abreast of his subject and maintain himself as a good teacher. It is in preparing for formal publication what he has acquired that the strain comes. Collecting the materials can be done at odd times, irregularly and in spite of interruptions; and later when the book has gone to press and the proof sheets come back thick and fast the author is chained to his work, and must keep up with it whatever else he may have to do. But to put his material into final shape in the actual writing of a book demands for most men much effort, and a considerable period of continuous attention — many hours a day for months and sometimes years. This is the stage where relief from the pressure of other work does most good, and is most likely to ensure definite production that might otherwise not be accomplished. If the function of a university is not only to impart, but also to create, knowledge, then it would be wise to aid professors at this critical period of production, by relieving them for a year or more of a part of their teaching, and perhaps also by supplying them, if necessary, with some expert clerical assistance. In working out such a plan certain conditions must, however, be kept in mind. The number of men who can in this way be helped to write must at any time be very limited; the selection must be made by such imperfect wisdom as can be brought to bear; and however wise the choice, those not selected will be disappointed. Moreover the funds of universities are not limitless, and what is spent for one object cannot be used for another. If departments are constantly pressing for an increase in instructors and courses, or, indeed, unless they are willing to give up some courses for a time, relief from teaching in order to help production will hardly be a possibility. Teaching and writing are both essential to a university, and neither of them should be pressed to the neglect of the other.

FROM THE ANNUAL REPORT, 1919–1920

The Relation between Faculties and Governing Boards

THE question of the organization of universities and colleges, of the relation between the faculties and the governing boards, has of late years provoked much discussion, and it may not be out of place to consider the problem from the point of view of our own history and traditions. The form of corporate organization with which we are most familiar is the industrial. Concerns of this kind are created by capitalists who take all the risks of the business, conduct it through a board of directors whom they select, and employ the various grades of persons who serve it. The rights and duties of all persons employed are fixed by a contract with the corporation, that is with the owners of the property, and extend only so far as they are contractual. The main reason for the present form of industrial organization is that capital originates the enterprise and takes the risk. For that reason the board of directors is elected by the owners of the capital. Other kinds of industrial organization can be imagined, and have existed. A body of workers may get together, secure the use of capital at a fixed rate of interest, and conduct the business themselves. But whatever other forms of corporate organization might exist, it is natural that we should take our ideas from the one to which we are most accustomed, and apply them to institutions of all kinds. Yet to do so in the case of universities and colleges, where the conditions are very different, creates confusion and does harm. In this case, there are no owners who take the risk of the business. The institutions are not founded for profit, but for the purpose of preserving, transmitting, and increasing knowledge. The trustees, or whatever the members of the governing board may be called, although vested with the legal title to the property, are not the representatives of private owners, for there are none. They are custodians, holding the property in trust to promote the objects of the institution.

In the Middle Ages, when the universities first appeared, their property was held and the enterprise conducted practically by the academic body. This is the condition today of the colleges in Oxford and Cambridge, where the property of a college is vested in, and all its affairs are conducted by, the Fellows. In most places this state of things has not continued. In continental Europe the property has become vested, as a rule, in the State, which has also the ultimate power of control. In the American endowed universities it has become vested in a board, or boards, distinct, for the most part, from the teaching staff.

The transformation at Harvard is interesting. The College was founded in 1636 by a vote of the General Court appropriating money for that object. In 1642 an act was passed for the government of the College, placing the control in the hands of a Board of Overseers, composed of the Governor, the Deputy Governor, the Magistrates, and the Ministers of the six adjoining towns. This was followed in 1650 by another act creating a corporation, after the pattern of an English college, composed of the President, Treasurer, and five Fellows, but acting under the supervision of the Overseers. In the early days a part of the five Fellows were resident teachers, or, as they were then called, Tutors. They could not all have belonged to that class, because it was three-quarters of a century before there were as many as five teachers beside the President. As a rule the Tutors seem to have been young men who served a short time while awaiting a call to a parish. Perhaps it was for this reason that more mature men from outside were elected to the Corporation. Certain it is that by the time the charter was twenty-five years old, if not before, we find among the Fellows ministers of the neighboring towns.

Towards the close of the seventeenth century several attempts were made to revise the charter and introduce outside members, but for various reasons they all failed of adoption, and in 1707 the original charter was declared to be in force and has remained so ever since. The number of settled ministers among its members continued, however, to increase, until in 1721 there had been for some time only one Fellow in the Corporation who was a teacher at the College. In that year two of the Tutors presented to the Overseers a memorial claiming places in the Corporation, apparently on the ground that they were resident fellows giving instruction in the College and as such were the Fellows intended by the Charter of 1650. The Overseers sustained their claim; so did the House of Representatives, and the controversy dragged on for several years until it was finally brought to nought by the opposition of the Governor, backed eventually by his Council. The question was interwoven with an acute religious quarrel and a desire to remove the ministers in the Corporation whose ecclesiastical views were unpopular. Although the Corporation was not overborne, and the obnoxious Fellows were not removed, it yielded so far as to elect Tutors to the next vacancies that occurred, so that by 1725 three of them were members of the body.

There continued to be two or three Tutors or Professors in the Corporation until 1779, when a notable change began. Save during the confused period at the close of the seventeenth century, when new charters were put into operation only to be defeated by refusal of the royal approval, the nonresident Fellows, that is those who were not teachers at the College, were always ministers of the neighboring towns. But the convulsion of the Revolution, the growth of the University, and the financial difficulties caused by the war "indicated to the Corporation," in the words of Quincy, "the wisdom of selecting men of experience in business, and practically acquainted with public affairs." The first man of the new type was James Bowdoin, elected in 1779; and after that time almost every choice was of this kind, the occasional clergymen elected being chosen not because incumbents of the neighboring parishes but for their personal value as counsellors. The only teachers in the University thereafter elected Fellows were Professor Eliphalet Pearson, who served from 1800 to 1806, and Professor Ephraim W. Gurney, who served from 1884 to 1886.[1]

The change, however, did not take place without subsequent protest. In 1824 a memorial signed by eleven members of the instructing staff, claiming that according to the intent of the charter the Fellows ought to be resident, paid teachers, was presented first to the Corporation and then to the Overseers. While it was under consideration, a war of pamphlets was waged between John Lowell in opposition to the memorial and Edward Everett, then a Professor, in support of it. Each of them dealt keenly with as much of the early history of the College as he could find in contemporary records; and the impression left on the reader today is that the framers of the charter had in mind in a vague way the organization of an English college, but that the word "Fellow" was at that time used loosely, and that no distinct limitation was intended to be placed upon the selection. On January 25, 1825, the Overseers voted unanimously: (1) "That it does not appear to this board that the resident instructors of Harvard University have any exclusive right to be chosen members of the Corporation"; (2) "That it does not appear to this board that the members of the Corporation forfeit their offices by not residing in the College"; and (3) "That, in the opinion of this board, it is not expedient to express any opinion on the subject of future elections." The Overseers seem, however, to have thought that the instructing staff should be represented

---

[1] Joseph Story and James Walker were appointed professors while Fellows and retained their places upon the Corporation. Alexander Agassiz, who was a Fellow 1878–84, 1886–90, although during all that time Curator of the Museum of Comparative Zoölogy, was not a member of the instructing staff of the University.

among the Fellows, for they refused to confirm the election
to the next vacancy of Judge Jackson, one of their own number, until the Corporation stated its desire and purpose to
elect a resident instructor a Fellow as soon as a proper occasion should offer. Within ten years Joseph Story and James
Walker were appointed professors while Fellows, and retained
their places on the Corporation; so that in a certain way the
instructing staff was represented there; but the proper occasion for electing a resident instructor did not come until 1884,
and the professor so chosen continued a Fellow for only two
years. In short, the question of giving to the instructing staff
a representation upon the Corporation was virtually settled
in 1825, has never been seriously revived, and there appears
to be no desire to revive it today.

The transition which has taken place at Harvard is an
example of the differentiation of functions that comes with
the growth in size and complexity of an institution. More
recent universities and colleges in America have not gone
through this evolution, but have started with a body quite
distinct from the instructing staff, and containing none of its
members except the President; yet a body in which the title
to the property and the complete ultimate control are legally
vested. This legal situation has no doubt led to the present
unfortunate tendency to regard the boards of trustees of institutions of learning as analogous to the boards of directors
of business corporations, their legal position being the same.
In spite, however, of a difference in legal organization, the
best and most fruitful conception of a university or college is
the ancient one of a society or guild of scholars associated
together for preserving, imparting, increasing, and enjoying
knowledge.

If a university or college is a society or guild of scholars
why does it need any separate body of trustees at all? Why
more than learned societies, which are obviously groups of
scholars, and have no such boards recruited outside their own
membership? One reason is to be found in the large endow-

ments of our institutions of learning that require for investment a wide knowledge and experience of business affairs. In fact, as already pointed out, the vast complexity of a modern university has compelled specialization of functions, and one aspect thereof is the separation of the scholarly and business organs. Another reason is that higher education has assumed more and more of a public character; its importance has been more fully recognized by the community at large; it must therefore keep in touch with public needs, make the public appreciate its aims and the means essential to attain them; and for this purpose it must possess the influence and obtain the guidance of men conversant with the currents of the outer world.

There is a further reason more fundamental if less generally understood. Teaching in all its grades is a public service, and the administration of every public service must comprise both expert and lay elements. Without the former it will be ineffectual; without the latter it will become in time narrow, rigid, or out of harmony with its public object. Each has its own distinctive function, and only confusion and friction result if one of them strives to perform the function of the other. From this flows the cardinal principle, popularly little known but of well-nigh universal application, that experts should not be members of a non-professional body that supervises experts. One often hears that men with a practical knowledge of teaching should be elected to school boards, but unless they are persons of singular discretion they are likely to assume that their judgment on technical matters is better than that of the teachers, with effects that are sometimes disastrous. Laymen should not attempt to direct experts about the method of attaining results, but only indicate the results to be attained. Many years ago the Board of Overseers, after a careful examination, came to the conclusion that the writing of English by Harvard undergraduates was sadly defective. In this they were acting wholly within their proper province, and the result was a very notable improvement in the teaching of English composition. But if they had attempted to direct how the subject should be taught they would have been hopelessly beyond their province. They would not have known, as the instructing staff did, how it should be done, and they would have exasperated and disheartened the teachers.

But another question may well be asked. Granted that there should be both expert and non-professional elements in the management of a university or college, why in a society or guild of scholars should the non-professional organ be the final authority? For this there are three reasons. In the first place, so far as the object is public — and where teaching is conducted on a large scale the object cannot fail to concern the public deeply — that object must in the final analysis be determined by public, that is by non-professional, judgment. In an endowed university the governing board does not, indeed, represent the public in the sense that it is elected by popular vote, but it is not on that account any less truly a trustee for the public.

In the second place, the non-professional board is responsible for the financial administration, and the body that holds the purse must inevitably have the final control.

Thirdly, the non-professional board is the only body, or the most satisfactory body, to act as arbiter between the different groups of experts. Everyone knows that in an American university or college there is a ceaseless struggle for the means of development between different departments, and someone must decide upon the relative merits of their claims. In a university with good traditions the professors would be more ready to rely on the fairness and wisdom of a well constituted board of trustees than on one composed of some of their own number each affected almost unavoidably by a bias in favor of his particular subject.

Let it be observed, however, that although the governing board is the ultimate authority it is not in the position of an industrial employer. It is a trustee not to earn dividends for stockholders, but for the purposes of the guild. Its sole object is to help the society of scholars to accomplish the object for which they are brought together. They are the essential part of the society; and making their work effective for the intellectual and moral training of youth and for investigation is the sole reason for the existence of trustees, of buildings, of endowments, and of all the elaborate machinery of a modern university. If this conception be fully borne in mind most of the sources of dissension between professors and governing boards will disappear. At Harvard it has, I believe, been borne in mind as a deep-seated traditional conviction.

The differences between the ordinary industrial employment and the conduct of a society or guild of scholars in a university are wide. In the industrial system of employment the employee is paid according to the value of his services; he can be discharged when no longer wanted; and his duties are prescribed as minutely as may be desired by the employer. In a university there is permanence of tenure; substantial equality of pay within each academic grade; and although the duties in general are well understood, there is great freedom in the method of performing them. It is not difficult to see why each of these conditions prevails, and is in fact dependent upon the others. Permanence of tenure lies at the base of the difference between a society of scholars in a university and the employees in an industrial concern. In the latter, under prevailing conditions, men are employed in order to promote its earning power. In a university the concern exists to promote the work of the scholars and of the students whom they teach. Therefore in the industrial concern an unprofitable employee is discharged; but in the university the usefulness of the scholar depends largely upon his sense of security, upon the fact that he can work for an object that may be remote and whose value may not be easily demonstrated. In a university, barring positive misconduct, permanence of tenure is essential for members who have passed the probationary period. The equality of pay goes

with the permanence of tenure. In an industrial establishment the higher class of officials, those who correspond most
nearly to the grade of professors, can be paid what they may
be worth to the concern, and discharged if they are not worth
their salaries. How valuable they are can be fairly estimated, and their compensation can be varied accordingly.
But professors, whose tenure is permanent, cannot be discharged if they do not prove so valuable as they were expected to be. Moreover it is impossible to determine the
value of scholars in the same way as that of commercial
officials. An attempt to do so would create injustice and
endless discontent; and it would offer a temptation to secure
high pay, from their own or another institution, by a display
wholly inconsistent with the scholarly attitude of mind. The
only satisfactory system is that of paying salaries on something very close to a fixed scale, and letting every professor
do as good work as he can. In an industrial concern the prospect of a high salary may be needed to induce the greatest
effort; but indolence among professors is seldom found. They
may, indeed, prefer a line of work less important than some
other; a man may desire to do research who is better fitted for
teaching, or he may prefer to teach advanced students when
there is a greater need of the strongest men in more elementary instruction; but failure to work hard is rare.

The governing boards of universities having, then, the
ultimate legal control in their hands, and yet not being in the
position of industrial employers, it is pertinent to inquire
what their relation to the professors should be. If we bear in
mind the conception of a society or guild of scholars, that
relation usually becomes in practice clear. The scholars, both
individually and gathered into faculties, are to provide the
expert knowledge; the governing board the financial management, the general coördination, the arbitral determinations,
and the preservation of the general direction of public policy.
In the words of a former member of the Harvard Corporation, their business is to "serve tables." The relation is not

one of employer and employed, of superior and inferior, of master and servant, but one of mutual coöperation for the promotion of the scholars' work. Unless the professors have confidence in the singleness of purpose and in the wisdom of the governing boards, and unless these in their turn recognize that they exist to promote the work of the society of scholars, the relations will not have the harmony that they should. The relation is one that involves constant seeking of opinion, and in the main the university must be conducted, not by authority, but by persuasion. There is no natural antagonism of interests between trustees and professors. To suggest it is to suggest failure in their proper relation to one another; to suppose it is to provoke failure; to assume it is to ensure failure.

The question has often been raised whether nominations for appointments should be made by the faculties or their committees, or by the president. It would seem that the less formal the provisions the better. Any president of a university or college who makes a nomination to the governing board without consulting formally or informally the leading professors in the subject and without making sure that most of them approve of it, is taking a grave responsibility that can be justified only by a condition that requires surgery. The objection to a formal nomination by a faculty, or a committee thereof, is that it places the members in an uncomfortable position in regard to their younger colleagues, and that it creates a tendency for the promotion of useful rather than excellent men. A wise president will not make nominations without being sure of the support of the instructing staff, but he may properly, and indeed ought to, decline to make nominations unless convinced that the nominee is of the calibre that ought to be appointed.

Attempts have been made to define, and express in written rules, the relation between the faculties and the governing boards; but the best element in that relation is an intangible, an undefinable, influence. If a husband and wife should attempt to define by regulations their respective rights and duties in the household, that marriage could safely be pronounced a failure. The essence of the relation is mutual confidence and mutual regard; and the respective functions of the faculties and the governing boards — those things that each had better undertake, those it had better leave to the other, and those which require mutual concession — are best learned from experience and best embodied in tradition. Tradition has great advantages over regulations. It is a more delicate instrument; it accommodates itself to things that are not susceptible of sharp definition; it is more flexible in its application, making exceptions and allowances which it would be difficult to foresee or prescribe. It is also more stable. Regulations can be amended; tradition cannot, for it is not made, but grows, and can be altered only by a gradual change in general opinion, not by a majority vote. In short, it cannot be amended, but only outgrown.

FROM THE ANNUAL REPORT, 1920–1921

TEACHING BY PROBLEMS

THE School of Business Administration has developed systematically the plan of teaching by means of problems. The aims and merits of this method are discussed fully in the report of Dean Donham, and the progress in preparing case books of business problems is therein described. The plan suggests interesting questions touching objects and methods in education.

There are many such objects which persist throughout the whole course of teaching from infancy to the professional school. Without venturing to touch upon the vexed question of the extent to which acquired capacities can be transferred from one subject to another, and without purporting to be exhaustive, one may mention among the specific objects of education in any given field or at any given level: the imparting of information; the training of memory; the training of observation, perception, discrimination, and taste; training the power of analysis and synthesis; and training the art of expression. All these qualities can be developed by various processes, of which we have far too little exact knowledge; and more than one of them is in fact stimulated by almost any method of teaching. Important, indeed necessary, as all of them are, there is no quality among them more valuable than that of analysis and synthesis, that is the capacity to sift from a number of facts or ideas those which are essential to the matter in hand, to discover their relation to one another, and thus disclose their significance. This capacity is of vital consequence in the domain of abstract thought and of pure science, and not less in the conduct of practical affairs. But it is one of the most difficult objects to attain, and like all others it is acquired mainly by practice. We learn to do by doing. Yet it would appear to have received until recent years less consideration in American study of education than it deserves. It would seem also that it can be effectively cultivated throughout the whole course of systematic training from the beginning to the end. If in what follows reference is made only to what is done here, it is not that similar methods are not pursued elsewhere, but that one must seek examples in the region with which he is most familiar.

For half a century, under the name of the case system, devised by Professor Langdell, the practice of presenting problems to be solved by discussion between the instructor and student has been applied in our Law School as the chief method of teaching. The problems are presented in the form of actual cases that have been decided in court; and these, selected and arranged in the order required to bring out the successive points in the subject matter of the course, are printed in case books, so that before the class meets the students may have read those that will come up for consideration. The discussion, keen and eager, conducted by a process of trial and error with many false starts on the part of the students, evolves the principle which the instructor designed to bring out. It is not a quick method of imparting the principles and rules of law. Ground can be covered much more rapidly by lectures or by reading text books, but this gives nothing like the same ability to deal with the kind of problem that confronts the lawyer in his practice. Nor do lectures or text books give the same intellectual stimulus. The vehemence with which students, meeting in their rooms, at meals, or on street corners, discuss actual or hypothetical cases is the glory of our Law School and accounts for much of its attraction and success. The case method does not appear to develop in a marked degree the imaginative quality that makes the original jurist; but it forms the habit and capacity of analysis and synthesis as nothing else does. Its value has been shown by the kind of practicing lawyers it has produced, by the application for our students on the part of legal firms, and by the spreading of the system throughout the better law schools of the country.

This is the method that has been adopted in a systematic form in the School of Business Administration, where the instruction has more and more taken the form of problems to be discussed and solved by the students under the guidance of the instructor. It is deemed the best preparation for active business life, because the decision of questions by the banker, the manufacturer, the merchant, or the transporter consists in discerning the essential elements in a situation and applying to them the principles of organization and of trade. His most important work consists of solving problems, and for this he must have the faculty of rapid analysis and synthesis.

.   .   .   .

The suggestion has already been made that the method of teaching by problems can be effectively applied throughout the whole course of education from the beginning to the end. But the difficulty in framing problems such that the information required for their solution is within the grasp of the pupil is much greater in childhood than in youth; and, therefore, in the elementary and secondary school a child has not usually the knowledge required for a solution of problems in history or economics, in literature, or in most of the natural sciences. But there are subjects within his range. To the writer it has seemed that, quite apart from the literary heritage of the classics, whose value to the student comes only after struggling with the language, one of the chief merits of the old school regimen of Latin, Greek, and mathematics lay in its constant presentation of problems that needed no greater knowledge than the child possessed. Mathematics is, of course, essentially a series of problems, beginning with arithmetic and running at school through algebra, geometry, and sometimes trigonometry. In fact it is almost impossible to teach mathematics except by the problem method. The same thing is true in the study of the ancient languages. The boy is confronted by a Latin sentence to be translated. He has to determine whether a word is a noun, a verb, or what other part of speech; if a noun in what number, case, and gender; if a verb in what mood, tense, and person. Then he has to consider what the distinctive part of the word should be, and look that up in the lexicon. From these words, whose sense and whose place in the syntax he has discovered, he must construct a sentence with a rational meaning. The whole process is that of solving puzzles or problems, at first by making the boy discover the meaning of a few words and put them together in simple sentences, but gradually involving more complex forms of speech, and leading up to the interpretation of the thoughts of authors of greater and greater difficulty, yet all the while within the scope of his command of facts. It has been said that the process, good for those who take a real interest in it, is not much use for others. But the experience of one who at that time was not much interested in study leads him to believe that almost all fairly intelligent boys derive no small profit from these efforts at translation; although it may be admitted that the profit is greater to those who have, or can be given, a purpose for their effort. Latin grammar learned by rote in the old-fashioned way has seemed to the writer of little or no educational value. Like the multiplication table, the grammar with its rules and lists of exceptions is doubtless necessary as a tool, and furnishes part of the difficulties encountered in solving the problems presented by translation. But it would seem to be the series of problems themselves that are of use in training the mind.

Modern languages can, of course, be used for this purpose instead of the classics, but their structure is less well adapted therefor, and the authors read less adapted to stimulate immature minds. Of the other modern subjects taught in the schools, physics is the only one that lends itself readily to teaching by problems. For various reasons many of them are highly important; some of them for the knowledge with which children should be equipped, others as tools for future use. But there is a danger of failing to cultivate the habit of independent analysis and synthesis, of solving without assistance problems simple enough for the elements to be grasped, yet difficult enough to require personal effort. This danger has been the greater by reason of the prevalence of direct instruction by the teacher, as compared with the earlier practice where study by oneself played a larger part. Men whose recollections of school go back fifty years will remember that in those days the lesson was set by the teacher and worked out by the pupil himself; the class reciting to the teacher, who corrected mistakes and gave explanations, but imparted little direct information. The recitation was more in the nature of an examination than of a lecture or demonstration, and the whole process had more the character of self-education than it has today. In later years mental nourishment was furnished to the pupil in a more predigested form, requiring less effort for assimilation than formerly. To change the metaphor, children were given their intellectual experience by seeing the country in an automobile instead of walking on their feet. The distance covered could be greater, but there is a doubt whether their muscles are as much developed by being carried as by exercise, and college teachers sometimes complain that Freshmen are deficient in the capacity to think for themselves.

For the less vigorous minds direct instruction has advantages. Fewer of them fall by the wayside; but for the more active-minded there is something lost. The selective function of education, the sifting out of those who can go farthest, is not so well performed where the pupils depend less on their own exertions. There are many ways of reaching a desired result, and in education there are many things that ought to be done without leaving something not less important undone; but apart from dogmatism one may deprecate the extent to which a neo-Herbartian philosophy has spread an impression that the value of instruction is in proportion to the smallness of the effort on the part of the pupil.

VALUE AND KINDS OF EXAMINATION

Connected with direct instruction in school seems to be the aversion of many teachers, especially in the West, to examinations. So far as these are not a test of memory, they involve in some form the solving of problems — a practice to which the pupils are not accustomed, and in which accordingly they do not appear at their best. If they are in the habit of absorbing rather than giving forth this comes hard. Teachers often feel that examinations are needless because they are aware how much knowledge the pupil possesses, since they know what has been imparted to him. But how much has been poured into a bucket is a poor measure of what it contains if it leaks, and children's minds always leak, one never knows how much. Many teachers regard examinations not only as needless, but as a sort of indictment of the pupil, to be used only in case there is reasonable ground for believing him deficient; whereas examinations not only furnish the teacher with an accurate measure of what the pupil knows and how far he can use his knowledge, but, if properly used, are an essential part of the educational process. They should test not only memory, but still more the capacity to apply the knowledge possessed. In other words, they should be to a very large extent in the nature of problems. If we learn to do by doing, then there is for the pupil no better way of learning than to be set occasionally to do things without assistance, in competition with others who are trying to do the same things. That is the essence of an examination.

FROM THE ANNUAL REPORT, 1921–1922

KINDS OF EXAMINATION

THE art of examination is beginning in this country to attract the attention of men engaged in education more than ever before. There are at least three distinguishable kinds of examination. First the disciplinary, whose object is mainly to ascertain whether the work required of pupils has been faithfully done. Since in our common schools oral teaching has to a great extent replaced individual study by the pupil of prescribed lessons in a text book, the need of constant examinations of this type has been felt less than formerly. The old-fashioned recitation was in part an opportunity for explaining matters that had presented difficulties, but chiefly a test of how thoroughly the lesson had been learned by the members of the class. It would seem to be against examinations of this kind, the most common and best understood type, that the repugnance of teachers is mainly directed.

A second kind of examination may be termed informational, its object being to discover the extent and accuracy of knowledge possessed by the person examined. Of this nature are the examinations for admission to college by those institutions that still employ them — now almost entirely conducted by the College Entrance Examination Board. Into the same class fall also for the most part, although by no means wholly, the examinations held at the end of college courses. Such examinations are valuable only in measuring knowledge which the person who takes them ought to possess. In a college course where the same ground has been covered by all the members of the class the questions can easily be made both fair and searching. But where precisely the same ground has not been covered, or has not been covered with equal thoroughness in all parts, such examinations lose much of their value and precision; and school teachers sometimes complain that even in an elementary subject the varying stress laid on its different parts makes the questions prepared by a stranger in some degree an unfair test of the proficiency of the pupil. A larger use of options in the paper might go far to meet this objection without impairing the strictness of the test.

The third kind of examination may, for want of a better word, be called potential, its aim being to measure the power or capacity to use and correlate knowledge. The object is not so much to find out what facts the student knows, but how far he has grasped their meaning, how fully he can apply them, how far his studies have formed a part of his being and developed the texture of his mind; in short not whether he has been duly subjected to a process, but what as a result of it he has become. This type of examination, while employed regularly for the doctorate of philosophy in universities, has not hitherto been used systematically in our colleges. Oral examinations, from their greater flexibility, have certain distinct advantages for this purpose, but they are by no means necessary. The psychological tests that have recently come into vogue are attempts to measure intelligence, that is to disclose the capacity of the persons to whom they are applied; and useful as they are so far as they go, they deal only with very elementary information. We are seeking for examinations that will measure the acquired ability to use specialized knowledge on a far higher plane. This the general examination undertakes to do, and in doing so it must strive to measure, not merely what has been included in formal courses, but the subject as a whole, because the object to be attained is fixing the student's attention upon the subject, not on those portions of it that happen to be included in any course or series of courses. Those are merely means to an end, and if the student does not so regard them he loses the true standpoint of higher education. It cannot be repeated too often that no one can be really educated from outside, or against his will. External agencies assist, but the essential thing is self-education, and the value of this depends much upon the object sought. If it is merely to do well in a course the value is far less than if it is the mastery of a field of thought. Now to cover any subject thoroughly would require far more time than the years in college permit. One student will be drawn more especially to one aspect of the field and another to something else. While all must show a grasp of the subject as a whole, each of them can be expected to be particularly strong in some part of it, and therefore the examination, if written, must contain a large number of options among the questions on the paper. Each question, moreover, should require for its answer a correlation of knowledge, an exposition of the relation between different sets of facts.

The reasons for a general examination have been stated more than once in these reports, but experience in its use has now continued long enough to say something about its results. Counting more than once those who failed and tried again, we have now examined one thousand and nine students in this way — certainly a number sufficiently large to justify drawing some reliable conclusions; and in fact during the single year covered by this report, the first in which the general examination was in use for subjects other than History, Government, and Economics, four hundred and twenty-four students were so examined, a number that will not be less in the years to come.

The examination is a real additional requirement for graduation, because the students who fail to pass it lose their degrees although they have passed all the seventeen courses which are still required, and which until the general examination was established were alone required. It is interesting, therefore, to note the number of failures. In the division of History, Government, and Economics, during the seven years it has been in use, there have been seven hundred and seventy-three men examined, of whom fifty-nine or 7.6 per cent have failed. A man who fails is allowed two more attempts at subsequent examinations if he so desires, without being obliged to reside in Cambridge; and in fact of the fifty-nine who failed nineteen have tried again, fifteen of them with success. Of the sixteen who failed for the first time in 1922 it is probable that some will present themselves another time. In other subjects, to which the general examination was applied for the first time in 1922, there were two hundred and thirty-six candidates, of whom sixteen or 6.8 per cent failed. Naturally the proportion of failures varied considerably in the different subjects. In English, which is not deemed by the students very difficult, and where the number of candidates was much the largest, being one hundred and twenty-five, the failures were thirteen, or more than one in ten. These figures show that the requirement of a command of the subject as a whole, beyond what is obtained from taking courses of instruction, is effective.

FROM THE ANNUAL REPORT, 1922–1923

Honor and Pass Degrees

RAISING the minimum is not a very difficult matter. It can be attained by making the easy courses more rigorous, and exacting a higher standard for remaining in college and for graduation. By such means the result is reached automatically. The problem of lifting the capable, but indolent or uninterested, students to excellence is far less simple; yet it is one that is insistent if our colleges are to accomplish the object for which they exist. We have sought, and are constantly seeking, to attain this result; but while we have made progress, much remains to be done.

One of the remedies suggested is that of creating distinct honor and pass degrees. As this plan is derived from Oxford and Cambridge, a few words about the practice there may clarify our ideas. The separation of the two kinds of degrees in those universities is based upon two distinct differences of treatment which are there applied together, but do not necessarily depend on each other. The differences relate to the grade of scholarship and to the content of the curriculum. In general the standard of scholarship required for the honor degree is much higher than for the pass; but this is not absolutely true, for there are several grades of honors, and it is commonly said that no more proficiency is needed to attain the lowest grade of honors than to get a pass degree. The divergence in the curricula is quite a different matter. The honor degree both at Oxford and Cambridge is awarded for concentration in a single field of study, which may be wide, but does not include subjects not regarded as germane to that field; whereas for a pass degree a distribution of studies is permitted at Oxford; and at Cambridge, where the difference between the two kinds of curricula is most marked, it is expressly required, and the subjects may be as far apart as the

most diverse realms of thought. For this reason it is said that
some students of honor quality there prefer to study for the
pass degree.

During the last generation two changes have been taking
place in Oxford and Cambridge. The requirements for the
pass degree have been made more rigorous, and the proportion of students seeking the honor degree has also greatly
increased. Now the object of awarding distinctions at graduation is not accomplished unless a large part of the students
are thereby provoked to develop their natural faculties, and
the success of a system of honors is measured not only by the
excellence of the candidates therefor, but also by the numbers
that it attracts. In the two great English universities this
result appears to be in large measure attained. A generation
ago a minority of the students sought the honor degree, a
proportion said to be about twenty-five per cent; but the
number has increased very much, until at the present day it
is estimated at not less than seventy-five per cent. It is
highly probable that if the pass degree were to be abandoned
altogether, the honor degree, with its varying grades, would
not suffer or be less effective.

In their efforts to stimulate scholarly ambition the English
universities have one great advantage. Graduation with
honors of a high class is believed there to open the door to a
successful career in after life. Not only do fellowships at the
universities, and church livings in their gift, depend upon it,
but admission to the higher grades in the civil service and
initial success at the bar are much promoted thereby; and
during the period when the respect for honors was being established this was true also of obtaining a start in political
life. Such an incentive for achieving a high rank in college
has not existed in this country, although there are signs that
employers are beginning to regard excellence in college work
as of more significance than they did formerly. Therefore it is
even more important here than in England that the colleges
themselves should find means to stimulate to better scholar-

ship students of natural capacity whose attitude is indifferent, or whose interests are inclined to lie too exclusively in other directions.

Several colleges in this country have established an honor degree, with methods of instruction and requirements for graduation different from those prescribed for the ordinary degree. In such cases the number of students who enroll themselves for the honor degree has been small, sometimes very small. It seems to appeal only to the few who have already a strongly marked desire for scholarship, and to have little influence upon the mass of undergraduates. Perhaps in time it may attract more widely, but we may well ask ourselves whether the manifest benefit of the honor degree cannot be obtained here without a sharp difference in curriculum which for various reasons is not wholly adapted to the American college. The lack of uniformity and solidity in secondary education makes the amount of specialization in the English honor schools inappropriate here, while the excessive importance attributed to athletic sports and other outside activities by the alumni and the public, and to a lesser extent by the undergraduates themselves, tends to smother the regard and desire for high scholarship.

With all this in view it has seemed to us, under the present conditions, wiser not to prescribe different kinds of work for honor and pass degrees, but one general method of instruction and study for all the students concentrating in the same field, each of them being obliged to concentrate in some field, and degrees with distinction being awarded to those who excel therein. By this process the student, instead of being compelled to choose at a comparatively early stage in his college life whether he will be a candidate for honors or not, — a choice that, with the relatively small esteem for academic distinction now prevailing, is likely to be negative more often than it should be, — can, as his interest in the subject grows, or as his tutor stimulates his ambition, determine to try for a standing that he would not have contemplated a year or two

earlier. Moreover, to require the same general examination
at graduation for all students whose principal work lies in one
field cannot fail to increase the regard for those who excel,
and does much to undermine the self-complacent attitude,
not uncommon in youth, expressed in the remark, "I suppose
that I could if I chose, but I do not care to." Every man has
some respect for the powers of another who surpasses him in a
fair contest, even if he believes the result due to more assidu-
ous training.

The students themselves understand the force of such a
motive better than their teachers, and it is noteworthy that
a couple of years ago the Student Council suggested to the
Faculty a change in the rank list that has been put into effect.
They said that the publication for each class of the list of
honor grades alone had little effect on the great mass of undergraduates, but that to publish the standing of all students
would be likely to improve the quality of their work. The
object they sought was to infuse into the whole body a desire
to do better; and this, if successful, has the double effect of
inducing some men of superior talents, but otherwise lacking
in scholarly ambition, to strive for distinction, and of producing a general respect for high scholarship without which no
school can truly fulfil its purpose. The criticism they made of
the old rank list applies in full force to a sharp division of the
student body into a small number who are working for an
honor degree and the greater mass who are looking only for a
pass.

To have the same method of instruction for all the students, and a common general examination at the end for all
those concentrating in the same field, does not mean that all
must be treated precisely alike, or that the final measure for
all is identical. The better scholars may be allowed various
privileges, as indeed they are now; among the courses open
to all they will naturally take the more advanced and difficult, as they do now; they will read more, and more profoundly, making a larger use of the summer vacations for the

purpose; and if there are tutors, these will be called upon for more attention by their most ambitious pupils. In the general examination also, where an option is necessarily given among the questions on the papers, some questions of larger scope may be included which are specially designed for aspirants for distinction. But all this is quite different in its effect upon the student body from a segregation of honor and pass undergraduates with distinct methods and subjects of study. It gives distinction to those who earn it, without creating a barrier dependent upon premature choice. Having regard to such considerations, we have preferred, in those departments that have adopted the general examination, to require it of all candidates for a degree, rather than for those alone who seek honors at graduation.

In discussing the advantages of a common procedure for all students it was suggested that the tutors may have an influence in stimulating the ambition of their pupils to achieve distinction, and this appears to be a fact. In April last the proportion of the students about to graduate who purported to be candidates for a degree with distinction in their several subjects were as follows:

In departments without a general examination and without tutors 10.5
In departments with a general examination and without tutors 7.9
In departments with a general examination and with tutors 21.5

All these men, of course, did not attain distinction, but the effect of the tutors in instilling a desire for it seems clear; and in fact, the proportion of undergraduates aiming at distinction is certainly on the increase.

MASTERS AND DOCTORS

THE Graduate School contains two kinds of students, not indeed sharply distinguished, but on the whole substantially different. The first are those who will not go beyond the master's degree, the others those who are working for the doctorate of philosophy. The requirements for the two degrees are quite unlike. For the former all that is required is the taking of four courses, more or less advanced in character, with a grade in each not less than B. The courses may be in the nature of personal research, but that is not required, and they are not infrequently such as any undergraduate might take in his last year. In that case the graduate student coming here from another college is continuing the type of work he has done as an undergraduate, in a form more advanced, but not more advanced than many a Senior does at Harvard; and he obtains the master's degree by completing it with uniform distinction. In fact, in many subjects the master's degree is in one respect inferior to the bachelor's degree, because there is no general examination. For the doctorate of philosophy, on the other hand, the candidate passes a rigorous general examination on his whole subject, a still more searching examination on his special field, and must prepare a thesis showing capacity to do highly creditable research. In short, one of these degrees measures the capable student, the other the competent scholar; the one qualifies for teaching in secondary education, the other for taking a place in the instructing staff of a univeristy.

On these facts two questions arise. First, whether it is wise to require, as is practically done at present, that a graduate shall take the master's degree on the road to the doctorate. There are, no doubt, many college graduates whose education has not been thorough enough to justify their be-

ginning at once on their preparation for independent scholarship; but there are also many others from the best colleges
who ought to be free from all further obligation to secure
credits in courses, who need to be set at once on their own feet
and march ahead with the guidance, criticism, and inspiration
that come from working at the side of eminent men. The
second question is, whether it is a benefit to either or both of
the two kinds of students to be classed and treated as a single
body, or whether it would not be better if the nascent scholars could be thrown together more intimately, each in social
contact with other ambitious young men in fields diverse
from their own. These are large questions, involving a departure from American practice, and likely to arouse difference of opinion, but they may be worth consideration. It is
important, not only that the future professor should, in the
years of his graduate study, be fitting himself for research,
but that throughout his life in the faculty of a university or
college he should be contributing to productive scholarship.
He should be in the tingling atmosphere of creative thought,
which is of quite as much consequence for his own mental
tone and that of the body to which he belongs as for the absolute value of what he succeeds in producing; and if this is true
of the professor's life, it is not less true in its preparatory
stage.

THE MEDICAL EXAMINATION

The report of the Dean of the Medical School is of unusual
interest because it considers two matters that are not, indeed, new in the School, but have not been treated in so
authoritative a way before. One of these is the system of
general examinations for graduation. It will be remembered
that this was introduced into the School thirteen years ago —
in fact, before it was adopted in the College. For some years,
however, it was treated as a review and therefore did not accomplish its object. Examination is the most difficult of the
educational arts, and its influence on both students and

teachers may be very great. After the war this art developed rapidly in the Medical School, and the general examination, used not to review but to correlate knowledge, became a potent force. It has affected both the laboratory and the clinical subjects, because the student must keep fresh, and be able to apply, his knowledge of the former when he graduates, and his whole medical training is ultimately directed to solving clinical problems by all the knowledge at his command.

A MOBILE FUND

In my annual report for the year 1917–18 I said, "Finally we need, perhaps above all else, what we have never had, a mobile fund, the income of which is not mortgaged to any one department or purpose. . . . An unpledged fund would greatly aid the University to do its work in a great way." The amount required for such a fund was thought to be a million dollars. Strangely enough, the dream has come true. Mr. William F. Milton, of the Class of 1858, left by his will, subject to his wife's life interest, a fund of about a million dollars, to be used in building a library if we did not have one; otherwise, the income to be used, "either in whole or in part, to defray the expenses of any special investigation of a medical, geographical, historical or scientific nature which said corporation may from time to time desire to make or prosecute . . . or for any other special or temporary object of the nature above stated, and not included in the routine work of the college, or any of its departments." Information about this fund has been sent to the members of the University, with a notice that applications must be filed by December 1st. The Corporation will then appoint a committee of experts to advise them in the selection of the applications. As these are so numerous that only a part of them can receive a share of the income, there will no doubt be many disappointments; but the Corporation, with the aid of the best advice it can get, will make the wisest guess it can in regard to the distribution of the fund. It is to be hoped that a number of researches will be greatly promoted in a way that would not otherwise be possible.

The Unity of Knowledge

Many years ago a thoughtful friend remarked that every original thinker strives to cut a new diagonal through human knowledge, and if so, it is important to place no obstacles to the cutting of such new lines across the field, but rather to keep the by-paths open and the fences in such a state that they can easily be knocked down. Knowledge has so increased that it is difficult for any man to master more than one subject in all its detail, and in fact subjects are becoming subdivided into plots to which, by the need of intensive cultivation, scholars are constrained to confine their labors. And yet the very extension of knowledge brings quite different subjects into close contact. An unknown region is explored and the explorer finds himself at the border of another's territory. At their foundations the frontiers of physics and chemistry are no longer sharply defined. In biology a new field of general physiology has grown up which deals with phenomena common to botany and zoölogy, while each of these is increasingly dependent upon both physics and chemistry. Moreover, where subjects do not strictly overlap they throw new light on one another, as is true of history and economics. The new field of psychology is also important for both of these, and is almost indispensable for philosophy, politics, sociology, and education. All this has its bearing upon the problem of teaching; but it is of far greater consequence for the other, and not less essential, function of a university, that of productive scholarship.

The growth of institutions of higher learning, with the multiplication of their instructing staffs, has inevitably caused a division into departments, each of which is more or less self-contained, for purposes not only of teaching, but also of administration, of purchase of books and supplies, and of common interests. One sees this in the desire to duplicate expensive and rarely used books that lie near the border line, and in the pressure for funds to enlarge the work of the several departments with little regard to the duly proportioned welfare of the institution as a whole. There is a danger that this may be carried too far, especially, perhaps, when the department becomes a distinct school with its own faculty. But it must not be allowed to take an exclusive form by closing doors, by dividing knowledge into tightly-shut compartments through which men are prevented from passing. All doors should be kept as wide open as possible, and scholars who like to plant their chairs in the doorways should be encouraged to do so, because they are in a position to see things from a fresh angle.

So far we have been on the whole peculiarly fortunate in avoiding such dangers; and, in fact, men bent on doing original work give that as a reason for accepting an invitation to come here. They are surrounded by others whose subjects touch the circumference of their own, and from whom they can get advice, suggestions, and sympathy. An illustration of the way the unity of knowledge may be expressed in material appliances can be seen in the arrangement of the Widener Memorial Library. In a number of university libraries the books are, or have been, segregated more or less completely by subjects, each directly connected with the seminar of a department, and not freely open to other readers except through that channel. Here substantially all the books are shelved as one collection, and every one who has access to the stack has almost everything that the library contains equally open to him. The seminar rooms on the upper floor are not as a rule for the segregation of the books on a subject, but convenient places to consult and work, often containing only volumes likely to be in constant use; while the professors' rooms and the readers' stalls are in the main stack, over which they may wander at will. That arrangement was not an historical accident. It was deliberately preferred.

FROM THE ANNUAL REPORT, 1924–1925

CULTURAL SUBJECTS

FORMERLY an opinion was often expressed that students in college could never be expected to have the same interest or desire for excellence as those in the professional schools, because the motive of general culture could never equal in force that of preparation for a definite career. It was said that the connection between distinction in college studies and subsequent achievement was too remote to be appreciated by undergraduates, and that the motives impelling the Oxford and Cambridge men to strive for honors could not be reproduced in this country. The subjects pursued in college are not all of the same nature. Some of them have a more obvious bearing than others on a subsequent vocation, and it is interesting to observe the proportion of candidates for distinction in the different fields. Of course no sharp line can be drawn, because one student may concentrate in a subject with a definite vocational intent while another does so for purely cultural reasons. This is true, for example, in the classics and mathematics. Still, there are clearly subjects in which the vocational motive has more influence than in others; and it is noteworthy that among those in which the proportion of candidates for distinction is large are to be found Fine Arts (52%), Philosophy and Psychology (53.9%), Government (55.5%), and History and Literature (75.2%), where the vocational motive is less than it is in Chemistry (42%), Biology (30.7%), Economics (39%), and Engineering Sciences (17.8%), where that motive is more common and yet the percentage of candidates for distinction is markedly smaller — the percentage being given in each case by the figures in parentheses.

FROM THE ANNUAL REPORT, 1925–1926

THE MEDICAL EXAMINATION

THE most distinctive feature in the education given in the Medical School is the general examination for graduation, to which reference has already been made. The committee that has it in charge lays down in its report three main ways in which this examination should serve the School: "first, by effecting an elevation of standards throughout all four years as a result of the existence of a better organized test for graduation; second, by affording the faculty an impartial source of information upon the methods of teaching now operative in the School; and third, by assuring a higher type of medical graduate through enforcing the necessity of correlating the work of all four years." The committee goes on to say that, as in previous years, it has "attempted to select questions which were designed in a broad way to test the ability of an individual to correlate his knowledge rather than to serve merely as a test of memory. Furthermore, the scope of the questions was such as to require considerable judgment in selecting the proper aspects for emphasis." It would be hard to describe better the object and nature of a good examination, especially of a general examination such as we use here; and an examination of this kind is of peculiar value in a Medical School by reason of the vast amount of facts that must be learned and the tendency to teach them in separate courses which have little connection with one another. The committee has kept its threefold objects very fully in mind, and has attained to a marked degree the results desired. Few men fail to pass the examination and thereby lose their degree — last year only one — because the promoting boards weed out in the earlier years those whose work is clearly defective. But the general examination has very distinctly affected the conception of the students about what is required to fit them for practice, and of the professors about teaching the various subjects as related to the whole body of medical science.

FROM THE ANNUAL REPORT, 1926–1927

THE READING PERIOD

THE president of another university remarked some time
ago that one of the impediments to be avoided by such an
institution was that of traditions; to which the reply was
made that there was one tradition of which the speaker
would doubtless approve, and that was the tradition of frequent change. We certainly have that tradition here, for
we have been continually making experiments, and we hope
wise ones. We have, indeed, some reason to suppose so, because they are being made in a definite direction with a constant object. That object, so far as the students are concerned, is to provoke an ambition and cultivate a habit
leading to self-education, — the only education that is later
self-starting and self-propelling. For this purpose another
departure has now been made, a somewhat surprising one,
yet designed for the benefit not of the students alone, but
also of the instructing staff. In last year's report it was
pointed out that the tutors' time was so absorbed by their
pupils as to make it difficult for them to pursue their own
studies and research, and a danger was felt of losing our
best men if they could not be given a better opportunity for
these things. They were asked whether limiting the time
when their pupils might confer with them to certain hours of
the day or certain days of the week would give relief, but
they replied that, so long as the regular routine of the college
proceeded, their relations of friendliness and helpfulness to
their pupils would be marred by anything that resembled
closing their doors. It was then suggested that certain
periods of the term should be marked off in which instruction
of all kinds would cease. The same problem, indeed, arose
in regard to all members of the staff, whether engaged in
giving courses or in tutoring. With the raising of the quality

of instruction the giving of courses has become a more laborious matter than in the past. The students are more keen, more ready to criticize and discuss, and a course given one year cannot be repeated the next with as little preparation as formerly. As compared with European universities our periods of lecturing are nearly half as long again, and the vacations, in which the professor has a full chance to do his reading and writing, are correspondingly shorter. The Division of History, Government, and Economics, which has had the problem of the tutors longest, discussed this matter, and presented to the Committee on Instruction a plan which that Committee, as a whole and through a sub-committee, worked over and presented to the Faculty in a slightly modified form. It was adopted by that body in February, and later approved by both governing boards. Almost all the departments have, with some adaptations, voted to put it into operation at once for all the courses not of an elementary nature. Its object is to create during the academic year two reading periods aggregating seven weeks, in which there shall be — except for Freshmen, for elementary courses and other peculiar conditions — neither instruction in courses nor tutoring. The teaching force will be relieved thereby, and the student will be engaged in educating himself by assigned reading, to which he will be held by subsequent examination. These periods are to be integral parts of the academic terms, in which neither students nor instructors are to be away without special leave of absence.

THE LAW SCHOOL

Formerly it was said that the Law School produced large numbers of admirable practitioners and few jurists. The first of these things it continues to do, and now it does the second also. Its professors have never ceased to make great contributions to the science of law, but until the graduate department was organized in 1912 no systematic training was given to juristic students. Advancing the knowledge of its subject by productive scholarship is as much the function of any professional school as training for the practice of the art; nor is this less needed in the law today than in any other matter affecting human welfare. Law is the crystallized expression of enforceable social obligations, the measure and framework of civilization, without which it cannot exist and by which it endures. It is a satisfaction, therefore, to record that, by the contributions to the two and a quarter million dollar fund, research in law has been placed upon a firm financial basis.

FROM THE ANNUAL REPORT, 1927–1928

DIVIDING THE COLLEGE

THE project of residential groups or Houses within Harvard College did not, as a practical question, fall within the period covered by this report; but this autumn the generosity of a benefactor, who desires to remain for the present unknown, has brought the matter within the sphere of action; and hence some remarks upon it seem imperative. Discussion of the subject is not new. A feeling has long been prevalent that the increase in numbers of the larger American colleges brings with it disadvantages. The personal contact of teacher and student becomes more difficult. Large communities tend to cliques based upon similarity of origin and upon wealth, a tendency that produced at Harvard the Gold Coast, as the private dormitories on Mt. Auburn Street were called until they were bought by the University. Great masses of unorganized young men, not yet engaged in definite careers, are prone to superficial currents of thought and interest, to the detriment of the personal intellectual progress that ought to dominate mature men seeking higher education. This drift of the American college has been the basis of much of the criticism leveled from outside, and of the dissatisfaction on the part of those intrusted with its management. It is the cause of the exaggerated importance of the secondary interests as compared with the primary object of education; of what Woodrow Wilson, when President of Princeton, called the overshadowing of the main tent by the side-shows. If this is less true of Harvard today than in the past, it is because of endeavors to make the intellectual life of the students more serious and more interesting. But the very fact that we have made some progress is a reason why we should be in a position to make a further advance in the same direction.

On the scholastic side progress took the form of requiring every student to concentrate his studies in some definite field selected by himself, while not wholly neglecting any of the great subjects of human thought. This was followed by the general examination and tutors in the student's field of concentration, beginning with the Departments of History, Government, and Economics, and, as the art was slowly perfected, gradually extending until it included, by voluntary adhesion, almost all the others. That the system has stimulated effort and interest on the part of students cannot now be doubted. It is, indeed, clearly shown by the result of the reading periods, which have been both another step in the path of developing self-education as the only enduring basis of intellectual growth, and a measure of the progress in this direction so far achieved.

Meanwhile, the question of dividing the College into residential groups was not left out of sight. For a long time it had been debated by people both inside and outside the faculties of American colleges. In 1906 the late Charles Francis Adams discussed it in a Φ B K oration at Columbia, afterward republished in his "Three Φ B K Addresses." He considered that such groups, or colleges as he called them, should be based largely on the subjects to be studied and also on the amount of the fees to be paid, suggesting one endowed or free college, and others for scholarship holders, for men of moderate means, and for millionaires. Surely this would be an unwise method of distribution. About the same time Woodrow Wilson strove to introduce at Princeton a subdivision into what he termed "Quads"; but his plan involved the abolition of the clubs, which seemed to us needless and undesirable. The question of the distribution of students among the groups has always been one of the difficulties of the problem and was discussed by men here at that time. It was foreseen that if the selection were purely arbitrary the students would be so dissatisfied that it could not be carried out; and that if voluntary on their part they would be guided by associations of origin, all those from one school or one type desiring to enter the same group. To lessen this obstacle it was suggested that if the students could be thrown together for a year they would, to some extent, form new associations, thereby making the selection of groups less difficult. That was the genesis of the idea of Freshman Halls, which was soon perceived to have independent merits of its own.

The conception of an ultimate formation of residential groups has been kept in mind, the construction of new dormitories having been so planned that they might be useful in that connection; and therefore we are, to some extent, prepared for such an evolution. It had seemed clear, however, that the change could not be made at a stroke; that the College could not be subdivided for purposes of residence by a sudden cleavage, but that this must be done by successive steps. The first approach was thought to be an honor group of men who had the capacity for intellectual achievement and could be stimulated to desire it. With this was appropriately combined a plan for a society of research fellows of the kind that has proved highly profitable at Trinity College, Cambridge, England. A project of this nature was submitted two years ago to the General Education Board, but did not meet with its approval; and we were hoping that some far-sighted giver might be found to make the plan possible.

Such was the situation when the anonymous benefactor, who had independently formed the opinion that a subdivision of large colleges into residential groups was of vital importance, came to Cambridge. He believed, as we did, that the division should not be based upon differences in the subjects studied or the career the members intended to enter; that, on the contrary, men interested in various fields of thought should be thrown together with a view of promoting a broad and humane culture. We explained our method of approach through an honor group or House, which we estimated would cost three million dollars, and he most generously agreed to give it. In a later conversation, having been informed of the attitude of the Corporation and the Faculty on the matter, he indicated that if the University would commit itself to the whole project, to be carried out in such time and ways as seemed to it wise, he would give the larger amount that we had deemed necessary; careful estimates to be, of course, prepared before a definite pledge is made. Thereupon the Faculty of Arts and Sciences passed unanimously the following vote: —

> "The Faculty welcomes the idea of dividing the undergraduate body into social units of appropriate size and rejoices that means have been found to carry out this plan."

The estimates are now being prepared.

It is proposed to build one or two, preferably two, such Houses at once, adding the remainder as soon as the first have become established, and using for the purpose existing College dormitories. Naturally the details have not yet been worked out, but certain general principles would seem to flow from the object in view. The aim is to bring into contact a body of students with diverse interests who will by attrition provoke one another to think on many subjects, and will have a corporate spirit. For this purpose their number must be considerable without being so large as to subdivide itself into smaller self-sufficient groups. Until tested by trial it is impossible to be sure what the best number will prove to be, but taking the experience in the colleges of Oxford and Cambridge, and allowing for the differences between English and American youth, it has seemed that the right number will be between two and three hundred, varying somewhat with the conditions, but averaging not far from two hundred and fifty.

Certain misconceptions are sure to arise. One is that Harvard College is to be superseded or rivalled. This has no foundation. Save so far as tutors may reside, or have their conference rooms, in a House instead of in a lecture hall or administrative building, there will be no change whatever in the methods of teaching, which will remain wholly under the direction of the Faculty of Arts and Sciences. The plan is expected to give an additional stimulus to scholarship and intellectual interest, but otherwise it is not an educational but a social one. The discipline of the Dean's office and the Administrative Board for deficient scholarship will remain unimpaired.

To a few men the plan may not offer any benefits that they do not now enjoy; but it is hard to see how, if rightly understood and intelligently carried out, it can be a detriment to anyone. To far the greater number of undergraduates it should bring serious advantages, part of which would accrue to all large colleges, and part apply to special conditions here.

The plan makes possible more personal attention to the individual. This is an end for which all colleges are striving, and which is attained here when the student comes to the Dean's office; but that means in most cases after he is in some trouble. For the young man who is liable to fall behind, or who is not developing his own natural gifts and qualities, foresight is better than cure. In that way the benefits of the small college may be combined with the rich offerings of a great university.

Then such a residential House, where members of the three upper classes live together, gives an opportunity for contact in cultured surroundings of younger with older undergraduates, and of both with instructors. This happens here now only to a limited extent; yet it is an extremely valuable factor in a true education. Strangers sometimes refer to the conversation about intellectual things among our college students, and so far as it exists it supplements and enhances formal instruction; but a House of this kind could not fail to promote it with all men not destitute of mental appetite.

The Graduate School

The whole system of the Graduate School needs to be revised in view of the changes here and elsewhere in undergraduate methods. It needs to be adjusted to the wide differences in the training of the students at their coming and in their aims; and it needs to be freed from formalities which hamper progress. Many men enter the School for a year to get what is here undergraduate instruction, and for them the taking of four courses in a subject provides what they seek. Others come with higher ambitions in scholarship, but are as yet unprepared for its pursuit, and must devote some time to preliminary study before beginning to work on their own account. Finally, there are not a few, including our own college graduates with honors, who should be set at once to read and explore for the Doctorate. In his report of 1925 Dean Lowes urged a separation of these types of students. If that were done, the first two classes described above would take the courses laid out for them; while the third class, that of men accepted as candidates for the Doctorate, would, indeed, attend such lectures as they or their advisers thought useful for them, but would not be given credit for courses. They would apply themselves to acquiring a general mastery of their subjects and to research on their theses. On such a plan some men, whose college graduation showed them to be capable of rapid progress, would be accepted as candidates for the Doctorate on entering the School, and others after a year or two of preparatory work. The methods of instruction, though differently applied, would not be greatly changed, save by the exemption of candidates for the Doctorate from all course credits, and their treatment as a distinct body, a great gain in their position and a distinct saving in time for the more intellectual men.

THE INSTITUTE OF BIOLOGY

Closely connected with the Faculty of Arts and Sciences, although by no means exclusively so, is the project of an Institute of Biology. The great importance of this has often been urged in these reports, and it has now been brought within reach by a gift from the International Education Board. Recognizing that the first requisite is a building in which the various branches of biology, now scattered, can be brought together and enlarged, the Board generously voted to grant two million dollars for that purpose.

. . . .

When the project is complete, the biological work of the University, which has hitherto been singularly dispersed, will be collected about one centre, near the laboratories of chemistry and physics, on which it is dependent in manifold and increasing ways. Some branches of study, like those conducted in the Arboretum, the Forest at Petersham, and the sub-tropical Garden at Soledad in Cuba, must always remain at a distance; but these already have been made useful for scientific research, and in the future will be still more so, by coöperation and supervision in Cambridge. The object is absolute freedom for the investigator, with the greatest convenience and stimulation by making easily accessible to him the sources he needs, and the colleagues laboring in cognate fields. No doubt the Institute will require hereafter a farm, tropical stations, and larger facilities for exploring marine life; but with the new laboratories, and the present staff enlarged by the endowment contemplated, it will have a marvelous opportunity for contributing to human knowledge and welfare in the realm of biological discovery.

THE MEDICAL SCHOOL

A new departure was taken in the Medical School by the building of Vanderbilt Hall, described in last year's report. The unfortunate living conditions of the medical students had been long a source of anxiety to many people, and above all to Dr. Joslin. He organized the movement for a dormitory; and with the help of others obtained the subscriptions of an extraordinarily large proportion of graduates of the School and the generous gift of Mr. Harold S. Vanderbilt, which made the Hall a possibility. That the objects of good housing and good food have been attained hardly needs to be stated. But the educational results that the Hall has produced were not foreseen. Instead of separating to their lodgings, for the most part lonely and unattractive, or at best to an undergraduate medical society house with little intellectual stimulus, the students who live, or take their meals, in the Hall come into companionship with their fellows in all the classes and with the instructors, especially the younger unmarried ones. Here, as it has proved, they discuss the subjects they are studying among themselves and with men of greater maturity and knowledge. No doubt the relief recently given from an excessive amount of highly specialized courses has contributed to the elasticity of mind and eagerness of interest in basic principles which mark the conversation in the Hall. Certainly the general opinion of the officers and instructors who come into close touch with the students is that a distinctly more active intellectual atmosphere has arisen in the Hall and tends to pervade the whole School. The attrition of mind with mind among contemporaries, and with older men, in an informal but eager contact is one of the most potent forces in the stimulus that makes for power; and this the Hall appears to have fostered in a notable degree.

Around the ceiling of the vestibule of Vanderbilt Hall is a quotation from Pasteur, "Dans les champs de l'observation le hasard ne favorise que les esprits preparés" — a principle of very general application. The dormitory has proved to be another step on the road we have been following, of making the students strive actively toward a conscious goal, that is the comprehension of medicine as the application of a complex biological science whose elements form one organic whole. The general examination, the loosening of the curriculum, the bringing of the men together in the dormitory, have had a cumulative effect in promoting the result. Dr. Edsall in his report, which reviews the progress of the School during the ten years since he became Dean, discusses these matters, as well as the gains in financial resources, the improvement in the relations with the hospitals, and the advance in research. He points out that owing to the De Lamar legacy, and other gifts for capital and for immediate use, the joint income of the Schools of Medicine and Public Health is four times as large as the medical income at the beginning of the period; that the hospitals are now making large appropriations to enable our professors in their clinics to extend the knowledge of disease; that all these things have greatly enlarged the possibilities of research, and enabled us to retain men, especially promising young men, who would otherwise have gone elsewhere. He states that ten years ago there were about a score of senior and as many junior members of the staff doing research, and that there are now about sixty of each, besides some thirty research fellows sent by other organizations from all parts of the country and foreign lands; making in all a body of about one hundred and fifty men so engaged in the two Schools. This has resulted in many discoveries, the most striking one being that of Dr. George R. Minot, mentioned in the last report, whereby the effects of pernicious anaemia, previously an absolutely fatal malady, are prevented by the use of liver. This disease, by which, at a rough estimate, two hundred and fifty thousand people were afflicted at a time in the United States alone, has practically ceased to be a cause of human infirmity and death. That one discovery is worth to mankind all our expenditure upon research, and it is not the only one that will bear much fruit.

Dr. Edsall is firmly convinced that the future of these Schools depends upon their close connection with the basic sciences pursued in Cambridge; not only with biology but also chemistry and physics. If so, there is an additional reason for raising as rapidly as possible the three million dollars for the endowment of the Institute of Biology, toward which the International Education Board has granted two million for the building and a million more if the three million is duly raised. Chemistry is now well housed, equipped, and endowed; but physics sorely needs enlargement, and the Board has promised half a million for the purpose if a like sum is subscribed. This also should be done without delay.

.   .   .   .

The new Astronomical Observatory for the southern hemisphere at Bloemfontein in South Africa is now in operation, and while preparing for the installation of the large telescopes the smaller instruments are being used; for the help cordially given by the public authorities there we are very grateful. On account of steadier atmospheric conditions, this is a much better situation than the older one at Arequipa in the Andes of Peru. The Observatory in Cambridge is continuing its vast work on variable stars, nebulae, and their spectra, to determine the constitution of the sidereal universe and our position therein.

FROM THE ANNUAL REPORT, 1928-1929

THE HOUSE PLAN

THE House Plan is a great experiment, in some respects the greatest tried since the College was founded; but it is the consummation of the changes that have been going on for many years. It follows upon that of the general examination, the tutors, and the reading periods, and without them might not be wise. They are all directed to giving the student more individual attention, and at the same time making him more dependent upon his own efforts; to enlarging self-education under guidance, with more guidance. This involves a serious and mature attitude of mind on the part of the undergraduate. It signifies the tone of a university as contrasted with that of the schoolroom. The problem of the college is a moral one, deepening the desire to develop one's own mind, body, and character; and this is much promoted by living in surroundings and an atmosphere congenial to that object. The Seniors are now a highly serious body, with a strong sense of personal and corporate responsibility; and much can be done by placing the younger classmen in close contact with the older ones. The Houses are a social device for a moral purpose.

THE GRADUATE SCHOOL

In the belief that we can do more good by giving an excellent education to smaller groups rather than a less thorough training to more numerous ones, the number of students in almost all the larger departments of the University is now limited. This is true of the College and of the Schools of Medicine, Law, and Business Administration; and the time has come to consider whether it may not be wisely applied to the Graduate School of Arts and Sciences.

.   .   .   .

The burden laid upon our instructing staff by so many men and women [1] is very heavy; and, as in other parts of the University, it may well be that the service to learning, and to the country, would be increased by expending the labor upon the portion best qualified to profit thereby. No one can suppose that all these thirteen hundred and more young men and women are capable of adding to human knowledge, or of attaining the higher grades in the field of education; and it may be observed that a diminishing proportion are devoting their whole time to their studies. Twenty years ago about 70 per cent did so, whereas last year it had fallen to 44 per cent. The remainder are by no means always the weaker students, for the University makes itself in part responsible by employing many graduate students in teaching. But it is by no means clear that this is good either for the graduate students or for those whom they teach. No other of our professional schools would be willing to have so large a portion of its students on part time, save the School of Education so far as it is giving courses for teachers in actual practice.

The question is not a new one, although hitherto it has not taken the form of a limitation of numbers. It has been urged for some years in these reports, and in those of the Deans, that men intending to become scholars, who are working for the doctorate, should be separated from those who do not propose to do so, or who are not sufficiently prepared to be candidates. Now the growth of the School has forced the question whether it would not be better to restrict ourselves to men who show some promise of going far. Nor would this be a hardship on those who have not the native ability, or whose preparation is defective, since the opportunities for graduate study in the universities and larger colleges of the country are almost limitless, and this is true in New England as elsewhere.

If such a limitation were adopted, its extent and method of application would require careful study. A drastic solution,

---

[1] In Radcliffe College.

and one well-nigh automatic, would be that of abandoning the degree of Master of Arts altogether, and admitting to the School only men who can at once become candidates for the doctorate. At present our bachelor's degree with honors in a special field, involving a general examination and a thesis, is a better measure of capacity than the master's degree, which requires four grades of B in as many courses in related subjects, and can be obtained with industry by a man of moderate ability. Yet there are every year many failures to win it. Proposals have been made to raise the standard by requiring a general examination or a thesis, or both. But the degree has a commercial value, being commonly required by school boards for appointment to teaching positions in high schools, and one may doubt whether much would be gained by raising our standard above that which is usually required. There is a tendency in America to make a fetish of degrees, which, in some of its effects, is not unlike the counting of credits in courses, whereof the evils, long denounced here, are coming to be widely felt. One of the results has been the academic impression that degrees must follow one another in a regular succession, that the master's degree cannot be conferred until after the bachelor's, nor the doctor's degree until the master's has been taken, so that many a man, otherwise qualified to proceed toward his general examination for the doctorate and his thesis, has been practically obliged to score credits for four courses. Surely the function of our Graduate School is to train scholars of the highest calibre; and we may well ask whether this would not be done better if we admitted only students apparently capable of attaining something near that aim, gave them greater freedom in doing so, and associated them together as a band of prospective scholars in a body not containing men with less ambitious aims.

FROM THE ANNUAL REPORT, 1929–1930

A SOCIETY OF FELLOWS

CLOSELY connected with the training of thorough scholars for the doctorate is that of recruiting young men of rare capacity for contributing to thought and developing their power early in life. This is, of course, one of the aims of the Graduate School; but after training its best students, and giving them a chance by writing a thesis to learn the mysteries of research, it cannot enable them to carry the subject farther. It has been suggested that a group of fellowships for men not over twenty-five on appointment, who should be members of a society that included scholars eminent in various fields, living where they are naturally much together and frequently meet for meals, would have a highly stimulating effect. This is what James Russell Lowell had in mind when in his oration at the two hundred and fiftieth anniversary in 1886 he said:

> "The friends of university training can do nothing that would forward it more than the founding of postgraduate fellowships and the building and endowing of a hall where the holders of them might be commensals, remembering that when Cardinal Wolsey built Christ Church at Oxford his first care was the kitchen. Nothing is so great a quickener of the faculties, or so likely to prevent their being narrowed to a single groove, as the frequent social commingling of men who are aiming at one goal by different paths."

The prize fellowships at some of the English colleges, especially at Trinity, Cambridge, are of this nature, and they have produced an extraordinary number of distinguished men, one half of the British recipients of the Nobel prizes having been holders of Trinity fellowships.

We hear much today about coöperation in research, and that is good in working out well defined problems which require great labor and often the collaboration of different specialists. But it is not all. It aids in solving difficult and intricate problems; yet it does not touch the greatest of all contributions to thought, that of discovering a wholly new problem to be solved. This, like a work of art or literature, is essentially the creation of a single brain. To select men capable of this, to set them at work in surroundings most adapted to entice and fructify imagination, is certainly worth while if it can be done. The plan would be to have the prize-men selected in any subject by a body of older fellows eminent in different fields, upon evidence of remarkable promise; to provide them with ample stipends; and to appoint them for three years, with a reappointment for three more if their work in the first term justified the renewal. Mr. Alexander Agassiz once told the writer that he had such a plan in mind; and the new Houses seem to provide an excellent opportunity for an experiment of this kind. One of them will, in fact, contain a suite of dining, common, and service rooms so planned as to be suitable for the purpose.

STORING KNOWLEDGE

In every decade the proportion of the resources and energy of the University devoted to increasing and storing knowledge grows larger, and this is as it should be in a nation that is gaining in population, in wealth, and, what is more to the point, in maturity. The great task of the people of the United States in the nineteenth century was filling a continent and creating its industries. That of the twentieth should be raising its civilization to the highest level attainable, and in this the universities and colleges can and must play an essential part. They must train the men, accumulate and enlarge the learning on which advance depends. Of that work we are seeking in many directions to do our share.

The Library, in the Widener Memorial building and in branches throughout the University, is a vast storehouse of knowledge. For scholars' purposes it is said to rank third in the world, and it is growing rapidly all the time.

.   .   .   .

The new Biological Laboratory, now being built, has been mentioned. Not only will this provide a means of bringing all the movable parts of biology together but, by taking out of the University Museum laboratories which occupy much space, and involve some fire risk, it will give to that over-crowded building and its vast collections greatly needed room. . . . It is, indeed, the policy of the University to draw together as much as possible related fields of work, and for that purpose to bring museums having kindred objects under the supervision of a single management.

FROM THE ANNUAL REPORT, 1930–1931

The College

ATTEMPTS at improvement wisely begin with the foundation rather than the superstructure, and this is true of a university where the foundation is laid in the undergraduate portion or college. If that is not sound, the graduate and professional schools are endangered. A revision of the instruction under the Faculty of Arts and Sciences began, therefore, with the College, and indeed with the Freshman class. In 1902 there was strong and just criticism among teachers of the older academic subjects that in the large lecture courses for the lower classes the amount and thoroughness of the work required were not what they should be. A "Committee on Improving Instruction" was appointed, primarily to investigate these courses, but by no means confined thereto. At its first meeting it decided to examine all the teaching in the College, and sent a circular asking many pertinent questions to both instructors and students. Replies were received from two hundred and forty-five of the former and seventeen hundred and fifty-seven of the latter — practically all those addressed. The labors of the Committee covered more than a year, and ended in a report in 1903 stating, among other things, that the average amount of study was discreditably small, and that there was too much teaching and too little studying. It urged also "the importance of encouraging a greater number of men to take honors at graduation, and of making honors something more than a purely scholastic distinction for young specialists; for the Committee believes that students in pursuit of general culture should be encouraged in a thorough and somewhat advanced study of subjects to which they do not intend to devote their lives." One of the immediate results was a stiffening of not a few courses, and the report was followed some years later by rules requiring concentration and distribution in studies, instead of an uncontrolled, and too often haphazard, election.

The requirement of concentration, that is of electing not less than six courses in one subject, paved the way for another change. Of late the public has heard much of general or comprehensive examinations for honor students in their special fields. This is an old story with us, such an examination having been prescribed for candidates for honors as early as 1871; and it has been in force ever since, usually taking the form of oral questioning before a committee of the department. The test was in addition to grades in courses, and was commonly used to ascertain both range of knowledge and originality in thought. The candidate for honors had been obliged to take at least a fixed number of courses in his subject; and when all men were required to do so the question was naturally presented of extending such an examination to all, one of the objects being to place men with intellectual capacity, but without sufficient stimulus to exert it, in a position where, having to pass for graduation a general examination on their field of work, they would be tempted to do it with distinction — a result now in large measure attained. The examination involved the use of tutors to cover the vacant spaces between courses, and to correlate the different parts of the subject. But this system has been discussed so often in these reports that it seems needless to do so again here. Suffice it to say that it was adopted first by the Division of History, Government, and Economics, and after experience there had proved satisfactory it spread to other departments, until now it has been voluntarily taken up in practically every subject, save that of Chemistry.

All human results come from a combination of causes, and those we see among our undergraduates may fairly be ascribed in part to the changes in educational methods. Our college students as a whole appear more mature than a generation ago, not only in scholarship, but also in their outside interests, and in the sense of proportionate values which is the flower of maturity; and this in spite of — perhaps to some extent because of — the fact that they enter a year younger than they did in the early nineties. Maturity is by no means wholly a matter of years. It depends much more on environment, and above all on responsibility. A youth who enters college at nineteen and is treated like a schoolboy matures less rapidly than one who enters at seventeen and is treated 'like a man. To enter at the appropriate age and be expected to be rather above than below his maturity is the best way to develop manly character. Although undergraduates have less freedom in the choice of electives, and are more rigidly held to a higher standard of work, they are induced to feel more responsibility than in the past for their own education and for the well-being of the college to which they have the honor to belong. The Student Council is constantly consulted, and through it undergraduate opinion is stimulated and considered. The Houses, by dividing the body into smaller groups with a distinct responsibility for their good name, seem to be valuable factors in the process. Nor has the fear entertained by some people that greater interest in scholarship would lessen athletic prowess been verified. A general desire to excel is likely to foster excellence in all things.

The Graduate School

An improvement in the mode of instruction and the standard of scholarly attainment in the College prepared, and, in fact, almost forced, consideration of the work done in the Graduate School of Arts and Sciences. Instead of the School taking the man at the point where the College had brought him, and carrying him forward as a scholar perfecting himself in his specific field, the two had come to overlap. For a man who, with the guidance of a tutor, has passed with distinction a general examination in a large subject to be set at the Graduate School routine of merely taking for a master's degree four courses of no higher grade than those he has had in college, is for him a step backward, and has become an anachronism. The courses under the Faculty of Arts and Sciences are divided into three groups — those primarily for undergraduates, those for graduates and undergraduates, and those primarily for graduates. All these are open to properly qualified students in Harvard College, and every man takes some of those in the two higher groups in his field of concentration. In short, our men are doing in their later college years work that in many colleges is not done at all, and in universities is often reserved for graduates.

.　　.　　.　　.　　.　　.　　.　　.　　.　　.

We may, I think, assume that the conditions at Harvard are not untypical, for we certainly receive as good a body of graduate students as are to be found anywhere. They are of several kinds, not of course sharply defined, but running into and overlapping one another, yet easily recognized as types. There are those ambitious and capable of high intellectual achievement. They are the élite of the School, the future leaders in their fields, destined for professorships, of whom we hear the complaint that we do not produce enough. Their aim is the doctorate of philosophy and they should be enabled to progress as rapidly as possible. Then there are those of less ability, earnest and industrious but not gifted with the qualities that will bring distinction in after-life, for they are better at absorbing than producing ideas. More numerous than the first type, they run from its border through all gradations to men who can never in any real sense be scholars and should be discouraged early from trying to be. Of this second kind no small number aspire to a doctorate, and some succeed, while others fall by the wayside or fail in examination. Many of them will be very useful, well worth all the effort expended by them and by their instructors on their education. This is especially true in the sciences, where the demand is constantly increasing in laboratories, both academic and industrial, for highly trained technicians who can carry out experimental work planned by their superiors. For such positions the originality and imagination that lead to discoveries and leadership are not essential. Thorough knowledge with careful and complete reliability is enough. Nor is this without application in other subjects, for a useful, or indeed an excellent, teacher may not possess the power of contributing to knowledge. No doubt we often tend to go too far in the selection or promotion of a teacher, even at a university, in requiring that he shall have written a book. Nevertheless, the glory of a university is the enticement and production of scholars destined to be eminent in their fields. Now while the line between the first and the second kind of student in the Graduate School is not a sharp one, and a number of men stand near the border line, it is usually possible to determine to which category a particular man belongs; and it may be wise not to treat them alike or make them all follow the same beaten path, but rather to guide them according to their needs — a matter by no means simple in a school that has grown to more than a thousand men.

As in all other graduate schools at the present day, there is a third kind of student here, the man seeking only the master's degree now generally required for teaching in the best public high schools. With us he comes mainly from colleges with less developed standards than our own, and his work here is usually comparable to that of our college seniors, but without the tutors and the general examination. He must take four courses of the kind seniors habitually take, and get a mark not less than B in each. In fact, his degree signifies no more than our bachelor's degree with distinction; and hardly that, for, although many of them do not succeed in attaining the required grades, one cannot assert that the B is invariably given on the same rating as undergraduate marks. To a graduate student anything less is a failure which costs him his degree — a fact that makes an appeal to clemency. Many years ago such men entered Harvard College for a year and took a bachelor's degree. They were few, and it was probably the best plan for them; but it is not now possible, both because for their purpose they need the degree of master, and because by reason of their number, and our system of tutors, general examinations and Houses, we could not receive them in the College. These men deserve what they are seeking, but in view of the many institutions ready to teach them we may ask whether we should do it, and if we do whether they had not better be treated as a class by themselves. The objection will be made that the best of them are fit material for going farther. If so, they can advance after taking the master's degree and reaching the level of graduates of colleges with higher standards; but surely their presence here should not be a reason for causing others more advanced to take four courses with a B, and thus retard their progress as is too much the case today.

The life of a professor in a university or college has singular advantages. His work is congenial, very free from worry, leaves more time for vacation than any other serious pursuit, is carried on in pleasant surroundings among other men of like nature, brings contacts with scholars in the same field in foreign lands, and is highly honorable and useful. There are, indeed, no large fortunes to be earned by the successful, salaries being in general nearly uniform for any grade, but this should not affect men of ample means with scholarly tastes and ability. To such men the academic life, and the Graduate School as its gateway, should be attractive. Yet it is a strange fact that of the men who do not need help in college few enter that School. No doubt some of them have not property enough to spend the rest of their lives as they would like, and prefer a more lucrative career; but to many others who are well off the desire to increase their income is not in itself a controlling motive.

The figures are suggestive. In the College the three upper classes are arranged in six groups according to the average of their marks in the preceding year. Those in the first group are of the highest rank, receiving the largest scholarships; and any man not applying for one, but whose grades would entitle him to it, is included in the list with an honorary John Harvard scholarship.   In the same way the second group of men with the next highest rank receive scholarships if they need them, and those who do not are included in the list with Harvard College scholarships.   It is noteworthy that nearly one half of the men of high rank are awarded these honorary distinctions without stipend.   Out of two thousand men in the three upper classes the holders of scholarships this year and last have been as follows:

```
1930–31  I Group scholars   43, of whom John Harvard scholars   17
         II Group scholars 142, of whom Harvard College scholars 71
1931–32  I Group scholars   46, of whom John Harvard scholars   13
         II Group scholars 166, of whom Harvard College scholars 79
```

In the Graduate School also John Harvard fellowships may be given to men whose standing would warrant their receiving a pecuniary fellowship if they needed it.   But it is not regularly done, the tradition of the School in this respect being different from that of the College.   In fact these honorary distinctions are usually conferred only on men who are going abroad, or for some other reason want a certificate of their standing here.   No statistical comparison of the proportion of high scholars of independent means in the College and the Graduate School can therefore be made by this process, but that it is far less in the School than in the College, or than in the Schools of Law, Medicine, and Business, is evident to any observer.   Probably a fair estimate would be rather under than over ten per cent among the students of the Graduate School.   Clearly the School is not alluring to such men who have ranked high as undergraduates.   It is often said that the salaries of professors are too small to attract, but that should have the least influence with those to whom it makes the least difference.   Many men moreover, prefer a life of action to one of thought, and seek it in other professions or in business; yet such men sometimes return to scholarly pursuits later to study and write. We have several of them in our faculties today. A fear of the drudgery of teaching may deter others; but there is drudgery abundant in every regular occupation, and here — no doubt the same is true elsewhere — we are glad to appoint an eminent scholar to a chair on part time, teaching as much as he pleases, and paid for what he does. We have often done so. The absence from the Graduate School of men who are not obliged to think of what they will earn is striking, not because they are more to be desired than others, but because their choice of calling being free the fact that they reject this one is significant as an index. Many things may contribute to their reluctance,.some of which we have power to change. One may be the rigidity, and in cases almost the pedantry, of requirements which suit the plodder better than the gifted man. To require the graduate, who has just passed a general examination with distinction and written a brilliant thesis, to take with men of lesser calibre four courses of the kind he has had already is not attractive. Another reason no doubt lies in the composition of the body he is to join. Some of the students are of the highest intellectual type, and almost all are at least fair scholars; but the majority are industrious rather than imaginative, and they are all shepherded as one flock.

Professor John Livingston Lowes, when Dean of the Graduate School, referring to the fact that the master's degree "is regarded as a more or less necessary half-way house to the higher degree," declared that "the two degrees stand, in the main, for different disciplines and different ends, and it is for the training of scholars equipped, on the one hand, to contribute to the advancement of knowledge, and skilled, on the other hand, to inculcate into the minds of others, vivified by their own research, the body of knowledge which has been already handed down — it is for this discipline that the School chiefly exists." The Faculty does not yet see its way to adopt and act upon this point of view; but it has decided to improve the quality of the students in the School, and remove some of the rigidity. In the year 1929–30 it voted to limit admission to men "who present satisfactory evidence of ability to pursue graduate work with profit; such evidence may be graduation with distinction or in the upper third of the class, election to Phi Beta Kappa or records that show distinguished work in a special field." The result has been that this autumn three hundred and eighty-one applicants have been admitted and one hundred and twenty refused. During the year covered by this report the Faculty took another step directed mainly to making the treatment of the students more personal and more elastic. The votes urge every department to study and report the best means of supervising the work of first year men; and provide that each division shall report the names of all students whose standing does not warrant their pursuing further work, that the degree of Master of Arts may be based on other tests than marks in courses, and that a year's work shall hereafter be measured simply in terms of progress in scholarship as estimated by the division in which the work lies. This last will permit men who enter well qualified therefor to study and do research as is best for them, instead of scoring four courses; but as Dean Chase says, "both teachers and students continue to think in terms of courses, not in terms of progress and mastery of a field of knowledge. It is hoped that the new definition will result in a change of attitude."

It is very much to be hoped, for in this matter the Graduate School, far from keeping ahead, has not kept pace with the College. These changes are wise and will do good; but they will not solve the problem of separating the future creative scholars into a distinct body that will have a greater attraction for ambitious men of talent; and I commend to the consideration of the Governing Boards, and of all others interested in the progress of the University, the plan for a Society of Fellows, composed of a limited number of the most brilliant young men that can be found, with the guidance and companionship of professors who have achieved eminence.

Such an atmosphere should carry intellectual contagion beyond anything now in this country. To be thoroughly effective the Society should be well endowed, but where conviction of value is strong and enduring the means of execution are sometimes forthcoming.

FROM THE ANNUAL REPORT, 1931–1932

LATTER-DAY TRENDS IN COLLEGE EDUCATION

As THIS is the last report I shall make it may not be amiss to refer to some of the latter-day trends in higher education that have been significant, not only here but in other places, These concern the colleges, the professional schools, and the progress of learning.

To start at the base of the structure we should begin with the College. On this, and on similar institutions elsewhere, almost all our other work rests. If the education of under-graduates is not serious and substantial all that follows is impaired; for habits of indolence or superficiality indulged in college are hard to overcome, and slow down the march of students in the professional schools. The trends in the College have been toward a less vocational objective, a greater correlation of knowledge, a recognition of the principle of self-education, and a stimulation of more vivid intellectual interests. These trends are not absolute, but relative; not the creation or substitution of new principles, but a change of emphasis and attitude on matters that have been familiar since education became self-conscious. Moreover, these four objectives are interrelated, the methods adopted to promote one of them having an effect upon the others also, so that it is fruitless to deal with any of them as a specific means for a single result.

"Less vocational" means regarding the purpose of college education less from the standpoint of its direct utility in a future career, and more from that of developing the faculties of the student; building the mind rather than storing it with special knowledge; teaching young men how to think accurately and comprehensively about large subjects, rather than how to use the tools of a restricted field. All this is, of course, a matter of degree about which it is not well to be too dogmatic; yet it expresses a reaction against the idea that all education should be essentially vocational, a conception that took a strong hold upon our people at the time our country was turning from a frontier and agricultural to an industrial condition. The vocational objective is natural among a people who must earn their living, and it was strengthened by the spread of universal schooling above the elementary stage. But a desire for men of a more broadly educated type has been gaining ground in the professions and in business, as well as among thoughtful people throughout the community, and the colleges are the places in America to which we must look.

"Greater correlation of knowledge" is to some extent the same thing regarded from a different standpoint. If the object is not so much to cram the mind with isolated facts as to learn how to use them, the student must be brought to compare them, to discriminate between their relative importance, to verify them, and must try to combine them into a system more or less consistent with itself. Feeding a living fowl is a different thing from stuffing a goose with chestnuts. No doubt every good teacher strives to make his pupils think about the matters with which he deals; but instruction in separate courses — especially in those subjects which are not in their nature progressive, and a subsequent course is not necessarily dependent upon the knowledge of the preceding one — is very far from equivalent to a process that compels correlating them in a larger unity. Of late there has come an increasing approval of the doctrine, long asserted here, that to accumulate credits in courses is by itself a defective method of education. The American tradition of courses with an examination at the end of each is excellent, and we shall not abandon it; but in college, and in some of the graduate or professional schools, it needs to be supplemented by some process that compels more extensive thought and a wider view of the whole subject. This we have sought in the general or comprehensive examinations and the tutors.

"Self-education" is based on the principle that, beyond the mechanical elements, no one can be really educated against his will, or without his own active effort. Teachers can impart facts — not, perhaps, better than an earnest student can get them from books; they can explain, present points of view, and, if the pupil is not too reluctant, they can stimulate and inspire; but unless the student desires, or is provoked, to learn he will profit little. He must be made to educate himself, working out things by his own effort. Here again the tutor comes in, for he meets the student alone, conversing with him, setting him work to do and problems to be solved in a personal way less possible for the instructor save in a very small advanced course. The tutor is not a success unless he makes the pupil feel that he is forming his own mind, or at least incites him to do it perhaps unconsciously. To absorb and give back the information and ideas of the teacher may win good marks in many courses, but for training and fortifying the mind it is less valuable than power acquired by voluntary exertion in pursuit of an object. In short, the essence of all institutions of higher learning should be self-education under guidance. Reading periods are a part of the plan of setting the student on his own resources, to work by himself along lines more or less laid down for him, but for the time without help and therefore independently.

"Stimulation of more vivid intellectual interests" is the most important point of all. It has, of course, always been the aim and despair of serious educators; despair, because it is the most difficult of all their problems in the absence of a strong vocational incentive. It is natural for teachers to pay most attention to the industrious and proficient students; and yet, while these usually obtain the greatest benefit, they are not always the ones that need attention most. This is particularly true of young men of superior ability whose intellectual tastes and ambitions have not yet been aroused, who are satisfied with a fair or merely passing grade, regardng college life as mainly valuable for other reasons. Few of the entering Freshmen come with an ardent thirst for knowledge of any subject. It must be acquired here.

The old fixed curriculum, the same for all, partook, as President Hadley remarked its name implies, somewhat of the nature of a race. Among those in the lead there was an ambition to excel, and they were held in respect by their classmates. Eighty years ago everyone knew who was the first scholar in his class, and usually for several classes before and afterwards; but with the inevitable adoption of the elective system the race over a common track became broken into many different and incommensurate parts; and the impulse of contest, dear to youth, with the attendant approbation of the victor, was much enfeebled. Moreover, the fame acquired, both in the College and with the public beyond, by intercollegiate games and other activities outside the range of studies, diverted ambition into other channels. Some people have thought that the condition could be improved by eliminating those contests, that is by abolishing intercollegiate sports; but ambition in one direction is not promoted by destroying it in another which is in itself good. Scholarly interest must be fostered as an end in itself, not by trying to remove other interests. It may be encouraged by placing before the student a distant object requiring a fairly long sustained and constantly deepening attention, and by close contact with men enthusiastic in its pursuit. That is what we have been trying to do by means of the general examination on a subject selected by the student, and by the tutors who counsel and cheer him on his way.

Our early prototypes, the English and Scottish universities, developed on different lines. The traditional policy in Scotland was that of requiring every student to pursue throughout his course the chief subjects of human thought. This resembled in principle our fixed curriculum, and there is much to be said for it. Some years ago an approach was made to the methods of Oxford and Cambridge, but there is not universal agreement that it has been wise. Leaving out details about Moderations at Oxford, the different parts of the Tripos at Cambridge, and the diminishing pass degrees, it may be said that the practice in both those universities is to have the student devote himself to a single rather broad subject, ending in a general examination thereon. Both the English and the older Scottish systems have merits, and each may be best adapted to a particular community. We have not thought it best to follow either absolutely; but, while requiring a main concentration on one subject, pursued with the aid of tutors and measured by a general examination, we have insisted that the student shall not be wholly ignorant of the chief branches of knowledge, and have left him latitude for taking other courses outside his chosen field. To us it has seemed that in this way we meet at the present time the needs of our students, and of the country we try to serve.

THE GENERAL EXAMINATION

The history of the general examination at Harvard is not without significance in view of the interest it has aroused in other American colleges. As early as 1871 the College Faculty, as it was then called, passed the following vote:

> Every candidate for Honors must, at or near the close of the Senior year, pass an examination on the subjects in which he applies for Honors before a committee of the Faculty appointed for the purpose. The examination may be either oral, written or by experimental work, as the committee shall determine.

Since the members of the committee were by no means necessarily instructors whose courses the candidate had taken, the intention was clearly a general examination on the subject; but, there being no tutors to guide the student on outside reading, the questions could hardly stray far beyond the courses and the conclusions to be derived from comparing them. So the matter remained for forty years, when, the principle of concentration for all students having been adopted, an obvious corollary was a general examination in their chosen field with tutors to enable them to cover the ground. The matter was first proposed to the Division of History, Government, and Economics; and after deliberation, running through the winter of 1911–12, they decided in favor of the plan, asking in the following autumn leave of the Faculty to adopt it. The motion, although affecting only the division that made it, was opposed, debated through three meetings, and accepted in principle on November 5, the detailed provisions being approved on January 21, 1913.

Clearly such an examination and the functions of tutors were experimental; and, when peace restored normal conditions, a suggestion was made that if the system was good it ought to be extended; if not, it ought to be abandoned. On December 3, 1918, a committee was appointed to consider the question, and in accord with its report the Faculty voted on April 15, 1919, that general final examinations be established for all students concentrating in divisions, or under committees, which signify their willingness to try them. From that time one division after another has adopted the plan until all have done so except Chemistry and Engineering.

All the more notable changes that have been made — the requirement of concentration in some subject, the general examination, the tutors, the reading periods, and the Houses — have been designed to promote the four trends mentioned at the beginning of this report, and especially the last of them, the stimulation of intellectual interest. They are merely means to an end, and others might be quite as effective; but these are the ones we have tried, and it would seem not without avail. Men familiar with the College in the present and the past assert that the undergraduates, although younger, are more serious than they were, more deeply concerned with scholarly pursuits, and have more respect for marked achievement therein. We do not hear the term "greasy grind" or "greaser," so commonly applied to men of high rank a generation ago. "C is the gentleman's mark" is no longer a phrase to express a belief, or excuse indolence.

That committees of the Student Council criticize present conditions, on the ground that undergraduate standards of scholarship are not so high as they should be, is noteworthy; for the Council is not chosen from the high scholars, but mainly from men who have made their mark in outside activities. That their fathers would not have been worried by a matter of this kind shows the distance we have travelled; and without'loss of interest in sports, which are eagerly pursued, although not rated by undergraduates at an excessive value.

Encouragement may be drawn also from the increasing adoption of our methods in other places; still more, perhaps, from the use of the names without the substance, for one hears much of general or comprehensive examinations which are by no means comprehensive of a subject; of reading periods which are merely a few days for review before course examinations; and of Houses which are little more than dormitories, without dining halls, without libraries, without tutors, and with no professors as Associates. We have reason to believe that we have made an advance in our own work, and in the regard in which it is held elsewhere.

In the higher branches of university instruction and in research, especially in the sciences, there has been a marked trend towards greater correlation. So far as professional education is concerned this has been particularly true of the Medical School, where the curriculum covers many biological subjects that have, to a beginner, no obvious relation to one another, and yet where the object is to make the practitioner regard his patient as an amazingly complex unity. For that purpose, following the practice of European medical schools, two general examinations were introduced in 1911, one at the close of the first two years on the laboratory subjects, the other at the end of the last two years on the clinical aspects of medicine and surgery. But it was found that the examinations had too much the nature of a review, and that they did not induce the most important of correlations, that between laboratory and clinical knowledge. A change was therefore made by having only one general examination at the end of the four years, each question involving both kinds of information. One of the best questions used consisted of a single work "milk." Any man who, without notice, can describe how milk is produced, how it is assimilated as nutrition, the functions it serves in the body, the diseases it may carry, their effects, the means of detecting and distinguishing them, and the treatment to be applied, must know much of anatomy, chemistry, physiology, bacteriology, and clinical medicine; in short, it is a good guarantee that he is fit to practice.

In the realm of scientific research the trend toward correlation has been proceeding apace. The sciences began at isolated points and were confined within more or less impassable compartments. Physics was quite distinct from chemistry, botany was one branch of science and zoölogy another; but from those isolated origins they have been reaching out until they have touched and overlapped one another's boundaries. No frontiers now separate them, and at their edges there is not a debatable but a joint territory. The growth of knowledge has made the ultimate factors of physics and chemistry identical, and has brought the sources of botanical and zoölogical life to a common base. Moreover each science needs the aid of others. Astronomy would be helpless without physics and chemistry, and in fact without the latter no modern science could progress. Fifty years ago it would have been thought incredible that the Medical School, the Massachusetts General Hospital, Chemistry, and a new School of Business Administration should be coöperating in a study of fatigue. Such a trend is universal, and we have been striving to assist it. The laboratories of physics, chemistry, and biology are housed for the most part in single buildings, all near together and close to the University Museum. Much of the work of the Bussey Institution has been brought to this group of buildings. The Arboretum, formerly somewhat apart, as a collection of living trees and herbaria, has now professors of pathology and cytology; and the Director, Professor Oakes Ames, keeps it in touch with the Bussey Institution, the Botanical Museum in Cambridge, and the Atkins Biological Garden in Cuba. The Astronomical Observatory, also largely detached in the past, is now through Professor Harlow Shapley, its Director, in intimate relations with the rest of the University.

The laboratory space and equipment, the various collections of books and of specimens, the number of men engaged in research, have all increased greatly since the beginning of the new century. Yet these are but means to the enlargement of knowledge and wisdom, which will depend in the future upon the capacity and fervor of the men who will hereafter be the pioneers of thought; and this again upon impressing on young men the delight, the dignity, of intellectual attainments, and the respect due to those who seek them. Everything in a university is a means to a distant end. The Houses, made beautiful by the skill of our architects, Mr. Charles A. Coolidge and his partners, are like mother-of-pearl, shells in which jewels may grow.

COMMENCEMENT, JUNE 22, 1933

AFTER REHEARSING THE GIFTS DURING THE PAST YEAR

WHETHER we have come to the end of great gifts for educational institutions, as some people say — which I had always thought would happen sometime — I do not know. But I do know this, that we are very comfortably off, and we are fairly comfortably off for a very good reason. For the last few years we have taken a lesson from the greatest business man recorded in history. Perhaps you recognize whom I mean. Perhaps you do not. His name was Joseph and he lived in Egypt. I call him the greatest business man for this reason — he knew that seven prosperous years would be followed by years with a lack of prosperity, and he looked forward with that expectation in mind. Consequently during the good years he laid up for the lean ones that were bound to come. We have done the same thing so far as laying aside a little money during the good years to cover the bad ones is concerned. The Corporation is a body that reads the Bible and knows something about Joseph, and the members followed his example and laid up some little surplus during the good years. The result is that we have not been obliged to reduce our academic salaries, and, with the help of God and good judgment, we shall not be obliged to reduce these salaries.

People say to me every little while, "What do you think is the best thing that has been done in the college? Is it this, that, or the other?" In the first place, I want to say that no man does anything. Everything is done by a group of men acting together. It so happens in this world that when a group of men act together some one of them gets the credit. And I think it is fair that he should, because he also gets the blame, and there is more of this than there is of the other.

Taking the period together, you get more blame than praise. As a matter of fact you are not entitled to all the blame you get, and you are not entitled to much of the credit.

The body of men who have been acting together here for twenty-five years, consulting one another and working together towards a common object, had a definite notion of what they meant to do, a definite object and definite ideas of accomplishing it; and no one thing in particular was of more account than any other. They had a whole in their minds, and all the things done were merely means to accomplish that whole. Totally different means might have been quite as effective, provided those means were coördinated in such a way as to point towards a common object. The common object has been to make students care about thinking on serious subjects, to make them think as a matter that is worth while; to make men more serious.

We have believed that the problem of Harvard College is really a moral problem. We want men to think, and think seriously. We do not want them to think alike. That is an entirely different matter. We have stood, and we always shall stand, for absolute freedom of thought under any circumstances, both with our professors and with our students. We do not want them made in a pattern. We want them to think. In other words, if I may parody the motto of the University, what we desire here is not truth, but the search for truth. A truth that is held at any one time by any body of men is always more or less defective. What we want is an interest in the pursuit of truth, in caring for truth. We want our men to realize that there is no delight so great in life as the exercise of the intellectual faculties in the pursuit of something which is hard to find; in other words, that the attempt to think and think purposely towards the solving of a problem is the most delightful thing there is in life. That is what we want of the college man from the day he enters as a freshman until as a professor he is the author of a book. That is what I understand the University has always stood for.

The University, therefore, must be always changing. It must change from one generation to the next, and change radically, change deeply, its ideas. But that does not prevent its holding on to the eternal thread that runs through all changes that occur.

Gentlemen, you have been good to me, and what I want to say to you as my final word, the last time, perhaps, that I shall ever speak to the alumni as a body, is this: You have as my successor a man extraordinarily qualified for the place. In my own estimation he is better qualified for the job than I ever was. I want you to realize that and to give him your support and help. And remember that he also will be working for a whole, which whole may not be exactly conceived in the same way that those of us who are now passing away have conceived it. Do not judge him on the details of what he tries to do. Wait until you can see the pattern, and then judge him upon that.

So I pass to him the work. This is a relay race. It has been going on for a long time, and I pass the flag to him, knowing not only that he will keep the pace but also that he will better it, and make up for the delinquencies whereof we may have been guilty.

COMMENCEMENT, 1934

A CENTURY and a half ago we won the independence of our nation, taking our destiny wholly on ourselves. That was a beginning, but also the end of a long period of preparation. The first declaration of independence was made six years after our forebears landed on this shore, when the General Court decided that the youth need not seek their education in English universities across three thousand miles of stormy sea, but should find it in a college of our own. To confer degrees belonged, by English law, to universities alone, which could be created only by the Crown, and for this they ventured not to ask. But the intrepid Dunster, then President and sole teacher in his little school, assumed, without objection from his fellow-colonists, the right to give them, and thus secured our first measure of autonomy, that of education, with which the mother country never interfered. Moreover he prevailed upon Oxford and Cambridge to recognize our degree as on a par with their own and those of other European universities.

Ancient Rome maintained, as one of its earliest institutions, a place where fire was ever burning, and anyone could find it. So here our ancestors' first care was of a sacred flame; but instead of intrusting it to Vestal Virgins — women's colleges were then unknown — they ascribed it to the Muses, whose servants, the teachers and administrators, were from the outset nearly, and at last entirely, free to tend it as they might decide. Ten generations of these faithful servants have now fed the blaze, growing ever brighter with the passing of the years; and others have taken of the flame to kindle beacons of their own, until the whole land is aglow with universities and colleges, like a field with the camp fires of an army on the march.

With such a host of places where anyone can go for knowledge, it has seemed that we should strive not for quantity but for quality; not alone for preserving and imparting what is known, but more than ever for extending it; and we have done so, not, we hope, in vain. A year ago a friend sent me the distribution of the two hundred members of the National Academy of Sciences connected with universities and colleges. Some of these had a single member, others two, three, five, eight, nine, and ten. Of the six that had the largest share, Chicago and Johns Hopkins had each fourteen; Yale sixteen; Columbia and California eighteen apiece; and Harvard led the list with forty. Take not a straw too seriously, yet it may indicate the breeze.

To maintain a pace, and better it, where many are striving to excel, is arduous; but to you, President Conant, and your colleagues, we look with confidence for an ever brighter future; for a greatness yet undreamed; and with this glowing hope we, who have passed off the active stage, can but repeat, "Morituri salutamus."

A DECLARATION OF PRINCIPLES

TO BE READ EACH YEAR TO THE SELECTED CANDIDATES RECEIVED INTO THE SOCIETY OF FELLOWS

You have been selected as a member of this Society for your personal prospect of serious achievement in your chosen field, and your promise of notable contribution to knowledge and thought. That promise you must redeem with your whole intellectual and moral force.

You will practice the virtues, and avoid the snares, of the scholar. You will be courteous to your elders who have explored to the point from which you may advance; and helpful to your juniors who will progress farther by reason of your labors. Your aim will be knowledge and wisdom, not the reflected glamour of fame. You will not accept credit that is due to another, or harbor jealousy of an explorer who is more fortunate.

You will seek not a near but a distant objective, and you will not be satisfied with what you may have done. All that you may achieve or discover you will regard as a fragment of a larger pattern of the truth which from his separate approach every true scholar is striving to descry.

To these things, in joining the Society of Fellows, you dedicate yourself.